CUENTOS TRADICIONALES

El flautista de Hamelin

edebé

ES PROPIEDAD DE EDEBÉ
© Edición Cast.: edebé, 2005
Paseo de San Juan Bosco, 62
08017 Barcelona
www.edebe.com

© Texto: Josep-Francesc Delgado, 2005
© Ilustraciones: Alicia Cañas Cortázar, 2005

Dirección editorial: Reina Duarte
Diseño: Lluís Vilardell

ISBN 84-236-7264-6
Depósito Legal: B. 8881-2005
Impreso en España
Printed in Spain
Talleres Gráficos Soler, S.A.

El flautista de Hamelin

*Versión de Josep-Francesc Delgado
realizada a partir del poema de Robert Browning*

Ilustrado por Alicia Cañas Cortázar

Había una vez un pueblo que se llamaba Hamelin.

El pueblo tenía ricas casas de piedra y un río que proporcionaba agua a sus habitantes. Los campos que lo rodeaban daban abundantes cosechas y todo el mundo vivía feliz.

En verano los niños se bañaban en el río. En invierno, cuando helaba, patinaban sobre él o jugaban a tirarse bolas de nieve.

Pero una mañana de verano, cuando los habitantes del pueblo se despertaron, se encontraron invadidos por las ratas. ¡Miles de ratas!

Se habían apropiado de casas y calles.

Se metían en las cocinas.

Mordisqueaban los quesos.

Se comían los embutidos.

Relamían los cucharones de los cocineros.

Vaciaban las despensas.

Asustaban a los niños pequeños en sus cunas.

Corrían sobre las mesas de la taberna.

Causaban escalofríos entre la gente con sus gritos de rata.

Y hasta habían roído la cuerda de la campana de la iglesia...

Todos los vecinos se reunieron delante del ayuntamiento para quejarse.

—¡Señor alcalde, gánate el sueldo que te pagamos y líbranos de esta plaga!

—Si no, olvídate de volver a cobrar.

—¿Es que no ves que las ratas toman el sol tan panchas en la Plaza Mayor?

—¡Parece que hayan montado una fiesta en el mercado! ¡Se ríen de nosotros!

—¡Incluso los gatos han huido del pueblo, muertos de miedo!

El alcalde estaba muy preocupado... Así que optó por reunir al Consejo Municipal para buscar soluciones entre todos.

Primero decidieron redactar un bando pidiendo ayuda y lo difundieron por todo el país.

Mientras tanto, pusieron un montón de trampas para las ratas, pero no tenían suficientes.

También trajeron más gatos, pero pronto volvieron a huir...

Por último, trataron de envenenarlas. Pero las ratas eran tan listas, que ni siquiera probaban la comida con veneno.

Al cabo de unos cuantos días, alguien llamó a la puerta del señor alcalde.

—¡Adelante!

El alcalde se quedó bastante sorprendido cuando vio ante sí a un joven muy alto y delgado, que vestía un traje de muchos colorines, con una bufanda amarilla y roja al cuello, y para rematar, una flauta bajo el brazo.

—¿De verdad que en este pueblo pagaréis mil monedas de oro a quien os libre de las ratas como dice el bando?

—Ehhh, sí... —respondió el alcalde con desconfianza, porque no podía creer que un individuo tan estrafalario fuese capaz de ayudarlos.

—Pues ya podéis ir preparando todo ese dinero —afirmó el flautista mirando al alcalde fijamente con sus ojazos de color verde, parecidos a dos grandes botones de abrigo.

—¡Para el carro, flautista! Primero tendrás que hablar ante el Consejo.

Y así fue:

—*Dignísimas autoridades, yo puedo libraros de las ratas.*

—*¿Tú?* —preguntó el consejero más anciano con extrañeza.

—*Ya he librado a muchos pueblos de otras plagas: de topos, de alacranes y hasta de ranas. Mi fama da la vuelta al mundo, aunque nunca desvelo mis secretos. En la India aprendí los mágicos encantamientos de un gran sabio de Oriente.*

—*¡Tú eres un farsante!* —le echó en cara el alcalde.

—*Os equivocáis al dudar de mí, señores. Os aseguro que soy capaz de vencer cualquier tipo de plaga de molestas criaturas. Para ello domino un amplio repertorio musical...*

Mientras la discusión tenía lugar, el consejero más anciano se había fijado en los dedos del flautista, que se agitaban veloces e inquietos al ritmo de sus palabras. Y le pareció notar que había en ellos algo extraordinario y mágico. Así que sugirió:

—Un momento, consejeros. ¿Por qué no le dejamos intentarlo? Después de todo, no tenemos nada que perder.

—De acuerdo... —acabó aceptando el alcalde, mientras una rata se paseaba sobre su sombrero—. Si nos libras de las ratas, te pagaremos las mil monedas de oro.

Poco tardó el joven en ponerse manos a la obra.

Los habitantes del pueblo no le perdían de vista, atraídos por los chillones colores de su indumentaria.

El flautista, desde la altura que su estatura le proporcionaba, también los observaba, siempre con una sonrisa pícara.

Entonces alzó su flauta y se la acercó a los labios.

Sus ojos de color verde brillaban como un mar ardiendo.

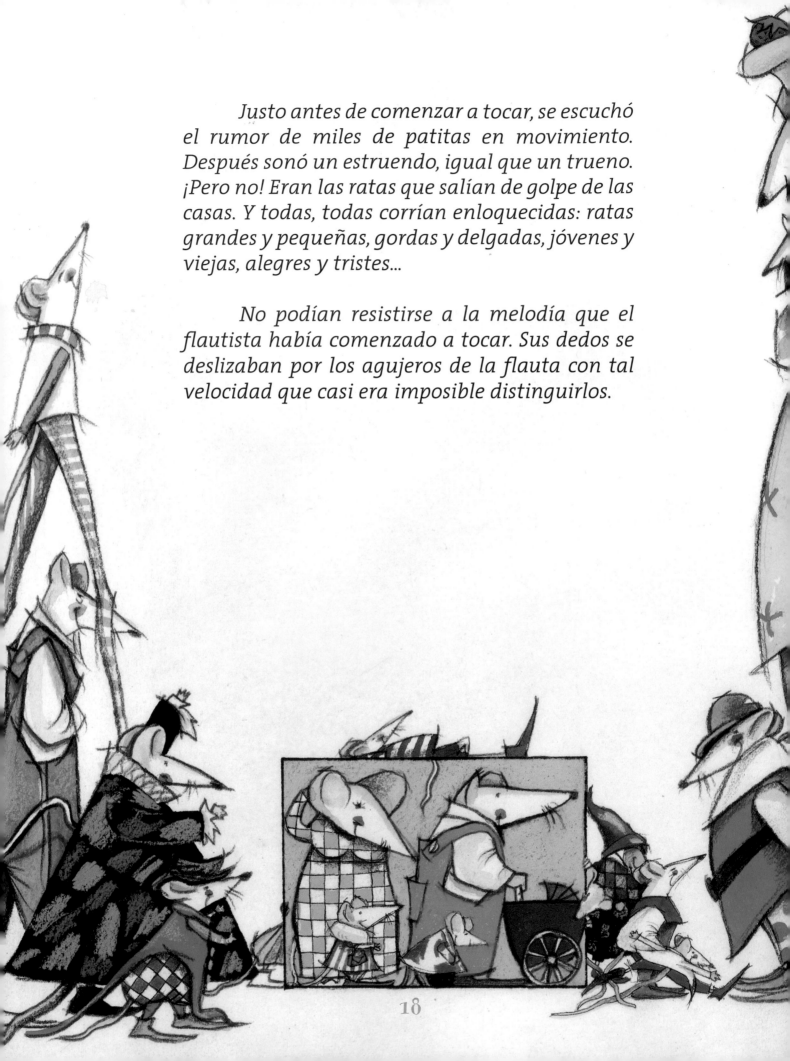

Justo antes de comenzar a tocar, se escuchó el rumor de miles de patitas en movimiento. Después sonó un estruendo, igual que un trueno. ¡Pero no! Eran las ratas que salían de golpe de las casas. Y todas, todas corrían enloquecidas: ratas grandes y pequeñas, gordas y delgadas, jóvenes y viejas, alegres y tristes...

No podían resistirse a la melodía que el flautista había comenzado a tocar. Sus dedos se deslizaban por los agujeros de la flauta con tal velocidad que casi era imposible distinguirlos.

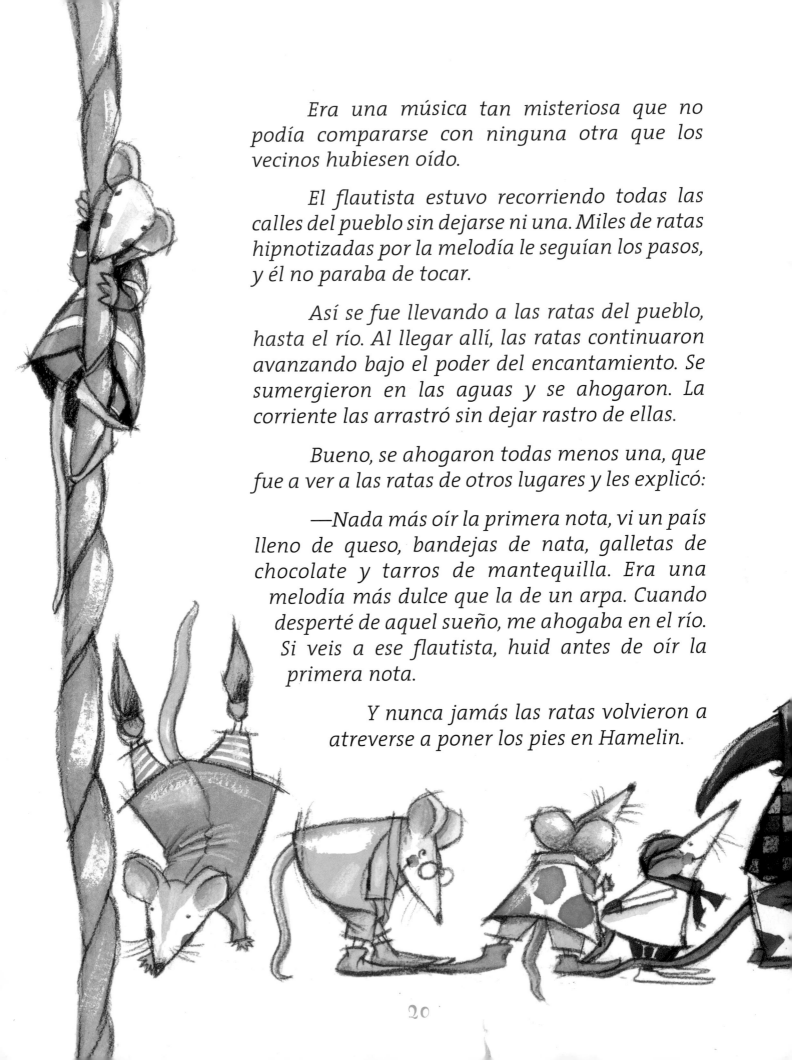

Era una música tan misteriosa que no podía compararse con ninguna otra que los vecinos hubiesen oído.

El flautista estuvo recorriendo todas las calles del pueblo sin dejarse ni una. Miles de ratas hipnotizadas por la melodía le seguían los pasos, y él no paraba de tocar.

Así se fue llevando a las ratas del pueblo, hasta el río. Al llegar allí, las ratas continuaron avanzando bajo el poder del encantamiento. Se sumergieron en las aguas y se ahogaron. La corriente las arrastró sin dejar rastro de ellas.

Bueno, se ahogaron todas menos una, que fue a ver a las ratas de otros lugares y les explicó:

—Nada más oír la primera nota, vi un país lleno de queso, bandejas de nata, galletas de chocolate y tarros de mantequilla. Era una melodía más dulce que la de un arpa. Cuando desperté de aquel sueño, me ahogaba en el río. Si veis a ese flautista, huid antes de oír la primera nota.

Y nunca jamás las ratas volvieron a atreverse a poner los pies en Hamelin.

Mientras tanto, el flautista había regresado al ayuntamiento para buscar al alcalde. Todos los vecinos que iba encontrando a su paso le felicitaban y le agradecían que los hubiese salvado. Él, a su vez, les sonreía con amabilidad y modestia.

—¡Buenos días, señor alcalde! Vengo a cobrar mi recompensa.

El alcalde lo miraba con la misma desconfianza del principio. Pensó además que las ratas ahogadas en el río ya no podían resucitar. Así que labor cumplida...

Y como los sabios consejeros se habían ido a poner orden en las casas, intentó rebajar el precio pactado.

—Toma.

Y le lanzó una única moneda.

—Pero si me prometisteis mil... ¡Yo he cumplido mi parte del trato! ¡Cumplid ahora la vuestra!

—¡Venga ya! No me negarás que te ha sido bien fácil... Sólo has tenido que tocar una musiquilla...

Entonces el flautista respondió:

—Traicionar a un músico es peligroso. No hablo de un músico corriente, sino de los músicos como yo, que únicamente tienen la música por hogar y el viento por camino. Yo no dispongo de grandes posesiones, pero cualquiera de mis canciones vale mucho más que la recompensa que me debéis. Mi música es más fuerte que una roca. Si consideras que mis melodías son fáciles de componer, que nacen sin esfuerzo, inténtalo tú, alcalde, o morirás solo y sin amor... Te lo advierto: todos pagaréis cara esta ofensa.

—Te quejas demasiado —dijo el alcalde—. Te puedes dar por bien pagado con una moneda. Márchate de aquí y no insistas, porque no soltaré ni un céntimo más.

—Tengo prisa porque me esperan en Bagdad. En esa ciudad el califa tiene una plaga de escorpiones en la cocina y me reclama. Él siempre me paga lo acordado. Sin embargo, retrasaré mi viaje por ti, alcalde sin palabra. Mereces un escarmiento.

Y sin más, se dio media vuelta y se marchó dando un portazo. La moneda quedó en el suelo.

Al llegar a la Plaza Mayor, el flautista tomó aire y volvió a tocar la flauta.

También esta vez, la melodía sonó rara, misteriosamente hermosa y encantadora. Era una melodía diferente de la anterior, pero igual de maravillosa.

De pronto, comenzaron a salir de las casas todos los niños y las niñas.

Los chiquillos se dirigieron al encuentro del flautista saltando y cantando alegremente. Reían y corrían. Estaban como hipnotizados y, en su entusiasmo, se empujaban unos a otros, siempre detrás del flautista.

Y el flautista los conducía fuera del pueblo.

En esta ocasión, el flautista no se encaminó hacia el río. Pero corría tan deprisa como el viento.

Los niños le seguían, y ni padres ni madres podían detener a sus hijos. Una fuerza de otro mundo los arrastraba, como si estuviesen atados al flautista.

—¡Volved! —gritaba un padre.

—¡Que alguien haga algo! —gritaba una madre.

Pero niños y niñas se alejaban más y más.

Ya estaban lejos del pueblo.

Los niños y el flautista habían llegado al pie de una montaña que se alzaba al fondo del valle. Cuando estuvieron todos, se abrió una gran cueva. Y el flautista penetró en ella sin parar de tocar la flauta. En cuanto entró el último, la entrada de la cueva se cerró y todos desaparecieron en su interior.

Únicamente un crío, que se había quedado muy atrás porque era cojo, no llegó a tiempo de entrar. Incluso un niño sordo, muy pobre, había entrado en la cueva contagiado por la alegría de sus amigos, aunque él no sufría el encantamiento, porque no oía.

Cuando vio que la montaña se había cerrado y la melodía se interrumpió, el niño cojo regresó poco a poco a Hamelin.

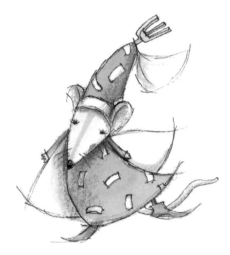

Sin niños, el pueblo era un lugar de tristeza. Todos lloraban.

El niño cojo explicó que, mientras escuchaba aquella melodía, veía una tierra llena de árboles frutales y ríos. El cielo estaba lleno de gorriones y jilgueros. Allí las abejas no te picaban nunca. Por los campos paseaban pavos reales. En los bosques vivían rebaños de ciervos y de caballos que nacían con alas. Y todos ellos vivirían en un palacio con las mesas siempre dispuestas como en un banquete con riquísimos pasteles.

34

Los vecinos fueron hasta el ayuntamiento para reclamar a sus hijos.

Iban armados con palos. Se habían enterado de que el alcalde no había cumplido su promesa.

—El flautista nos ha retado a tocar una melodía que los haga regresar.

Primero lo probó el mismo alcalde. Pero no tenía ni idea de tocar la flauta y la gente se tapaba las orejas.

El consejero de más edad solicitó ayuda a todos los músicos de la región, y los pobres tocaron día y noche. Pero la cueva no se abría.

Desesperados, pidieron ayuda al rey, que les envió a su propio compositor acompañado de toda la orquesta real. Pero tampoco dio resultado.

—Alcalde, acércate tú hasta la cueva y deja allí las mil monedas de oro —le exigió finalmente el consejero más anciano.

Y el alcalde no tuvo más remedio que aceptar.

Llegó al mediodía.

—¡Toma, flautista! Falté a mi palabra pero ahora te dejo aquí las mil monedas de oro —gritó el alcalde en dirección a la montaña.

El anciano consejero también estaba allí, con el niño cojito. Gracias a aquel niño sabían el punto exacto donde la montaña se había cerrado.

Sin embargo, la montaña no se abría y todos tenían la preocupación en el rostro.

Dentro de la cueva, los niños empezaron a rogar al flautista que saliese. Como estaban encantados, no sentían ningún sufrimiento, pero notaban que el flautista estaba enfadado. El niño sordo le preguntó:

—¿Qué te pasa, flautista? ¿Estás enfadado?

El flautista dijo que sí con la cabeza.

—Pero, flautista, tú amas la música. ¿Y verdad que también quieres a los niños?

El flautista volvió a decir que sí con la cabeza.

—Pues sal y recoge tu dinero, flautista, que bien te lo has ganado. Mira, yo solamente poseo esta moneda de cobre de cinco céntimos y nada más. Es todo lo que tengo, pero creo que tu música es tan buena que vale todos mis ahorros. Toma, quédate con mi moneda y toca tu música. Y si tuviese todo el oro del mundo, te lo ofrecería simplemente a cambio de oír unas notas tuyas, pero no puedo porque soy sordo.

Y el flautista no supo decirle que no.

Entonces salió acompañado del niño sordo a ver qué pasaba. Mientras, los demás niños y niñas se quedaron esperando en la cueva.

Como el flautista todavía dudaba, el consejero le sugirió:

—Flautista, no debes juzgar a todo un pueblo por un solo hombre de corazón mezquino. Está claro que todos reconocemos que tus melodías son extraordinarias. Coge lo que te pertenece.

Y el niño sordo dijo:

—Flautista, no deberías estar enfadado. ¿Quién posee un tesoro como el tuyo? ¿No ves que tu música es el tesoro más grande del mundo?

—El chico tiene razón, flautista —añadió el consejero anciano—. Tendrías que habernos visto tapándonos las orejas cuando el alcalde ha tocado la flauta...

El alcalde, naturalmente, estaba colorado hasta las cejas.

Y por fin, las puntitas de los delgados labios del flautista se alzaron un poco y dibujaron una sonrisa. Se le había pasado la pena.

Entonces cogió el oro y lo repartió entre el niño cojo y el niño sordo, que se quedaron maravillados viendo cómo brillaban las monedas.

—¡Acércate, pequeño! —le indicó al niño sordo.

El flautista sabía que los sordos podían sentir la música a través del tacto:

—Ahora soplaré muy fuerte y será como si me oyeras.

Subió al niño sobre sus hombros y le colocó las manitas sobre sus mofletes, que se hinchaban y deshinchaban al ritmo de la música. Y así volvió a tocar la melodía mágica.

La montaña se abrió y todos los niños salieron bailando y cantando.

Justo cuando el sol se ponía tras el horizonte, los chiquillos llegaron a Hamelin. Las madres salían a recibirlos, y todo eran lágrimas de alegría y abrazos.

Los niños explicaban lo que habían visto y los padres los escuchaban felices de volver a verlos. Las familias del niño cojo y del niño sordo, cuando vieron todas aquellas monedas de oro, se pusieron muy contentas. Eran pobres y así podrían pagar una educación a sus hijos.

El niño sordo cogió unas cuantas monedas y se las dio al alcalde:

—Toma, alcalde. Son para que tu hijo estudie música y aprenda a tocar algún instrumento.

El Consejo Municipal decretó que en Hamelin se fundara una escuela de música. En la puerta de entrada escribieron:

«Si bien aprendes una melodía,

quizás te sea útil algún día.»

Y en el balcón, grabaron esta frase con letras de oro:

«Seas rey, alcalde o ratón,

no olvides dejar cumplido

lo que hayas prometido.»

For the Petaccio sisters, Lilliana and Giuseppina

DARIO FO
& FRANCA RAME:
ARTFUL
LAUGHTER

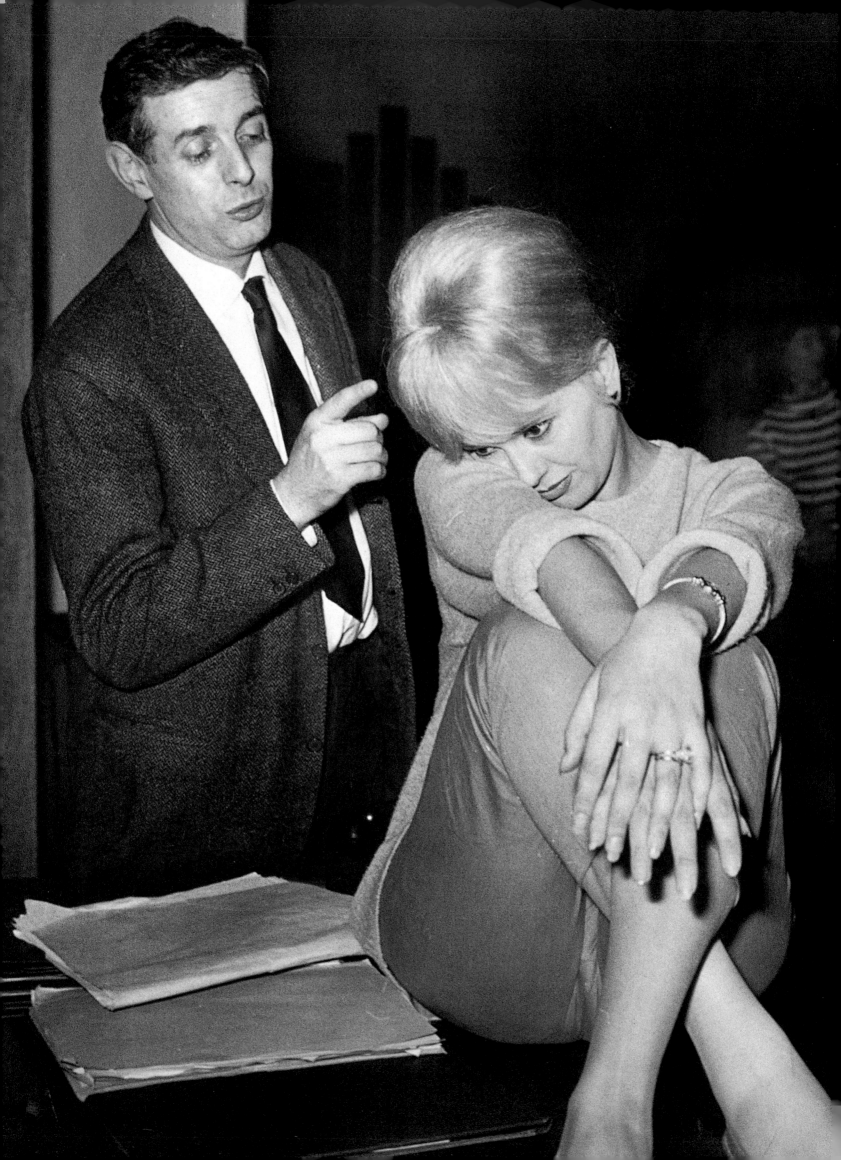

DARIO FO
& FRANCA RAME:
ARTFUL
LAUGHTER

BY RON JENKINS

APERTURE

ACKNOWLEDGMENTS

It is humbling to consider how many people have helped me in my ongoing efforts to understand the work of Dario Fo and Franca Rame. First, of course, I owe a tremendous debt to Dario and Franca themselves for welcoming me into their home, trusting me to translate their texts, granting me endless interviews (Franca insists that by now I must know everything about her except the year she started menopause), and making fun of me whenever I take my work (and theirs) too seriously. I am also indebted to my friend Joel Schechter, who first suggested that I might find Fo's plays intriguing without realizing the lengths to which I would go in proving him right. Harvard University made the initial phases of my research possible by awarding me a Sheldon Traveling Fellowship to spend a year with Fo and Rame in Italy in 1985. Walter Valeri helped me to locate them. Anna Maria Lisi, Cristina Nutrizio, Lino Avolio, and Piero Sciotto, members of the Fo/Rame company, befriended me during my first months in Italy, when I needed all the help I could get, and have continued to be generous in their support ever since. Marina de Juli, Deborah de Flammineis, Eliel Ferreira De Souza, Chiara Bonfatti, Mario Pirovano, Sylvia Varale, and Marco Scordo have gone beyond expectations in facilitating my research at the Fo/Rame archives in Milan, as well as providing invaluable assistance while the company was touring throughout Italy. Jacopo Fo, Fulvio Fo, and Bianca Fo Garambois have also been helpful in providing valuable perspective on their family's accomplishments.

Bob Brustein of the American Repertory Theater, the first artistic director brave enough to present Fo and Rame in the United States, gave me the opportunity to serve as the onstage translator for their American premiere and later produced two of my translations of their plays. Thomas Derrah proved that it was possible for an American actor to play Fo's roles with wit and distinction when I directed him in Fo's monologue *The Story of the Tiger*. He then tackled the text of *We Won't Pay! We Won't Pay!* in collaboration with Ken Cheeseman, Caroline Hall, Will Lebow, Karen MacDonald, and Marisa Tomei to prove that an ensemble of American actors could bring Fo's plays to life with a collective virtuosity that delighted audiences night after night. Tomei used her superb comic timing and intelligence to introduce Rame's monologue on orgasms to America, an effort that was continued admirably by Deborah Wise. My sister Tamara Jenkins graciously agreed to lend her considerable comedic talents to acting in the American premiere of Fo's play *Eve's Diary* before embarking on her glorious career as a film maker. My brother Robert Jenkins impressed Fo in person with his Harvard student production of *Accidental Death of an Anarchist* before embarking on his glorious career as a political scientist. Leora Rivlin brought new dimensions to Fo's words when I directed her in *Eve's Diary* in Israel, as did Kathleen Donohue, who also played the role with playful passion. Arvidas Dapsys brought political bite to *The Story of The Tiger* when I directed him in the play during the Soviet occupation of Lithuania. Sally Schwager made countless contributions, on stage and off, to my translation of *Archangels Don't Play Pinball*. Lloyd Richards assembled a talented cast to produce my translation of Fo's *Elizabeth* at the Yale Repertory Theater. I would never have fully understood the multiple dimensions of the plays discussed in this book without the impressive artistry shown by all these actors and directors in bringing the works of Fo and Rame to the stage.

Despina Mouzaki provided cinematic insights into the American tour of Fo and Rame by making the first documentary of their work to be broadcast on American television. Marina Kotzamani helped me to understand Aristophanes' connection to Fo and Rame during their visit to Delphi, Greece. Gloria Pastorino provided me with new perspectives on Fo when she introduced me to *Ho Visto un Re*. Stefania Taviano deepened my understanding of Fo's language during our collaborative translation work on *Johan Padan*, as did Cristina Nutrizio during our translation work on *Eve's Diary*. Marisa Pizza shared her enormous knowledge of the working process of Fo and Rame. Jules Frawley donated her audio equipment. Kathy Wilson generously offered her observations on the visual nuances of Fo's paintings. Howard Gardner proved to be a

4

valuable critic and mentor in more ways than he imagines. Eugenio Barba and the staff of the International School of Theater Anthropology (ISTA) have been constant sources of information and inspiration, especially Professors Claudio Meldolesi, Nando Taviani, Nicola Savarese, Cristina Valenti, Kirsten Hastrup, Franco Ruffino, Mirella Schino, Marco de Marinis, Ian Watson, Janne Rissum, Jean-Marie Pradier, Eugenia Casini Ropa, Jonah Salz, Mark Oshima, Clelia Falletti, Giovanni Azzaroni, Tom Leabhart, and the Odin Teatret company members Kai Bredholt, Julia Valery, Iben Nagel Rasmussen, Torgeir Wethel, Frans Winther, Jan Ferslev, Roberta Carreri, Patricia Alves, and Rina Skeel. Teaching a seminar on Fo's work with Nando Taviani at the ISTA meetings in Germany while writing this book was particularly valuable, as were the comments of the participants in those sessions. I also appreciate the questions and comments that were raised when I presented unfinished portions of this book to the Columbia University Seminar on Modern Italian Studies, the Boston University Translation Seminar, the Brown University Humanities Lecture Series, the New York meetings of the American Society for Theater Research, the Paul Desjardins Memorial Symposium at Haverford College, the Tufts University Spring Colloquium, and the Conference on Dario Fo and Franca Rame at Cambridge University in England.

Special thanks should be given to the dedicated community of international scholars and translators whose writings have become fundamental to understanding the reception of the work of Fo and Rame around the world. These include Joel Schechter, author of *Durov's Pig* and *Satiric Impersonations*; Joe Farrell, translator of *Tricks of the Trade* and author of a forthcoming Fo/Rame biography; Antonio Scuderi, author of *Dario Fo and Popular Performance* and editor with Farrell of *Dario Fo: Stage, Text, and Tradition*; Walter Valeri, editor of *Franca Rame: A Woman on Stage*; Claudio Meldolesi, author of *Su un Comico in Rivolta*; Christopher Cairns, author of *Dario Fo e la Pittura Scenica*; Tony Mitchell, author of *Dario Fo: People's Court Jester*; Tom Behan, author of *Dario Fo: Revolutionary Theatre*; Marisa Pizza, author of *Il Gesto, La Parola, L'azione*; Ed Emery, translator of many Fo plays in Great Britain; Peter Chotjewitz, translator of Fo's plays in Germany; Bent Holm, translator of Fo's plays in Denmark; and Carlo Barsotti, translator of Fo's plays in Sweden. While my choice to focus chiefly on primary sources means that not all of these works are specifically cited in this book, I wish to make it clear that I am indebted to each of these authors for their impressive research and their generous collegiality.

I also want to express my deep gratitude to the John Simon Guggenheim Memorial Foundation for providing me with the fellowship that made it possible for me to write this book, and to my colleagues at Wesleyan University for providing me with the time to write it. I am particularly grateful to President Doug Bennet, former Vice President Richard Boyd, and to Professor Jack Carr, who graciously took over the responsibility of chairing the theater department during my absence. The unique photographic skills of Mario Tedeschi helped make this book visually coherent as did the extraordinary talent of my designer, Yolanda Cuomo, along with the visionary efforts of my editor Melissa Harris, whose dedication to the project since its inception has been exemplary. Finally I give my heartfelt thanks to Hanne Mogensen, who supported me lovingly through everything.

NOTE ON TRANSLATION

Except where otherwise noted, I have translated all Italian texts, interviews, and sources myself. In most cases I have left the word *"giullare"* (plural *"giullari"*) in Italian. This is a key term, used frequently by Fo and Rame to describe the medieval street performers, storytellers, and satirists who are important role-models for their vision of theater. The term could be loosely translated as "jester," but because this is associated in English with court jesters performing under the patronage of royalty, it is best to avoid oversimplification by using the more evocative Italian word, which refers to improvising comic performers who, in the words of Fo's Nobel Prize citation, are known for "scourging authority and upholding the dignity of the downtrodden."

Aperture gratefully acknowledges
the generous support of:
The Olivetti Foundation, and
The Italian Cultural Institute, New York,
and its Director, Paolo Riani

TABLE OF CONTENTS

TRANSLATING PARADOX INTO ACTION

P R E F A C E

I'm interested in discovering the basic contradictions in a situation through the use of paradox, absurdity, and inversion. This enables me to transform one reality into another reality, not as a trick, but so people will understand that reality is not flat, but that it is full of contradictions and reversals, and that often absurdity is a reality which is closer to the truth than those things which seem to be sacred and absolute, but are almost always false. —Dario Fo[1]

Like all tricksters, Dario Fo envisions the world in a state of flux. He sees paradox, absurdity, and inversion as tools of transformation that underscore the contradictions of everyday life. Resurrecting the traditions of Aristophanes, Harlequin, and Molière, Fo uses these tools to probe beneath the placid surface of a situation and turn it into a kinetic comic event. Fo's comedy is kinetic in the sense that it pulses with physical actions that complement its verbal complexity. He is an artist who thrives on action. "I always walk to get ideas," says Fo. "Movement stimulates my thoughts." When Fo takes a walk, the results are usually eventful. He has an unassuming but charismatic presence that draws people toward him. In Italy, where he is an instantly recognizable celebrity, Fo is regularly approached for autographs and graciously engages his fans in conversation. But even when he goes abroad, and walks in relative anonymity, Fo often talks to local residents about the architecture of their town, gossips with shopkeepers, or invents ironic stories about the history of whatever region he happens to be visiting. Fo's antennae are always out, scanning his environment for new ideas. The restless landscape of his comic imagination manifests itself in texts, drawings, and physical performances that explode with action. The swirling figures he draws on paper propel him to write language that is charged with physicality. His vibrant syntax in turn inspires stage performances of acrobatic virtuosity, in which the actor's body nimbly twists, bends, and contradicts itself as it aspires to the muscular truth of slapstick.

This book is an exploration of the dynamic relationship between words, images, and gestures in the theater of Dario Fo and Franca Rame, who has been his indispensable collaborator for half a century. Working as their translator since 1986 has convinced me that the plays of Fo and Rame cannot be fully appreciated without acknowledging the visual images and physical actions that are encoded in the language of their texts. I came to understand this through translating their plays, sometimes onstage as their simultaneous interpreter. From this privileged vantage point, I watched them sculpt language into a form that achieves an extraordinary equilibrium between spoken words, graphic design, and bodies in motion.

Unlike other forms of theater, comedy provides the translator with an immediate measure of failure or success. Having performed their material around the world for decades, Fo and Rame know they are funny. When the audience doesn't laugh, there is no one to blame but the translator. This harsh test compelled me to grasp the essence of their art as quickly as possible. After three months working as the onstage interpreter for their 1986 American tour, I learned that Fo and Rame build their comedy out of action, and that maintaining the rhythmic momentum of that action is crucial to the successful translation of their texts. I gradually began shaping the words of the translation to fit the gestures they used in performance. As the years passed and I began translating their texts for productions with other actors, I found myself referring more and more not only to those remembered gestures but to the drawings that Fo sketched while writing his plays. These sketches captured the choreography of the performance in a primal blueprint, a score for movement that somehow had to be incorporated into the translation.

When Fo introduces me to people he often says, "This is my American translator. He makes very creative mistakes. Sometimes his mistakes are so interesting, I translate them into Italian and put them into the original." Fo's joke reverses our roles and mocks the concept of translation, just as he did during his 1986 American tour of *Mistero Buffo*, when I stood next to him onstage and struggled to translate his live and often improvised performances. Defying the skeptics who said that this awkward arrangement would kill the humor of his plays, Fo found unorthodox ways to use the presence of a translator to his advantage, and ended up playing to rave reviews and standing-room audiences in New York, New Haven, Baltimore, Cambridge, and Washington, D.C.

Inevitably there were times when I would falter and interrupt the relentless flow of Fo's comic cadences. Initially these moments terrified me, but eventually I came to look forward to them. Whenever Fo sensed me hesitate or alter the timing of our closely synchronized deliveries, he always found a way to turn the mishap into a source of laughter. If I shortened a long list of commedia dell'arte characters, Fo joked that "synthesis is the principal talent of the average American." If I used an invented word instead of a literal translation, Fo noticed the onomatopoeic quality of the sound and repeated it several times in English like a child playing with a new toy. "Popemobile" was one of his favorites. If I asked him to repeat a phrase, he teased me by telling the audience how he stayed up all night looking in the dictionary for arcane words to stump the translator.

By calling attention to our relationship, Fo made the act of translation a part of the performance, strengthening his sense of complicity with the audience by inviting them to participate in what was happening onstage. Wanting to remind the public that words are not flat and lifeless but malleable and full of contradictions, Fo implicitly urged them to step out of their role as passive listeners and become active participants in a game of bilingual Ping-Pong. The reliability of words is usually taken for granted in the theater, but Fo transforms language into an elusive living entity, teeming with paradoxes and absurdities that leap out at you with the unpredictability of a time bomb. "Some of you will laugh when I speak in Italian," Fo tells his audience. "Some of you will laugh when you hear the translation, and some of you won't get the jokes at all until you leave the theater, but then you'll laugh all the way home."[2]

Franca Rame is equally adept at turning translation into an active element of her art. When I was the onstage interpreter for her 1995 Toronto performance of a play she wrote with Fo called *Sex? Don't Mind if I Do!*, Rame played with the fact that her jokes about the male sex were being translated by a man. At the beginning of the show she apologized to the audience on my behalf: "You'll have to forgive Ron if he makes any mistakes," she announced. "We've been rehearsing for two days straight and talking about nothing but sex. By the time we're through he's going to need a psychiatrist."[3] In 1986, when we first worked together on a production of Rame's play *It's all about Bed, Home, and Church* at the Kennedy Center, a Washington Post reviewer noted that Rame often made her translator blush. "You see," Rame told me, "The audience likes that. You have to blush all the time."[4] When I told her I was not accomplished enough as an actor to blush without actually being embarrassed, Rame took it as a personal challenge to find a new way to embarrass me onstage every night, and to the delight of the audience she always succeeded.

The ease with which Fo and Rame exploit the comic potential of mistakes is rooted in the improvised medieval and Renaissance traditions that inspire their work. Their finely honed improvisational skills allow them to assimilate the potentially troublesome presence of an onstage translator into the fabric of their performance as smoothly as if it had been written into the script. Traveling players in the Middle Ages and commedia dell'arte actors of the Renaissance relied on a similar style of improvisation that incorporated random events into a performance. For example, a dog wandering onto a commedia dell'arte stage would not be seen as an interruption, but as an opportunity for Harlequin to invent

new jokes and interact with the audience. Fo explains the nature of this technique in an anecdote about the seventeenth-century actor/playwright Molière, who was deeply influenced by the improvisational style of his era's traveling commedia troupes. When a commedia actor asked Molière's performers what they would do if the roof of the theater began to crumble, they said that they would stop the show. "That's the difference between our theater of improvisation and a theater that relies entirely on a written script," replied the commedia actor, as paraphrased by Fo. "You drop the curtains and close down in the face of the unexpected. . . . For you an accident is problematic. For us it is an advantage. We perform the accident. The collapse of the theater frightens you. For us it would be a stimulus to create something new."[5]

Fo and Rame adhere to the same principle of readiness. They thrive on the unexpected occurrences that make live theater unique. Fo often begins his performances by ushering spectators to their seats and inviting some of them to sit onstage with him to get a better view. He also makes a show of asking the technicians to change the microphone levels, even if there is nothing wrong with them. These actions help to create a rapport of intimacy with the audience, establishing the performance as something that is being spontaneously created with the public's participation.

Fo attributes his success in improvisation to what he has learned from working onstage with Rame, who was born into a family of traveling players that had performed in the commedia tradition for generations. "My work in the theater would not be possible without Franca," says Fo, "because Franca was born in the theater. But she was not born in the theater seventy years ago, which is her age. She was born in the theater 400 years ago. This woman has at least 400 years of life in the theater, maybe 500. In her DNA is the memory of all her ancestors, grandparents, and great-grandparents who worked in the theater. Her family has the entire history of European theater in their collective memory: the itinerant theater, puppets, melodrama, Shakespeare, the commedia dell'arte, circus, epic theater, pantomime theater. When I have an idea and write it down and read it to her, this is the most delicate moment for me. It is as if it were Molière who was judging me, together with about thirty actors from the commedia dell'arte. If Franca tells me that it doesn't work or that the situation lacks comedy, I cry and go into my room. Sometimes I get mad and say, 'No. It's good.' But she is always right."[6]

Fo's explanation of his relationship to Rame is typical of his epic approach to comedy: it is full of absurdities that clarify the truth of the situation by putting it in a wider context. He blurs time frames, conflates history, and invokes biology to create an image of his wife's DNA as a container for caravans of circus acrobats, Shakespearean actors, puppeteers, and pantomime clowns; he pictures himself trembling before a tribunal of seventeenth-century commedia dell'arte actors overseen by Molière; he even throws in the sound effects of comic wailing, asking his listener to imagine him weeping inconsolably in his room at the harsh judgment passed down by his 500-year-old wife. In a few short sentences he conjures up the verbal equivalent of an epic film with period costumes and science fiction special effects. For all its absurdity, this slapstick summary captures the essence of his respect for Rame's talent with crystalline precision. His images are outrageous, but they succeed in converting complex ideas into visually exuberant arguments that are vivid, memorable, and persuasive.

One reason Fo adapts so easily to the rhythms of translation is that he is a master translator in his own right. In performance he frequently shifts back and forth between Italian and a variety of local dialects, but besides his fluency in linguistic translation, he has a gift for transforming the mundane world around him into the visual language of comic paradox. In Copenhagen, Fo mesmerizes an international gathering of anthropologists by translating the cadences of an obscure Italian folk song into the rowing gestures of the medieval boatmen who first sang it, linking the breathing pauses in their gestures to the rhythmic structure of the melody.[7] In Milan's most prestigious business school he gives lessons in communications to executives from all over the world, translating the body language of sixteenth-century aristocrats into practical advice for modern businessmen. "Relax and never raise your voice," counsels Fo with a grin. "People with real power never exert themselves."[8] At the site of the Delphic Oracle he translates classical Greek poetry into an onomatopoeic simulation of ancient Greek so convincing that classics scholars claim to understand what he is saying.[9] Fo is obsessed with transformation. He is always translating past history into current events, ancient dialects into modern vernacular, and obscene anecdotes into epic fables.

At the core of Fo's transformative imagination is his ability to visualize the world in drawings and gestures. He trained as a painter and architect at Milan's Brera Academy of the Arts, and he has continued throughout his career to use drawing to visualize his thoughts, rendering the basic characters and situations of his plays into sketches that capture the absurdity of their predicaments. The people in Fo's drawings fly through the air, hang upside down, and sprout the body parts of exotic animals. Like his stories, Fo's drawings are capable of capturing multiple time frames in a single epic collage, suggesting a narrative sequence that has been stopped in mid-action. The figures in Fo's artwork seem swept up in a whirlwind of motion, and Fo often animates his characters onstage with the same swirling gestures that appear in his designs. The pictographic language Fo uses is inextricably linked to both the drawings that inspire his stories and the physical gestures of the actors who bring them to life through movement.

The relationship between Fo's drawings, texts, and gestures is fundamental to his comic vision. The dynamic interaction

OPPOSITE PAGE: Lecture at Columbia University, 2000; THIS PAGE, TOP: Fo in dialogue with comic mask; THIS PAGE, BOTTOM: "Mannequin of Pope John Paul II with Face of Dario Fo," a prop from *The Pope and the Witch*, from the exhibition *Fellini and Fo*, Milan, 1999; PAGE 14: From a performance of *Fit to be Tied*

between these elements is most apparent when he is in the early stages of creating his work. At Fo's home in Milan I've watched him paint for hours as he prepared shows on Leonardo da Vinci and Saint Francis of Assisi. The walls of his apartment are covered with artwork. Masks from Africa, Asia, and Europe hang over the passageway from the living room to his study. An eighteenth-century statue of the Madonna cradling Christ sits on a table next to the bust of a medieval jester. Planted in the middle of these treasures is a wide-screen television with a remote control that Fo uses to switch channels incessantly back and forth between news stations, sporting events, and old movies, creating the same kind of dizzying montage on his home screen that he does in the theater. When Fo asks why I never get tired of watching him draw, I tell him it is like watching him rehearse a new play. He agrees, and continues drawing. Fo rarely rehearses his solo performances, preferring to try them out directly on an audience, so that drawing becomes a subliminal rehearsal process in which he acts out his scenarios on paper as a prelude to translating them to the stage.

Sometimes the images in Fo's performances come from visual sources other than his drawings. He has borrowed scenes from Bosch, Goya, and Giotto, among others, and just as frequently he turns to newspaper photographs and television news broadcasts for images that link the past to the present. During his 1986 American tour of *Mistero Buffo,* Fo immersed himself in the imagery of the United States, incorporating observations on late-breaking current events into the improvised prologues to his medieval stories. Ronald Reagan was a recurring subject. In the early 1980s, Fo and Rame had been denied entry into the United States by Reagan's State Department, which invoked the McLaren Act to declare the couple a threat to national security. Finally granted a visa to perform, Fo toured with *Mistero Buffo* and commented ironically on the controversy and the media coverage it had generated: "President Reagan offered us all that free publicity as a professional courtesy," quipped Fo. "It was the least he could do for a fellow actor."[10]

Fascinated by Reagan's blatant use of theatrical rhetoric, Fo watched the president regularly on the television news in his hotel. The image that remained with him most strongly, however, was a giant cardboard cut-out photograph of Reagan that he saw on the streets of Washington, D.C. An urban entrepreneur was charging tourists a fee to have their picture taken next to Reagan's likeness. Near the cardboard president, homeless people were eating out of garbage cans. That night in his performance Fo translated the scenario into a commentary on hunger in America. Having read Reagan's opinion that the only thing hungry people needed was information about where to find government food programs, Fo decided to include it in his introduction to a piece about hunger in Renaissance Italy: he put a variation of Reagan's declaration into the mouth of the fifteenth-century doge of Venice, who had ruled over one of his era's richest empires and had denied that there was hunger in his realm. "It's only a question of information," says Fo's doge, echoing Reagan. "The poor people don't know where the garbage cans are located." Fo also mocked Reagan's dependence on his wife by imagining a summit meeting with Gorbachev in which Nancy Reagan hid under the table to give the president advice. "Nancy pulled on his left pant leg when she wanted him to say yes," claimed Fo, "she pulled on his right pant leg when she wanted him to say no. And when she wasn't sure, she pulled in the middle. This was the origin of Reagan's well-known prostate problem."

The musical rhythms of Fo's delivery are crucial elements in his comic architecture, and I soon discovered the necessity of translating them as faithfully as I translated his language. Often the tempo of his language is linked to the visual pictures he paints with words and gestures. During the 1986 American tour, in a passage describing the arrival of Pope John Paul II at the Madrid airport, Fo compared the once athletic pontiff to a hero of American popular culture. "There he was in all his magnificence," said Fo. "Blue eyes. Big smile. Neck of a bull. Pectoral muscles bulging. Abdominal muscles well defined. And above all, a red cloak that fell down to his knees. Superman!"[11] The staccato beat of each physical detail built a momentum that climaxed in the punch line "Superman," which Fo delivered in English. Then his description soared into a spiral of lyrical absurdity that ended with the assembled crowd imagining the pope taking off into the air without a plane: "They could already see him in their imaginations. His cloak billowing in the wind.

Skywriting streaming out from under his gowns. In yellow and white smoke that read: 'God is with us . . . and He's Polish.'" The passage was accompanied by vivid movements that shifted from crisp hand gestures during the staccato description of "Superman" to full, flowing body movements that suggested the pope's airborne trajectory. These gestures had to be taken into account in the word choice and timing of the translation's delivery. Some gestures were intertwined in the words that inspired them; others required a beat of silence to achieve their intended comic effect. I often stepped to the back of the stage, when I sensed that Fo needed room to execute a particularly large movement sequence like the flight of the pope. Following Fo's imagination from the fifteenth-century doge of Milan to the modern American welfare system to Ronald Reagan's prostate gland, my job was to remain as invisible as possible while standing in plain view.

Working onstage with Fo was like entering the landscape of one of the paintings he would frequently sketch in his dressing room before a performance. His drawing technique is similar to his writing style: starting with an image that is real and concrete, he gradually transforms it into something fantastical and absurd, but slyly believable. The pope really did appear at the airport in Madrid wearing splendid cloaks and robes. His love of athletics is well known, and his followers do attribute all kinds of supernatural powers to him. The idea of their imagining him as Superman in flight was built on a foundation of fact, with Fo's fantastical details added on one at a time, so that the absurdity seemed a natural consequence of the truth. It is a process Fo uses regularly in his paintings, adding colors and details that heighten the intensity of a scene until it bursts into something surreal, like colored kites that metamorphose into flying horses and angels.

In performance Fo's flying-pope scene employed a similar kind of transformation. The realistic descriptions of the pope's "blue eyes" and "big smile" were part of a list that inched into absurdity with "the neck of a bull" and "well-defined abdominal muscles," so that by the time Fo got to the long red cloak, the image of Superman in flight became almost inevitable. In staging the pope's flight, Fo's words and gestures coalesced into the theatrical equivalent of an epic documentary film, a zany montage of images that juxtaposed fact and fantasy with a seamless flow of close-ups, long shots, and dissolves. And as Fo zoomed in on the pope's smile, panned to a long shot of the crowd watching the pontiff fly, and dissolved into skywriting that proclaimed the Polish origins of God, it was my responsibility to provide spoken subtitles for it all, a job that reminded me of the film *Sherlock Junior*, in which Buster Keaton steps into a movie screen and has to learn to survive the jump cuts that keep pulling the scenery out from under him. Like Keaton's bumbling protagonist, I was forced to anticipate and adapt to the ever-shifting viewpoints of a visual imagination that leapt from scene to scene with childlike comic abandon.

This book grew out of my experiences as a translator for Fo and Rame, and in a sense it can be read as another of my attempts to translate their elusive work. This time, though, instead of translating their texts, I have tried to translate the techniques they use to bring those texts to life, techniques that are themselves a form of translation, rendering images, gestures, and words from life, literature, and history into the stage language of epic comedy. Together Fo and Rame have invented a muscular theatrical vernacular that is dense with poetic allusion and political metaphor. They integrate the visual, verbal, and visceral dimensions of performance in a style that may be inspired by medieval and Renaissance theater traditions but owes much of its power to their own unique imaginations and the particular circumstances through which they developed their performance skills. In the introductory prologue that follows, I will discuss the trajectory of the couple's career in the context of an exhibition that Fo and Rame organized as a visual recapitulation of their life together in the theater. The exhibition is the couple's idiosyncratic artistic autobiography, and it provides an overview that lays the groundwork for the book's opening chapter on the origins of Fo's narrative techniques, and for subsequent chapters that analyze the use of those techniques in the couple's performances.

Fo and Rame have created over fifty plays together. Instead of offering an encyclopedic presentation of these works, I have chosen in this book to examine a few crucial plays which exemplify the couple's dynamic method of integrating words, images, and action. Outside Italy, the richness of these plays is often diluted in productions that focus single-mindedly on either the farce or the politics of

Fo's and Rame's work. It is my hope that the observations offered in this book may be of use to actors and directors who wish to stage more fully realized versions of the plays, as well as to general readers who are looking for a more complete appreciation of the multiple layers of meaning in these epic texts.

The performances of Fo and Rame are epic in both the standard and the theatrical usage of the word. They are bigger than life in that they present stories of individuals in the context of larger issues and events, but they are also epic in the sense of the word as it was used by Bertolt Brecht, who championed a non-naturalistic theater that actively engaged the audience's attention by presenting familiar events in a surprising manner (*Verfremdungseffekt*). Fo and Rame often refer to Brecht's ideas, but they understand that epic performances existed long before Brecht's time, and their plays are more directly inspired by the traditions of ancient Greek comedy, medieval theater, and the commedia dell'arte than by theoretical discussions of epic comedy.

Like the traditional comic actors they emulate in their performances, Fo and Rame make the familiar seem strange by highlighting the comic contradictions inherent in the stories they tell. This technique of epic comedy is designed to provoke audiences to thoughtful laughter, laughter that awakens outrage at injustice and indignation over the abuse of power. Fo and Rame unleash the epic dimension of their stories by presenting them from multiple points of view: the tyrant, the victim, the anonymous onlooker, and others. These changing perspectives ask spectators to perform a series of mental double-takes, re-examining events that they had accepted unquestioningly, but that are actually riddled with paradox. Is the pope Superman? Is God Polish? What are the limits of the power of the Catholic Church? Fo and Rame examine events from historical perspectives, political perspectives, religious perspectives, social perspectives, moral perspectives, and ironic perspectives. Their work superimposes all these frames on one another in an epic montage of paradoxical action that sometimes seems anarchic but is in fact the product of an artful comic vision rooted in the deft teamwork of a clown trained in architecture and an actress who was born on the stage.

OPPOSITE: Fo's Tribute to Franca Rame, from the exhibition *The Life and Art of Dario Fo and Franca Rame*, 2000

BORN WITH A PAINTBRUSH

"When I came out of my mother's belly," claims Dario Fo, "the first thing I said was 'Paintbrush!'"[1] To illustrate his natal memory, the Nobel laureate re-creates the event with comic gestures that suggest a baby crawling out of the womb and drawing colors in the air. His body comes alive with an incandescent delight that seems to erase his seventy-three years and render him newborn. Fo's blue eyes widen wildly as he waves an imaginary paintbrush in circles over his head, and his mouth bursts open with a grin so large that it leaves his rabbit-toothed over-bite dangling gleefully in the middle of his ageless rubbery face.

Fo's impromptu re-enactment of his birth takes place in January 2000 as he leads a group of schoolteachers through an exhibition of his artwork that has opened at the Citadella dei Musei in Cagliari on the Italian island of Sardinia. The exhibition traces the theatrical career of Fo and his partner Franca Rame through paintings, photographs, and puppet installations. Although Fo is the winner of the 1997 Nobel Prize for Literature, the volume and variety of his visual output is impressive. "Writing is just a hobby for me," he quips. "My real profession is painting."

The visual complexity of the Fo/Rame exhibition makes it clear that there is truth in his joke. Fo trained as a painter and architect, and his kaleidoscopic display of acrylics, watercolors, tapestries, and pencil sketches reveals the pictorial foundations of his theatrical artistry. The words in Fo's texts are often rooted in visual images with specific historical and political contexts. (For instance, while writing his iconoclastic farce about the "discovery" of America, Fo made drawings of Christopher Columbus and Queen Isabella linked to each other by epic scenes of the slaughter, shipwrecks, and wars they unleashed on the New World.) The playwright's wordplay mirrors the visual dynamics of his graphic art, which in turn reflects his undulating use of gesture on the stage. The shadings of his chiaroscuro paintings are matched by the use of paradox and contradiction in his writing, which parallels the way his vocal tone shifts from a gravelly bass to falsetto when he gives voice to his characters in performance. Realistic details that anchor unexpected flights of fantasy are fundamental to both Fo's drawings and his plays, all of which display a surrealistic slapstick sensibility. The most striking aspect of Fo's artwork is its swirling sense of movement. Angels dance, peasants fly, horses gallop, bacchants revel, and bicycles float through the air. Action is, of course, central to all theater, but few playwrights are as deliberate as Fo in their pursuit of kinetic physicality.

"Sometimes I draw my plays before I write them," he explains, walking through the exhibition with the same restless pulse of perpetual motion that seems to animate the fluid figures in his paintings. "And other

BIBBIA DEI VILLANI

ZIRA 7

LIMONE LERCIO

CANTA LA DUMMANNA
ALLERO ALLERO
QUANNO ARRIVAMMO
ALL'ARTA SPONNA
EN FAZZA ACCA'
CE DICIMM'
"SIMM' ARREVATI
IN PALESTINA,
ALLERO
ALLERO

¡E ROBAMMO!

MADONNA SALVAGGE

UN MATO
TE VEGNE A
LIBERA'

times, when I'm having difficulty with a play, I stop writing, so that I can draw out the action in pictures to solve the problem. It's like a comic book where one frame of movement leads to the next. If the thread of the action gets lost in the words, I use drawings to help me connect one scene to another, and then the words fall into place. Drawing helps, because for me it is almost an animal instinct. I learned to draw before I could speak."

Fo's sketches for his plays resemble a film director's storyboard, but Fo's inspiration comes from his training as a painter, when he studied medieval frescoes based on religious themes. One corner of the exhibition includes drawings from *The Peasants' Bible*, in which Fo paints Bible stories in a narrative sequence from multiple perspectives, mirroring the style of medieval artists who made frame-by-frame depictions of the Creation and the Passion Play. Fo imagines these stories as they might have been told by the medieval *giullari*, itinerant storytellers and satirists who challenged the official Gospels of the Church with tales that grew out of the folk tradition. "These are based on the so-called 'apocryphal' Gospels," says Fo, as he shows the crowd his pagan version of Genesis in which an earth mother suckles a baby on one breast and a cow on the other. "I made these drawings in the style of the medieval *exultet*, painted sheepskin scrolls that were unfurled during Easter to tell the story of Christ's Resurrection as part of springtime fertility rituals." The *exultet*, the apocryphal Gospels, and the religious frescoes all merge in Fo's imagination as elements of medieval popular culture that were transformed into iconoclastic entertainments by the traveling *giullari*. Fo imagines the *giullari* as storytellers who mixed Bible stories with current events like medieval town criers, and he looks to them as role models for his visually-inspired narrative techniques.

Fo is often branded a "political satirist," but the density of his visual and historical reference points demonstrates the inadequacy of that glib label. He does in fact write satirical material with a political dimension, but his texts are also rich with intertwining allusions to religion, history, archaeology, folklore, classical architecture, Renaissance art, ancient mythology, and current events. Engaging his audiences in a multifaceted conversation on all of these subjects, Fo transforms simple stories into dizzying entertainments that function simultaneously as provocative farce, populist history, and pointed social critique. His drawings for *The Peasants' Bible* recall his play *Mistero Buffo*, a 1969 collection of mostly satiric monologues based on religious themes. Both works humanize the stories of Christ and the Madonna while calling attention to the unchecked power of the medieval papacy, the injustices

PAGE 19: Poster for Viareggio Carnival (detail), 1985; OPPOSITE: Drawings from Fo's notebook for *The Peasants' Bible*; THIS PAGE, TOP: Puppets from the exhibition *The Life and Art of Dario Fo and Franca Rame*, 2000; THIS PAGE, BOTTOM: Mannequins from *The Devil with Boobs*, from the exhibition *Fellini and Fo*, Milan, 1999

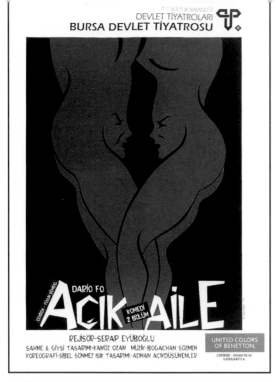

of the feudal system, the pictorial roots of popular entertainment, and the modern moral and political legacy that we have inherited from the Middle Ages. Fo covers all of these themes as he walks his guests through the maze of his collected works. "Medieval times mirror the conflicts, injustices, and problems that we are still living with today," notes Fo, as his listeners gather closer to get a look at the drawings he describes. One depicts Adam and Eve expelled from Paradise by a comically vicious angel. Another presents Mary Magdalene, looking far sexier than she ever did in Sunday school. "She was very popular in the Middle Ages," claims Fo, who has written wryly suggestive passages about Magdalene's carnal relationship to Christ. "Peasants revered her with the same love they had for the Madonna, but the cults in her honor have been ignored by the official Church historians who did not approve of her profession."

The gray, time-worn stone walls of the twelfth-century arsenal that houses the exhibition provide a fitting location for Fo's incursions into forgotten crevices of history, but the medieval era is only one of his stopping points. Fo's artwork and plays also take their themes from ancient Greece, Elizabethan England, Renaissance Europe, and modern times. The winding passageways of the exhibit take visitors to all of these eras, creating a maze of historical memory that overlaps with personal recollections that trace the shifting phases of Fo's and Rame's career.

Near the entrance to the show are a series of self-portraits of the artist. "I painted this one when I was eighteen," chirps Fo, "and there I am at twenty-eight. Over here I'm seventy-three. I just painted that last week. There was an empty space on the wall, so I thought I'd fill it up." The last-minute addition to the exhibition is typical of Fo's restless creative energy: he constantly re-writes his plays during rehearsal and continues making changes long after opening night. Often these alterations respond to current events. Inserting an allegorical reference to a contemporary political crisis is a way for Fo to maintain the vital dialogue between past and present that is a trademark of his work. He resorted to a similar tactic the day before the opening of his exhibition in Cagliari. Noticing that the town's archaeological museum was almost empty of visitors, he decides to stir up interest in Sardinia's past by creating a collage of ancient Sard icons that he cut out of the museum's catalogue. He arranges them in patterns suggested by an archaeological poster borrowed from the window of a local restaurant, then paints a background that links the figures together, creating the illusion that they are re-enacting a sea battle from the island's history. Fo's finished piece is five feet wide by four feet high, and he hung it in the foyer of his exhibition, so that visitors would encounter their own history on their way to viewing his. "This is my contribution to the publicity department of your archaeological museum," quips Fo. "Tomorrow I'll put a caption on it: 'Visit your Sard history museum. It is the least visited museum in the world.'"

Like all of his drawings, Fo's collage of Sard history is part of an evolving narrative. The story he has painted does not begin or end with the battle scene he has constructed to give life to the inanimate icons; he imagines it all as part of a larger epic going back to the mythic times of ancient Greece, when King Minos of Crete is said to have attempted to bring the island of Sardinia under his rule. "Minos asked his court inventor, Daedalus, to fabricate a giant who would stand guard over Sardinia in the king's name," Fo conjectures, weaving a tale that combines the murky history of the island with his own recurring narrative compulsions. "But when the people of Sardinia invited the giant to their feasts and dances, he was so moved by the beauty of their culture that he set them free. Minos then commanded Daedalus to concoct a potion that would make people forget their past, and put it in the drinking water of Sardinia, so that it would be easy to conquer them once they had forgotten where they came from. And still today the young people of this island do not remember their history. Forgetfulness is the world's most dangerous disease."

It is no surprise that the central figure in Fo's parable of cultural memory is an architect, a profession that Fo studied in his youth, acquiring skills he still uses regularly as a designer of his own stage sets. Daedalus, the architect and inventor who constructed the famous labyrinth of King Minos, appears frequently in Fo's work and conversation. Daedalus and the wings he made for his son Icarus are the subjects of one of Fo's monologues, and even when the mythical inventor is not evoked by name, one can see his spirit in many of Fo's paintings and stories, where humans fly through the air with surprising regularity. This recurring visual metaphor is fitting for a playwright whose characters are always struggling to liberate themselves from political or social oppression. "Perhaps all the flying in my drawings comes from a need to be free," muses Fo, "to win the battle against gravity in all senses. That's what an actor is always asked to do, to be light and never give the impression of being fatigued."[2]

An entire area of the exhibit is devoted to another artist/architect who tried to invent a mechanism enabling man to fly—Leonardo da Vinci. Fo painted a series of Leonardo-inspired designs in 1999, when he was asked to give a public lecture in Milan to celebrate the unveiling of the newly restored *Last Supper*. Characteristically, Fo chose to emphasize the movement embodied in Leonardo's play of perspective, using diagrams and arrows in

THIS PAGE AND OPPOSITE: Posters for international performances and a film

schematic reproductions of the painting to explicate Leonardo's technique for luring the spectator into the fresco. "He calculated the perspective points to give the viewer the illusion of floating up to the table as they walked toward the painting," explains Fo, who cheerfully suggests that everyone spend at least one afternoon of their lives walking back and forth in front of Leonardo's work to transform their picture-viewing into an experience of flight.

In Fo's interpretation of history, Leonardo is linked to Daedalus as an ingenious trickster who uses his wits to challenge authority. (One of Fo's Leonardo-inspired drawings is a long cannon called "The Phallus of the King.") Fo's exhibition is full of similarly resourceful tricksters, all of them aspiring in their own way to break free from the constraints of their times. Sometimes the protagonist is named Christopher Columbus or Jesus Christ or Shakespeare or Johan Padan (a fictional fifteenth-century explorer whose picaresque story Fo adapted from the journals of Cabeza de Vaca), but often he appears simply in the archetypal form of Harlequin. The masked trickster of the commedia dell'arte is the prototype for many of Fo's comic heroes, and the exhibition abounds with mannequins dressed in Harlequin's motley colors, performing acrobatics in defiance of the natural laws of gravity and anatomy. Harlequins are everywhere, as if they had broken free from the picture frames or sprung to life from Fo's plays. Puppet Harlequins stand on their heads, soar through the air, and grab the breasts of buxom servant girls. "Every character I have ever played was really Harlequin in disguise," confesses Fo.

One of Fo's Harlequin puppets lies prostrate at the feet of a gorgeous woman. Fo painted the blond beauty on a wooden backdrop as a tribute to Franca Rame, his wife and theatrical collaborator. When Fo first created the life-sized portrait of Rame, he was disappointed that he had not captured the true beauty of her long slender neck, and ended up sawing off the head, gluing in an extra plank, and re-painting his wife in all her swan-necked glory. Fo is possessed by a similar spirit of exuberant devotion as he describes Rame to the crowd of onlookers at the exhibition. "None of the work you see in this room would have been possible without Franca," he states, pointing out the dozens of portraits he has sketched of her over the years. "I painted this one for her seventieth birthday last summer," says Fo, gesturing proudly to a five-foot canvas that hangs majestically from the ceiling. "I imagined her as the personification of the Greek goddess of spring, and the branches full of fruit above her head are from the garden behind our summer house." All of the smaller portraits of Rame are signed with loving dedications, like the one dated 1992: "This is the way you looked when I first met you. You are even more beautiful today."

Fo often asserts that he owes his career to his wife. "Franca is a child of the art form," explains Fo. "Never having had formal training as an actor, I feel fortunate to have learned so much from Franca and her family. Her theatrical heritage was the dowry she brought to our wedding." The extent of Fo's artistic debt to his wife is suggested by an alcove in the exhibition devoted to "*La Famiglia Rame.*" Crumbling posters in faded colors attest to the diversity of her family's skills as the "Foremost Italian Company of Grand Spectacles." Their repertoire included operatic scenes from *Aida* and *Faust*, as well as "The Passion Plays of Jesus," "Mister William on the Gymnastic Trapeze," a "Human Serpent," and "Eccentric Clowns," a roster paralleling that of the Fo/Rame company, which has also included Passion plays, circus acts, stories about the devil, and more than a few eccentric clowns. The eighteenth-century marionettes in the "*Famiglia Rame*" alcove have been passed down through her family for generations, and provide a historical counterpoint to the contemporary puppets scattered through the rest of the exhibition. One of the latter, a modern Harlequin, kneels by the edge of the "*Famiglia Rame*" marionette theater, cradling a portrait of Franca Rame's mother that Fo painted as a tribute to the matriarch of his wife's family.

Having led his audience through a visual retrospective of his career with Rame in the theater, Fo guides them onto a large balcony dominated by a wall-sized tapestry he painted as part of the set for his play about the relationship between Queen Elizabeth and Shakespeare (*Elizabeth: Almost by Chance a Woman*). The group has been on their feet for almost an hour, and Fo senses their weariness. "It would be wonderful if you all had the courage to sit on the floor," he suggests, and suddenly the room is transformed. As they seat themselves the teachers begin whispering with the kind of buzzing anticipation one hears in crowded theaters before a play begins. An instinctively generous showman, Fo can see what the audience wants, and cannot resist giving them a taste of performance. There had been no promise of a show, so part of the crowd's murmuring is an expression of surprise that they are about to witness Fo's theatrical artistry against the backdrop of his graphic artistry.

Fo begins his build-up toward performance mode in soft

unassuming tones. He starts by recalling the controversy that erupted when he won the Nobel Prize. "Many scholars and experts have a fixed idea of what literature should be," says Fo calmly, "and my work does not fit their definition of literature as a text that begins and ends with the writing of a word on the page." Fo's body becomes more animated as he speaks. He mimes the action of writing a word mechanically on a page over and over again, and then stops as if freeing himself from a film loop. "But if you focus only on the word as it exists on the page, you lose the sound of the words, their rhythmic structure, the timing of the phrases, and the pauses between them." Now Fo's body is loose. He lets his limbs flow with the meaning of his phrases, stopping for pauses and sketching the flow of his words in the air with his arms as if he were an orchestra conductor. "These sounds and rhythmic structures of language were key to the works of Shakespeare and Aristophanes and Molière, because they were actors who knew that words were more than something that was written on a page." Fo's discourse on the physicality of language is an improvisation on the themes that he raised in his Nobel Prize acceptance speech in 1997. Framed on the walls around him as he talks are his notes for that speech, their pages full of cartoon-like drawings that praise Shakespeare, Aristophanes, and Molière as the great clowns and *giullari* of their times. As Fo speaks, his body assumes gestures that mirror the Nobel-lecture sketches in the frames behind him, but they also echo other drawings throughout the exhibit that are inspired by theater traditions across the centuries: Fo's architectural rendering of the ancient Greek theater where the plays of Aristophanes were performed; Fo's epic tapestry of Elizabethan intrigue for his play that suggests Hamlet is a transvestite satire of Queen Elizabeth; Fo's sketches for a mise-en-scene of Molière's *Flying Doctor* at the Comédie Française. (Fo was the first foreigner to direct Molière at the venerable French theater.)

As if channeling the energy of the Elizabethan characters on the wall above him, Fo makes his point about the rhythmic power of language by improvising a scene in Shakespearean cadences, loosely based on an episode from *Henry V.* "Imagine that you are soldiers on a battlefield by the sea," says Fo to the schoolteachers, "and you hear the waves crashing as your commander urges you to fight for the honor of your country." Fo then launches into a cascade of heightened prose that ebbs and flows like waves on a stormy beach. He finishes with a long pause and a punch line: "That's Shakespeare." There is no argument, just laughter and applause. Feeding off this enthu-

THIS PAGE, TOP: *Self Portrait*, 1965. Painting appears in the exhibition *The Life and Art of Dario Fo and Franca Rame*, 2000; THIS PAGE, BOTTOM: Fo and Rame in an early farce *The Three Experts*

THIS PAGE: Fo's rendering of an actor in the ancient Greek theater. Painting appears in the exhibition *The Life and Art of Dario Fo and Franca Rame*, 2000; PAGE 30: *Pig in Shit*, drawing from Fo's notebook for *The Peasants' Bible*; PAGE 31: *Adam and Eve*, drawing from Fo's notebook for *The Peasants' Bible*; PAGE 33: A poster from an international production

who speak no French at all will have a great advantage and will have no trouble understanding everything I say."

Fo sets up the story by explaining that it is being told by Scapin, one of Molière's comic servant characters, the French equivalent of Harlequin. Scapin is advising the son of his master on how to conduct himself properly in the world of French aristocracy. After this brief introduction, the words stop and Fo begins his musical montage of sound and gesture. It begins with an eloquent stream of pseudo-French that is clearly meant to warn the young aristocrat about the dangers of wearing long cloaks in the blustery streets of Paris. Fo inflates his cheeks to mimic the wind as he pantomimes the billowing of a huge cloak that carries a hapless aristocrat over the rooftops of Paris. The pinched vowels of Fo's pitch-perfect French grammelot become ever softer as the figure drifts farther and farther away into the distance. In the end there is nothing left but a shrill whisper as the tiny imaginary man crashes to the ground and one of the only real French words of the piece is spoken: "*Foutu!*" ("Screwed!") In just a few minutes of nearly wordless performance, Fo has managed to convey a

siastic appreciation, Fo takes his discourse on language to another level by performing a story in French without using words. "I will use a technique invented by the actors of the commedia dell'arte called 'grammelot,' in which the performer uses only the cadences and ono-matopoeic sounds of a language to make meaning clear. You will hear the illusion of French, but I won't be using real French words. Those of you who speak French and try to make out the words will get confused. But those of you

narrative that reflects class conflict in the reign of Louis the XIV, illuminates an obscure vocal technique of Renaissance popular theater, explores the nature of seventeenth-century French haute couture, and provides a cautionary tale about the puncturing of overblown pomposity. The single spoken word at the story's end is artfully imbued with the power of all the pictures Fo's body has painted in the air, and all the sounds he has orchestrated, to build to the story's simple climax: "*Foutu!*"

SOMETIMES DRAW MY PLAYS BEFORE WRITE THEM," FO EXPLAINS. AND OTHER TIMES, WHEN 'M HAVING DIFFICULTY WITH A PLAY, I TOP WRITING, O THAT I CAN RAW OUT HE ACTION IN ICTURES O SOLVE THE ROBLEM. USE DRAWINGS O HELP ME CONNECT ONE SCENE TO NOTHER, ND THEN THE VORDS FALL NTO PLACE. RAWING HELPS, ECAUSE FOR IE IT IS ALMOST N ANIMAL NSTINCT. LEARNED TO RAW BEFORE COULD SPEAK."

The delighted audience awards Fo a standing ovation. As the teachers file out of the museum, past paintings depicting Fo's visions of centuries past, they need only look up toward the ceiling to be jolted back to the present: an effigy of Pope John Paul II in a white robe floats over their heads, as if offering a benediction to the proceedings that have taken place below. Inspection of the papal figure reveals that it bears the face of Dario Fo, a playful response to the Vatican's labeling his plays blasphemous. The mannequin is a prop from a satire, *The Pope and the Witch*, which featured Rame as the witch and Fo as the pope.

The exhibition is entitled *The Life and Art of Dario Fo and Franca Rame*, but its labyrinth of memories covers more than the careers of two singular theater artists. Fo's drawings provoke reflection on the same social issues that are raised in his plays: abuse of power, economic injustice, the exploitation of religion, the power of faith, the cruelty of prejudice, and the indomitable dignity and ingenuity of the powerless. These themes are invoked in both the past and the present tense, so that the relevance of history to contemporary problems is always evident.

The wider resonance of the exhibition is revealed in the variety of visitors who are attracted to it and the level of their involvement. After most of the school teachers have gone, three of them stay behind to talk with Fo about one of the paintings in the exhibit, a six-foot-high watercolor of a Chinese lion painted by their students at Cagliari's fine arts high school. Fo has included the students' work in his exhibition because it is an enlargement of an acrylic that he himself had painted of a Chinese New Year celebration. When the art students arrive to join their teachers, Fo gives them an impromptu lesson on technique. "You have to add more color and shades to an image when you enlarge it," advises Fo. "Like a composer who transposes a violin solo to a full orchestra. The other instruments need more notes." Fo takes a sponge to the canvas, smearing the colors together in new shadings. "For the plasticity of this line, I should sing a song," says Fo, as he moves the sponge and begins to warble a funny tune inspired by a fifteenth-century poem. Fo handles the sponge with the same ease of movement he displays in performance, making long wavy curves on the canvas that echo the willowy gestures he uses on

stage. "You have to teach your students how to use a sponge," he tells the teachers without lifting his eyes from his work. "When Leonardo da Vinci moved to Milan, the only thing he brought with him was his sponges."

Seeing the subtlety of the results Fo achieves, Francesco Madedou, a teacher at the art academy of Cagliari, promises to institute a course on sponges as soon as possible. "When you first look at these paintings, they seem casually thrown together, as if anyone could have done it," notes Madedou. "But when you watch Fo explain to the students the difference between their version of the lion and his, you realize that there is an incredible amount of discipline and technique behind every line, behind every brush stroke. For example, look at the curve of the lion's thigh. I thought it was just there to delineate the shape of the lion's body, but it is actually an expression of the lion's movement as it twists around itself, showing three parts of the lion's body from different angles. That is the line that brings the lion to life in three dimensions. Without it the whole thing is flat."[3]

The art teacher's observation could be applied with equal truth to Fo's plays, especially when he performs them himself, with an effortlessness that suggests his words have been invented on the spot. In fact the structure of Fo's seemingly casual phrasing is shrewdly designed according to theatrical principles developed over the course of a half century's experience. Directors who cut apparently superfluous lines from his texts often re-insert them when actors discover in rehearsal that the lost words are essential to giving the characters a fully three-dimensional reality.

While the teenage art students and their teachers ponder Fo's lesson, the playwright retires to another alcove to greet the gray-haired rector of the university of Cagliari, who has heard about Fo's interest in Sard history and wants to propose that Fo work with the university on an illustrated history book like the one he has recently created with the students at the academy of fine arts in Ravenna.[4] In Italy the heads of universities have the formal title of "Rector, the Magnificent," so Fo welcomes him by that title and jokingly introduces himself as "Fo, the Stupendous." The rector barely has time to make his proposal

ABBIAMO SCELTO LA

BIBBIA DEI VILLANI

ADAMO

POESIA

STORIA DEI 2 GA

AMOROSI INTORCI

DENTRO

I BACCELLI COME

FAGIOLI

before Fo begins regaling him with stories of the demonstrations the playwright has recently organized with Rame to protest what he calls Italy's "Culture of Forgetfulness." Fo shows the rector a notebook of photographs documenting a week-long demonstration in December of 1999, during which he and Rame gathered hundreds of students aboard a "Train of Memories" to protest the political massacres that have been perpetrated in Italy over the last thirty years. Initially attributed to "left-wing terrorists," the massacres were actually instigated by right-wing extremists and the Mafia, but their victims are now all but forgotten. "Young people in Italy don't know anything about these massacres," laments Fo. The photographs in his notebook show huge banners that he has painted in collaboration with students from art academies all over Italy. Each banner depicts a different massacre, from the bombings in Milan's Piazza Fontana in 1969 to the 1995 murders of the anti-Mafia judges Paolo Borsellino and Giovanni Falcone in Sicily. In Fo's passionate battle against the "Culture of Forgetfulness" painting is a key weapon in memory's defense.

Later that evening, at the exhibition's official opening, Sergio Pernaciano, an official in Italy's railroad worker's union, remarks that "Fo and Rame are part of our country's history. We remember them in Sardinia because Dario was arrested here for saying things in his plays that others were afraid to say."[5] Fo did indeed spend a day in jail in Sardinia in 1983, for refusing to submit to the Italian government's censorship of a play he had written about the revolution in Chile. Pernaciano has recently demonstrated his allegiance to Fo and Rame by arranging to obtain the permits that allowed their "Train of Memories" to stay on the tracks to Rome, even during one of Italy's infamous railroad strikes. "People were shocked," recalls Rame. "It was the only train in the country headed to Rome that day. Everybody wanted to get on. Suddenly the whole country wanted to join our demonstration."[6]

While Rame and Pernaciano talk at the opening reception, Fo sits with a group of disabled children who are displaying their artwork at a table near the door. Rame has devoted extraordinary efforts to set

up a foundation called "The Nobel Committee for the Handicapped," which distributes the money from Fo's Nobel Prize to disabled children throughout Italy. As Fo autographs the numbered lithographs he has put on sale to raise more funds for disabled children, a boy with Down's syndrome begins to laugh hysterically. His outburst disturbs a teacher with the group, who tries to silence him, but Fo stops her. "Joy is a child's greatest gift," he says quietly. "Don't take it away from him."

In another corner of the exhibition hall, Fo's brother Fulvio recalls moments from his sibling's childhood on the shores of Lake Maggiore in Northern Italy. "Dario and I used to put on puppet shows when we were kids," Fulvio reminisces. "Dario would write the scenarios and I helped him build the puppets. I was always amazed by the stories he came up with. Even at home on Sunday mornings when our mother came into the bedroom to ask us all what we dreamed about the night before, Dario's dreams were always spectacular. He had dreams about cowboys and Indians where my sister and I would be part of the story, or pirate adventures where we were part of the crew. Then one day my mother took me to town to see my first movie, and as I was watching it I felt like I had seen it before. After a few minutes I realized that I had heard the story the previous Sunday when Dario told us his dreams. He had put us all into his movie."[7]

The stories Fo borrowed from films as a child set him on the path he still follows today. He continues to concoct fables from a great variety of sources, and to fill them with characters so engaging that audiences continue to recognize themselves in his work even when the action unfolds in another century. Using storytelling techniques gleaned from classical painters and medieval street-singers, Fo creates epic narratives full of pictographic language, onomatopoeic soundscapes, and kinesthetic impulses. The cinematic verve of his stories leads audiences to share his brother's suspicion that Fo has "put us all into his movie," assembling each scene with a swirling palette of colors so artfully designed that one almost believes his contention that he was born waving a paintbrush at the world.

... IN MANY OF FO'S PAINTINGS AND STORIES HUMANS FLY THROUGH THE AIR WITH SURPRISING REGULARITY. "PERHAPS ALL THE FLYING IN MY DRAWINGS COMES FROM A NEED TO BE FREE," MUSES FO, "TO WIN THE BATTLE AGAINST GRAVITY IN ALL SENSES. THAT'S WHAT AN ACTOR IS ALWAYS ASKED TO DO, TO BE LIGHT AND NEVER GIVE THE IMPRESSION OF BEING FATIGUED."

FRIA TEATERN

DEN OMVÄNDA VÄRLDEN
AV
DARIO FO

REGI: CARLO BARSOTTI
GYCKLARE: JÖRGEN LANTZ

ORIGINS:
SMUGGLERS, ART SCHOOL, AND MEDIEVAL MOVING PICTURES

SMUGGLERS ON THE LAKE

Of this I'm sure. Everything begins from where one is born. As for me, I was born in a little village on Lake Maggiore near the Swiss border, a village of smugglers and fishermen who were more or less poachers, two professions which require, in addition to strong doses of courage, a lot of imagination. It is known that those who transgress the law through the use of their imaginations, always save a bit of it to use for bringing pleasure to their intimate friends. That's why, growing up in an environment like that, where every man is a character, where every character is looking for a story to tell, made it possible for me to go into the theater with unusual skills that were, above all, alive, immediate, and true.... Maybe everything in my work doesn't begin there, but I'm sure that I learned from my fellow villagers how to read things in a certain manner. When I arrived in the city (in Lombardy that means Milan) I couldn't help but see things the way smugglers saw them, which is to classify everything in terms of characters and a chorus, in terms of the fabricators of stories (authors) and those who recounted stories (actors), with the addition of taking enormous pleasure in recognizing the grotesque, the inverted, and the irrational. —Dario Fo [1]

Dario Fo's theatrical sensibilities were shaped by the smugglers, glassblowers, and fisherman who told stories in the village of San Giano, in the Northern Italian province of Varese where he was born on March 24, 1926. Inspired by storytellers who used their imaginations to outwit authority, Fo developed the aesthetics of an outlaw. From poachers he learned the rudiments of improvisation, sensing the right moment to seize an opportunity. From glassblowers he learned how to shape raw materials into delicately structured objects of admiration. From fishermen he learned the patient art of give-and-take that informs his instinctive understanding of audiences. "An actor should treat his audience the way a fisherman handles a fish on the line," says Fo who is a master at building rapport with his public. "You have to maintain just the right amount of tension. If you relax too much the line grows slack and you will lose them. If you try to pull them toward you too abruptly you can snap the line and they are lost. The trick is to bring them close to you gradually while keeping them on the hook." [2]

The stories Fo remembers from his childhood mirror the tone of the plays he has written as an adult. They are told from the perspective of outcasts who do not accept the norms of society, and who use their imaginations to satirize convention in a grotesquely comical fashion. "The key to these stories was always paradox, opposition, contrariness," says Fo, in an assessment of the tales he heard in San Giano that could also serve as a characterization of his own work.

These inversions come from a deeply felt refusal to accept the logic of convention, from a rebellion against a simplistic morality that places good on one side and

"Memory... everything begins from there," muses Fo. "Not only for remembering things but for learning the significance, the place, and the time that are inside and behind every word. I'm an actor...for me memory has to enter through the mouth...to listen means to move your lips, your feet, articulate your face, stretch your throat, learn to speak...to become the instrument of your own memory, as if you were looking for a piece of music on a guitar..."

evil always and only on the opposite side. They take great fun in tossing aside the rules of the game that were put in place to affirm the position of people in power: Cain is evil, Abel is good, Goliath is a tyrant, David is a liberating hero . . . Adam is a bumbler, Eve is an intriguing whore . . . etc. Why? Who says so? Who decided it? Where are the witnesses? It could be just the opposite. In fact it surely is just the opposite. And laughter is the liberating entertainment that comes from the discovery that the opposite of what we have been told to believe makes more sense than the old stereotypes . . . that the opposite is more true . . . or at least more believable. And then there is also the great pleasure of de-sanctification, of tearing down the sacrosanct monuments of sacred tradition, everything that the canonical texts have supported, codified, blessed, and glorified.[3]

Fo views the fables of his birthplace as the community's mechanism for coping with the collective memory of tragic events from the past. One of the local stories describes a band of thieves who lead a donkey up a bell tower, tie his tail to the bell, and leave food just beyond his reach. All the villagers come to the town square, believing the clanging of the bells to be a gathering signal, and while they are away from their homes, the thieves steal everything they own. "The story is true to history, except for the part about the donkey," says Fo. "The variation of the donkey was a grotesque key inserted to exorcise through laughter the memory of the fear, the terrible memories of pirate-like barbarities, of ongoing massacres and rapes that were repeated on the shores of the lake for centuries whenever armies passed through in transit."[4]

One fisherman always told stories about people who had lost their minds. Fo believes these tales were rooted in the high incidence of brain damage in the glass-blowing factories, where workers breathed in poisonous amounts of silicon dust and often became deranged. "There was the story about a man who got it into his head that he could fly, or about a guy who went around naked with clothing painted on his skin, the story of another who threw himself from a bridge after burning down his house and hanging all the chickens. They were stories of madness . . . but the madness was just a pretext for talking about the people who were around them: the priest who wanted to bless or exorcise them, the doctor who said it was a matter of sexual depression, all the way up to the mayor, his wife, her lover."[5] Tales like these spoke directly to the concerns of the storyteller's audience. Fo calls them "theatricalizations of events that actually happened, sometimes recently, and were therefore still in everyone's memory."[6]

PAGES 35–36: From performances of *Harlequin*; THIS PAGE, TOP: From a performance of *Harlequin*; THIS PAGE, BOTTOM: Drawings for Fo's notebook for *Harlequin*; PAGES 40–41: "The Hunger of Zanni" in *Mistero Buffo*; PAGE 42: Dario Fo and his mother, photograph appears in the exhibition *The Life and Art of Dario Fo and Franca Rame*, 2000; PAGE 43: Fo's sketch of the spectator with a movie camera in his head; PAGES 44–45: From a performance of *Isabella, Three Sailing Ships, and a Con Man*; PAGE 49: Fo in "Harlequin: The Phallic Exhibitionist"

What struck Fo most powerfully about these fictionalized village chronicles were the ways in which the storytellers would adapt them for the particular audiences to whom they spoke. This is another of the theatrical principles that Fo has incorporated into his work: the direct and indirect integration of the audience into the narrative as a means of forging a connection between the spectators and the stage. "These fishermen were improvising," he says,

it was obvious that they were concerned with adapting the various passages to the world around them. I listened to the same story told ten different times and the skill of the ones who told it depended on their ability to adapt it each time to different situations in current events, including local facts and gossip. . . . They succeeded in incorporating into the story every dimension, every situation from their surroundings, even the physical and psychological climates. If there was a party, if there were bells ringing, if it was raining, they never lost a single detail, even chance occurrences; they never lost sight of a character, even an external one who might serve as a counterpoint to their story. And above all they never lost sight of the importance of those who were present, the listeners. If there was someone who laughed out of place or reacted badly, they would tease him with ironic anger and keep returning to him as a comic scapegoat. The same thing would happen to a spectator with slow reflexes who didn't get a joke, or one who expressed some sarcasm toward the narrator. All of this served to propel the narrative and render it more varied and immediate.[7]

All these remembered techniques are devices that Fo has used throughout his career on the stage.

When Fo observed the storytellers of his village he noticed that not only would they adjust the stories to the response of the audience, they also devised narrative methods that were naturally suited to the environment in which the tale was being spun. "What fascinated me the most and has always stayed with me was the mode, that is to say the technique of their storytelling," says Fo.

For example there was another storyteller who loved to play billiards and did so often. The billiard table was his space, his stage set. At a certain point, with the pretext of a phrase tossed out by one of his opponents, he would stop the game for a moment . . . and begin a story. He would walk around the billiard table, look at the balls, and tell the story at the same time, playing it out in pantomime. The game didn't exist any more, only his story existed. This billiard player was named Bratel. He was tall and thin and he always wore overalls with suspenders. He was imperturbable, scrutinizing the green table cloth and never putting down his cue stick, which while he told the story became a sword, a spear, a staff, a woman, a violin, a musical instrument . . . it was everything.[8]

The theatrical transformations of the billiard cue are similar to the transformations Fo observed when watching fishermen tell stories while cleaning their nets. As a group of fishermen collectively passed around the webbing of the nets, they would tell each other pirate stories and employ parts of the net to represent storm-tossed waves or billowing sails. The undulating arm movements they made as they manipulated the nets became a source for the willowy gestures that characterize Fo's performances onstage.

In Fo's recollections of San Giano, the stories were linked to the particulars of language as well as of space. "I learned the dialect of these storytellers," Fo recalls, "it was an archaic dialect. It was what was spoken by the elderly who would never allow themselves to Italianize the dialect the way people do now. Obviously they knew the idiomatic forms, the metaphors, the actual structure of the language. So that's how I learned the structure of dialect, which is different from speaking the dialect. Above all I learned the structure of a primordial language in its entirety. This structure and this language is what is found in my theatrical monologues today."[9]

The storytellers of Lake Maggiore are part of Fo's theatrical heritage, a source of inspiration that helped to shape his vision of theater as the physical embodiment of memory. "Memory . . . everything begins from there," muses Fo. "Not only for remembering things but for learning the significance, the place, and the time that are inside and behind every word. I'm an actor . . . for me memory has to enter though the mouth . . . to listen means to move your lips, your feet, articulate your face, stretch your throat, learn to speak . . . to become the instrument of your own memory, as if you were looking for a piece of music on a guitar. . . . Then your imagination takes you a step further. It enables you to remember more."[10] Fo sees imagination as an extension of memory, a fictional mechanism for remembering things that might never have happened but are nonetheless essential to telling the story of the past. "There is not only a mechanical truth," says Fo, "there is also a mythical truth that is sometimes more important than the truth of facts and numbers."[11]

Perhaps the most revealing indication of the influence that Fo's memories of his birthplace have had on his art can be seen in the tender precision with which he weaves the story of his childhood, mythologizing his village into a paradise of creative energies. His tales of storytelling fisherman, smugglers, and glassblowers are as picturesque and fantastical as the tales he remembers them telling. Listening to Fo's elaborate accounts of the characters who inhabited San Giano, one suspects that he is shaping his memory of the storytellers as much as that memory has shaped him. The storytellers of San Giano have become characters in a fable told by San Giano's most famous fabulist. The village by the lake is a kingdom of stories, nestled in an imagined landscape of paradox and inversion that seeps into everything Fo writes. "My universe of images is there," Fo insists, "especially when I tell the mountain stories from the province of Gian Petro, or of Icarus, or even the Chinese and Tibetan tiger story with its rivers and immense cave, or of the shouting Medea and her flight on the magic chariot. I have never left the lake, the valleys, and the rivers where I was born and where I heard my first stories."[12]

LEARNING TO THINK VISUALLY

I have had the great fortune to come to the theater by way of an education in art and architecture. I began to study at the Brera art academy when I was fourteen years old. . . . Theater came a long time after that and my view of it was greatly influenced by the cultural perspective of this training. Even today, when I conceive a play, when I write it, I think in terms of "frontal and aerial views," two dimensions that are fundamental in architecture and are often referred to in painting as well. . . . When I write a play, before I think about the text, I think about the physical space, the place where it will be presented, where the actors will find themselves, where the audience will be placed. In the development of a work it is difficult for me to be uncertain or not to know where the entrances and exits will take place. For me, it is important to have a clear idea of the sequence of changing positions, colors, and perspectives of the actors' movements in relation to the objects around them. . . .

I had a passion for the Renaissance, not just in Italy—I studied the great Flemish and French painters as well. I was always attracted to figure drawing. That's where I got my interest in lighting, in designing stage lights and projecting images from the stage to the audience. I draw hundreds of sketches for each of my plays. I make sketches while I write. The sketches help me to establish the foundation of the writing, to move ahead with the development of the work. — Dario Fo[13]

If Fo's narrative instincts were nurtured by the storytellers on the shores of Lake Maggiore, the visual rigor of his theatrical

technique was sharpened in Milan, where he studied painting and architecture at the Brera art academy. One of the reasons Fo's Nobel Prize was so controversial was that traditional experts in literature and theater could never categorize Fo's visual, physical, and architectural approach to writing. "Authors refuse to accept me as an author. Actors refuse to accept me as an actor. The authors say I am an actor who writes. The actors say I am an author who acts. The only ones who accept me are the set designers."[14]

The confusion over Fo's true profession is less a factor of his choice to both act and write than it is a response to the manner in which he conducts both those activities. He acts and writes with the visual sensibilities of a painter and architect, which can be disconcerting to actors and writers who are not accustomed to such an approach. Set designers, on the other hand, embrace Fo as one of their own, because he sees the theater in visual terms that are similar to theirs.

The pictographic precision of Fo's language can easily be missed by those who read his texts without reference to their performance, but in the hands of a physical actor, like Fo himself, the scripts of his plays become architectural blueprints waiting to be realized in three dimensions. Because they are based on visual scenarios that Fo either sketches or imagines before he writes, their language is dense with images. This is particularly true of his monologues, which condense multiple characters, changing landscapes, and epic conflicts into short passages of densely layered text. Encoded in this text are structural clues that the actor can use to develop gestures and movements that create the visual effects Fo imagines as he writes. Fo's deftness in telling stories from multiple perspectives and shifting viewpoints is the theatrical equivalent of cinematic montage. In recounting events as diverse as the resurrection of Lazarus, a medieval riot, or a shipwreck, Fo strings together sequences of changing first-person voices that create the illusion of a documentary film or an eye-witness television news account, complete with fast editing, cross cuts, and shifting camera angles. To modern audiences these effects may seem cinematic, but Fo traces their origins to the techniques used by painters of religious frescoes in the Middle Ages who borrowed the narrative structures of medieval theatrical representations. "I have studied the camera movements of the cinema," Fo acknowledges,

but what I am really trying to create is the effect that was employed by medieval painters of the Mystery processions. When painters tell a story they are outside language. They don't show the perspective of

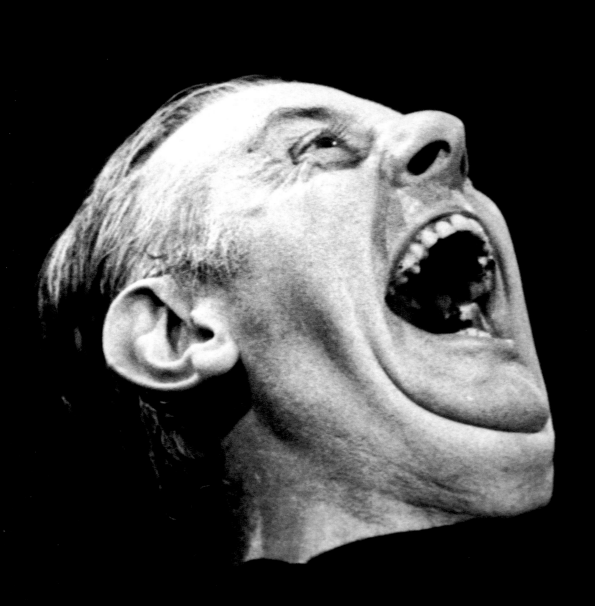

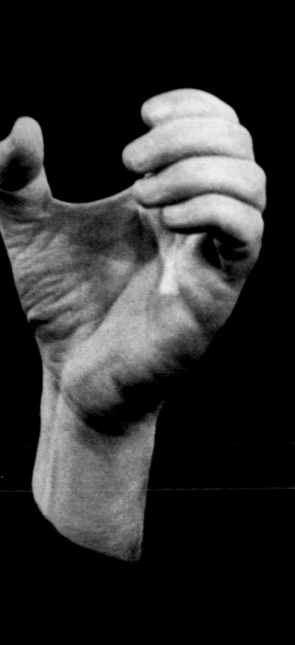

FO'S DEFTNESS IN TELLING STORIES FROM MULTIPLE PERSPECTIVES AND SHIFTING VIEWPOINTS IS THE THEATRICAL EQUIVALENT OF CINEMATIC MONTAGE. IN RECOUNTING EVENTS AS DIVERSE AS THE RESURRECTION OF LAZARUS, A MEDIEVAL RIOT, OR A SHIPWRECK, FO STRINGS TOGETHER SEQUENCES OF CHANGING FIRST-PERSON VOICES THAT CREATE THE ILLUSION OF A DOCUMENTARY FILM OR AN EYEWITNESS TELEVISION-NEWS ACCOUNT, COMPLETE WITH FAST EDITING, CROSS-CUTS, AND SHIFTING CAMERA ANGLES.

Fo's study of architecture at the Brera academy also spurred him to re-examine the churches and monuments built in the villages of his childhood. His research uncovered documents that led him to believe that the artisan builders of the provinces had made innovations that predated the work of famous urban architects who were given credit for the advances. "I discovered that the structural and decorative innovations were brought directly from the Orient by local bricklayers, all from the Como area, who in these centuries worked all over the Mediterranean and beyond, from Sicily to Syria, from Turkey to Persia. So when they came home they incorporated into their work the strange forms from abroad that fascinated them. These bricklayers, in their own home towns, were the first to experiment with the mixed use of diverse materials, stone and bricks of different chromatic values, to create a decorative texture that was very appealing and original."[17]

Constructing an epic story of past injustice to go with the intricately structured masonry, Fo became indignant on the behalf of the anonymous bricklayers who were denied credit for their innovations, and this indignation played a role in his developing sense of outlaw aesthetics. The smugglers of Lake Maggiore had told him stories that celebrated the value of circumventing authority, and now his research into other areas of folk culture was reinforcing his suspicion of official culture. "It was a shock for me," reflects Fo, "to discover this mystification of history. They always had taught us that everything flows from the top down, but on the contrary I was starting to realize that many important inventions and intuitions come from the bottom. When I came to the theater, this 'fixation,' almost an obsession to find the path of ascent rather than descent, has remained at the foundation of my research: if you tell me something, I don't have faith in it until I go out and verify it. And I have been right many times not to have faith."[18]

only one person, they show diverse points of view. In the sacred presentations of the Middle Ages, people would play a variety of scenes from the life of Christ, showing the actions of Jesus, the Madonna, the devils, etc. And when the painters designed their religious frescoes, they re-created mechanically the things that they had seen in the theater of the religious festivals. The painters show the processions as they are seen from different points of view: the same scene from behind, from the front, from a distance. The techniques of cinema were not born with the invention of the camera. They have been used by painters and storytellers for hundreds of years.[15]

At Brera, Fo's immersion in the narrative techniques of medieval painters and performers led to his re-evaluation of the storytelling tradition he had observed in the villages near Lake Maggiore, which he began to see as an oral tradition whose roots were hundreds of years old. "I was born a medieval story teller without knowing it," he marveled. "I didn't know I was talking about things whose origins went back to antiquity, because up until that time I had just listened to the stories and was never interested in investigating their dates."[16]

This principle of creative skepticism would guide Fo throughout his career. Whenever he needed source materials for his plays, he made a point of rejecting official documents, basing his research instead on unofficial sources like oral tradition and folk art. To write *Mistero Buffo* Fo went beyond the Bible to the apocryphal Gospels and medieval folk legends. To write *Accidental Death of an Anarchist* he went to court transcripts that recorded information ignored in the major media's accounts of a scandalous court case involving acts of police brutality. In art school Fo began to see details that others did not notice, weaving them into startling stories that took form in words as well as in pictures.

The connection between techniques used in painting and those used in theater was seminal to Fo's understanding of narrative. He was particularly intrigued by the art of the fresco, because of the speed and dexterity with which the paint had to be applied before it dried. For Fo, the fresco painter's skill was parallel to the nimble wit of a comic actor:

> I work in comic theater and comedy is derived from a mechanical fact. The halting of a phrase, of a speech, done with a certain timing in a certain way, will evoke hilarity. There is no book that can explain these things. If you don't try it you can't come to terms with it. To clarify it, let's take an example from painting. The rapport between a dramatic author and an actor could be the same as the relationship between the designer of sketches and the executor of a tapestry: the invention is credited to the painter who designs the sketch; the one who executes the tapestry has to be a talented artisan, one who knows his profession but nothing more. But everything changes in the case of a fresco. A painter prepares the sketch, but the one who executes the fresco is also in his turn a creator. It will be up to him to imbue the work with style, as is true of a comic actor, who can follow the outline of a play but has to be the author in his turn of the gags that he introduces and executes. [19]

The fresco painter was an appealing role model to Fo because of his quickness. There is an element of improvisation in the speed with which a fresco must be created. It is not the haphazard improvisation of a novice, but the prepared improvisation of a skilled artist who has a grand plan but is flexible enough to adapt to the needs of the situation at hand.

Fo also found this art of prepared improvisation in the works of Pablo Picasso, and believed that actors could learn a lot from that artist about the creative use of accident. Fo lamented the fact that teachers scold children for spilling paints and staining their drawings. In a passage from his book of advice to actors, Fo attributes the following remark to Picasso: "A stain can turn into a moment of invention. A stupid painter is painting, and some paint drips from his brush. A visible stain marks the paper. The stupid painter tears up the paper in desperation and starts over again. On the other hand I, who am, if I can permit myself to say it, a painter of talent, whenever I make a stain, I laugh, I look at it, I turn the paper around and around, and am moved to find a way to exploit the accident with a shout of joy. And from the stain is born my inspiration." Fo then goes on to suggest that teachers help children to learn about art by saying, "Yes, dirty the paper, paint with your hands, with your nose, use all the colors you want, use water, milk, coffee, anything goes. Just let whatever comes out be authentic, alive, and hopefully entertaining and funny." [20] Fo has a similarly raw and sensory approach to performance. His texts are full of onomatopoetic sounds, grunts, squeals, and growls, which seem to be thrown together by accident but have been artfully sculpted into the aural landscape of the story to give it authenticity, life, and humor.

Fo's fascination with Picasso led him to orchestrate a highly theatrical hoax during his art school years. "We announced that Picasso was coming to Milan," Fo recalls, "and scheduled a press conference in Brera where we said he would give advice to the art students. One of the school janitors bore a striking resemblance to Picasso, so we dressed him up in an old overcoat and told him to respond to questions with only gestures, because anyone who heard his Milanese dialect would know immediately that he was not Picasso." [21] Years after this escapade, Fo continued his ironic tribute to Picasso by painting mock imitations of Picasso's work. Hanging in the studio of Fo's apartment in Milan are a series of portraits of his wife, painted in Picasso's style, with a dedication to Franca signed jokingly by Fo with Picasso's name.

"Painting," says Fo, "is a way of thinking concretely. When I have a problem, I paint through it. I'm happy to have been trained in the professions of painting and architecture. They taught me everything I needed to know as a writer, director,

43

FISHERMAN HANDLES A FISH ON THE LINE," AMOUNT OF TENSION. IF YOU RELAX YOU WILL LOSE THEM. IF YOU PULL THEM TOWARD YOU TOO ABRUPTLY YOU CAN SNAP THE LINE AND THEY ARE LOST. THE TRICK IS TO BRING THEM CLOSE TO YOU GRADUALLY WHILE KEEPING THEM ON THE HOOK."

and designer of theater. That training gave me the skills to do everything, in all aspects of the theater, from costume design, set design, and lighting to acting and the use of space on the stage." [22] The fact that Fo had no formal training in acting or play-writing freed him to create a theater of pictographic texts and gestural images that bypasses the traditional rules of realistic drama and resurrects a theater where visual narrative is as important as words. Fo's education in the visual arts dovetailed with the rich gestural tradition of the storytellers he heard as a child on Lake Maggiore, resulting in a narrative style that blends medieval performance traditions with a cinematic sense of visual montage.

HARLEQUIN AND THE MEDIEVAL GIULLARE WITH A MOVIE CAMERA IN HIS HEAD

Montage in the theater is linked to the ability that an actor or director has to use the movie camera that every spectator has unknowingly installed in his brain. This phenomenon is even more astonishing when one realizes that even before the invention of modern cinematographic technology, all talented actors succeeded in utilizing the technique of the movie camera to give sensitive spectators the illusion of close-ups and reaction shots and even long shots with wide-angle panoramas, all before the Lumière brothers were ever born. Therefore it is only as a matter of convenience that in discussing examples of my work I refer to the techniques of cinema and its vocabulary. — Dario Fo [23]

The cinematic complexity of Fo's theater is most fully revealed through the monologues he writes in the style of the medieval storytellers known as *giullari*. The quickly shifting points of view, the overlapping sound effects, the jump cuts, close-ups, long shots, and crowd scenes seem modern in their apparent borrowing of motion-picture technique, but Fo takes the *giullare* as his model, attributing to this medieval entertainer the technical sophistication of a cinematic auteur. It is impossible to understand Fo's approach to theater without examining his self-invention as a modern-day *giullare*. The fact that there is little concrete historical documentation of the *giullare's* performance style frees Fo to create his own vision of the *giullare* as a subversive medieval street performer who became a prototype for Harlequin, a principal character of the Renaissance commedia dell'arte troupes. Fo imagines *giullari* as forefathers to the storytellers he grew up with on the shores of Lake Maggiore. He also believes that they used narrative techniques borrowed from medieval paintings like those he studied at Brera. These speculations on the theatrical methods of the *giullare* are rooted in Fo's idiosyncratic origins as a student of storytelling and visual arts, but he transcends the theoretical aspects of his arguments by testing them out on the stage, where the persuasiveness of his logic is unassailable.

Beginning with the fact that most medieval audiences were illiterate, Fo notes that Bible lore was communicated and passed down through visual pageants and church frescoes that told stories with few words. While the pageants have not survived, many of the religious frescoes have been preserved. These are structured so that events are seen in a frame-by-frame succession, using a style that might be viewed today as a forerunner of the comic strip narrative or the film director's storyboard. Fo believes that medieval *giullari* used these religious frescoes as guides to storytelling technique, employing shifts in gesture and vocal tone to create the narrative illusions that were used by the painters of their times. When Fo wrote his first "*giullarata*" (monologues performed by a *giullare*) he embedded in their language the visual narrative strategies he imagined had been used by the medieval *giullari*. Images, gestures, sound effects, and shifting points of view are all encoded in the texts in a form that is designed to come alive in performance. Onstage Fo was able to achieve the theatrical resurrection of the medieval *giullare* by combining the methods of the storytellers he grew up with on Lake Maggiore with the techniques of the painters he studied in Brera.

Fo's self-invention as a modern-day *giullare* is a triumph of imagined historical narrative that is as ingenious as the stories he tells onstage. According to Fo, the theatrical techniques of the medieval *giullari* were passed down through oral tradition to storytellers like the ones he listened to on Lake Maggiore. Meanwhile, these same narrative techniques, borrowed by the *giullari* from the visual artists of their time, survive in pictorial form in the paintings he studied at Brera as the cornerstones

of Western art. In the end, Fo's leaps of logic are no more fanciful than the speculations of academic historians, and they are rendered more convincing than most historical theories by his skill in bringing them to life onstage. His performances as a modern *giullare* do in fact create the intimacy of a fisherman telling a story by the lake at the same time that they employ the sophisticated visual illusions of perspective and point of view usually associated with paintings. Most surprisingly, Fo achieves all this onstage with a theatrical dexterity that seems entirely natural to a contemporary audience. There is nothing archaic or cobwebbed in his stage presentation. His stories are entertaining to modern audiences who have no knowledge of the historical antecedents of his style. To the general public, Fo's theater is as accessible as watching a movie.

The cinematic fluidity of Fo's theater is no accident. His skill at concocting complex visual narratives is rooted in his training as an architect and painter, while his manipulation of language goes back to the vernacular dialects used by the storytellers he heard on Lake Maggiore. This gives the texts of his monologues both the pictorial density and the conversational quality of screenplays. Though performed by a single actor, they unfold as miniature epics, giving voice to dozens of characters who appear in settings that shift with dizzying velocity. When Fo describes his performance technique, he often resorts to the language of film: "We have a movie camera in our brains," he explains, arguing that even before the invention of the camera, actors always took advantage of that internal mechanism when crafting the visual dimensions of their performances. "It's a question of the mode in which the public is conditioned by the actor to focus on a detail of the action or its totality," says Fo, "using the lenses which we unknowingly possess in our brains."[24]

Fo demonstrates the actor's natural use of "the movie camera in the brain" by analyzing his own performance of a monologue he wrote entitled *The Hunger of the Zanni*. A precursor of Harlequin, the Zanni is a commedia dell'arte character who evolved out of the performances of the medieval *giullare*. The commedia scenarios that survive in written form contain references to bits of comic stage business known as *lazzi*. One of these *lazzi* describes Harlequin as so famished that he resorts to eating a fly. Fo takes this fragment of historical documentation and fleshes it out into a virtuoso performance sketch that depicts the Zanni in such a desperate state of hunger that he cannibalizes his own body and eats himself alive. Fo enacts this horrific medieval comedy with the virtuosity of a master cinematographer. "When I perform The *Hunger of the Zanni*," explains Fo, "I create an ample space around myself to give the spectator a complete view of my body—a body which after a certain point is forgotten when I intentionally rigidify the lower half of it (rendering it uninteresting) and lure the audience into a close-up that brings them to focus only on my face. In fact, my gestures take place within a range of no more than thirty centimeters, without going outside of an imaginary frame . . . so as not to cause the public to lose their concentration."[25] Fo thinks of the space he inhabits onstage in terms of "frames," a concept he brings from his background in painting, and that is equally relevant to his cinematic vision of storytelling. The full-frame body shots that Fo describes occur when the Zanni is eating the parts of his body one by one. Eventually there is nothing left but a mouth chewing. By immobilizing the rest of his body Fo creates the humorously spooky illusion that the disembodied mouth is floating in the void, as if he were a one-man special effects team on a low-budget horror film.

Soundtracks are an important element in Fo's cinematic theater. He creates surprisingly elaborate sound effects using only his voice. After the Zanni awakens from his nightmare of self-cannibalism, the groans of his hunger pains metamorphose into the buzzing of the fly that he tries to eat. The sound of the body's hunger becomes the object of its desire.

> All of a sudden the attention shifts to a close-up, which is my face. The lament becomes acute and is transformed into the sound of a fly, which annoys the Zanni. The Zanni turns from side to side, for which I enlarge the space a little. Then I shrink it again at the moment when he catches the fly, so that the frame is reduced to just the space in front of his nose, with all eyes converging, fixed on the fly. Here the spectators are forced again to limit the focus of their attention down to a micro-frame, within which the fly's wings and feet are plucked off. The progression, naturally calculated, has to be executed with a precision measured in millimeters, and must be done with a sense of rhythm that gives the illusion of space, which if it is too limited will leave the public fatigued and distracted.[26]

Far from generating fatigue and distraction, this meticulously choreographed re-enactment of a fifteenth-century stage direction never fails to fascinate Fo's audience. He has performed it in over a dozen countries, sometimes in theaters of more than a thousand seats, and the public always follows the sequence of close-ups that Fo has engineered, laughing and gasping until the final moment when the Zanni eats the fly as if it were a gourmet meal and declares, "What a feast!" *The Hunger of the Zanni* is one of Fo's signature performance texts. It celebrates the storytelling and narrative painting techniques that enable an actor alone on a stage to rival the effects of cinematic illusion.

Fo's protagonist in "The Hunger of the Zanni" is an ancestor of Harlequin, the wily servant and masked trickster of the Renaissance commedia dell'arte tradition. A variation of this prototypical everyman has been the central figure in most of Fo's plays. "I have been playing Harlequin all my career," says Fo. "It's incredible that I was born with the face of that mask. I put it on and it looks just like me." Fo was associated with the Piccolo Teatro in Milan during the early 1950's when Giorgio Strehler's famous production of Carlo Goldoni's *Harlequin, Servant of Two Masters* was part of the repertory, and he was impressed with the title character's gift for transformation.

Like the *giullare*, who embodies many characters in the course of his storytelling, Harlequin is a master of impersonation. Even when Fo's plays are set in modern times, his characters often possess the protean skills associated with Harlequin. In Fo's contemporary farce, *Accidental Death of an Anarchist*, the protagonist is diagnosed as a "histrio-mani-ac," a compulsive actor of roles, who impersonates policemen, psychiatrists, politicians, and clergymen with farcical abandon. Today Harlequin survives in the popular imagination as an elegant character in a colorful diamond-patterned costume, but when Fo wrote a play called *Harlequin* in 1985 he played the central role in an outfit that was ragged and motley. The diamonds were replaced by more primitive patches in the shape of leaves, to give the impression of a wild man of the forest. "This is what Harlequin looked like before he was castrated,"[27] says Fo. His earthy characterization of the role included a sketch in which Harlequin attempts to hide the grotesquely inflated size of his penis. The enlargement results from his disobeying his master by drinking an entire bottle of a magic love potion, and the story climaxes with a gargantuan comic ejaculation.

The grotesque comedy that Fo finds in the Harlequin tradition is much more than simple buffoonery. Fo attributes a wry subtext to the comic narratives he encounters, as he does to the Rabelaisian stories he heard as a child. According to Fo, the tall tales of the fishermen on Lake Maggiore were rooted in their ongoing struggles against pirates, war, and natural disasters. Likewise, the *giullari* recounted allegories of injustice that mocked the feudal lords and religious hypocrites of their time.

Fo believes that Harlequin too had deeper motives for his slapstick behavior, epitomizing the struggle of the powerless who rely on their wits to survive. "Harlequin and Pulcinella battle against death," muses Fo, "because they are the loftiest of heroes, on the levels of those in ancient Greece. There is a reversal and the character succeeds in becoming immortal by using folly, paradox, and turning situations upside down."[28]

Throughout his career Fo has studied, written about, and embodied so many incarnations of the *giullare* that the boundaries between his identity as a storyteller and the identities of his characters have begun to blur. Most of them possess the traits that Fo attributes to Harlequin and the *giullari*. In Fo's plays Columbus becomes a dreamer and a weaver of fantastic tales; Queen Elizabeth's maidservant (played by Fo in drag) is a devotee of Shakespeare who invents fantastic stories, as if she were a transvestite reincarnation of Lear's fool; and Christ is a spellbinding orator with a sense of humor who blesses the world's first *giullare* with a kiss on the tongue that empowers him to satirize injustice. Fo's eccentric characterizations of historic figures are also influenced by his narrative approach to visual arts. Fo presents Leonardo da Vinci as a subversive satirist, explicating paintings like *The Last Supper* as if they were epic films rather than static artworks. And the life of Saint Francis of Assisi is performed by Fo as if the frescoes of his life painted by Giotto had come to life and run amok.

To fully appreciate the historic, visual, and theatrical dimensions of Fo's work, his texts are best read as blueprints for performance, encoded with information that actors, directors, and designers can use to make them come alive onstage. This is true of all writing for the theater, but in Fo's case the words are so densely packed with visual images, physical gestures, and stage actions that they can be seen as a self-invented form of hieroglyphics. Always visualizing and sometimes actually painting his scenes before he writes them, Fo has developed a pictographic language that seems deceptively simple when read casually but acquires deeper dimensions onstage, or in the imaginations of readers who are prepared to enact each scene in the movie camera of the mind's eye.

Like all the role models who contributed to the origins of his artistry, Fo attempts to engage his audience in active participation. A fisherman telling a story tries to hook his listener. A *giullare* teases the crowd. Harlequin leaps off the stage into the audience. A painter calculates the tricks of perspective on the eye of the beholder. Reinventing these visual and verbal traditions, Fo invites the public to join him in a collaborative investigation of history, fiction, memory, and farce that uses laughter to turn the world upside down and see it fresh. "The audience," says Fo, "is my co-conspirator."[29]

The most representative characters in Fo's repertoire are either directly or indirectly related to the mask of Harlequin, a figure Fo sees as a descendant of the medieval *giullari*. It is fitting that an actor/playwright/painter whose work stands at the intersection of the visual, verbal, and physical arts would gravitate to the mask of a clown as a recurring motif. A clown mask is a three-dimensional sculpture that inspires heightened speech and gestures. It is a source of paradox, revealing human features at the same time that it conceals them, signifying a character who ingeniously commands power from a position of utter powerlessness. The mask of Harlequin is particularly suitable to Fo's professional obsessions and personal history: Harlequin is a master storyteller, outlaw, and smuggler. His protean figure has inspired countless painters, from Tiepolo to Picasso. And his acrobatic performances conjure up the shifting perspectives of a human movie camera. Like Monsieur Jourdain, the Molière character who one day realized that all of his life he had been speaking prose, Fo has come to understand that the sum of his artistic influences has led him to a career in which he has always played variations on the Harlequin role. Although he rarely wears the actual mask of Harlequin, he sees the character as an inexhaustible metaphor for all the stage tricksters he has portrayed and for all the foibles of humanity that inspire their wit. "Research on Harlequin has shaped the arc of my life," reflects Fo. "Harlequin is a mask that represents all of society, with all the vices and maybe all the virtues of being human. But inside this Zanni is above all the voice of our passions: hunger, sex, and the spirit of play."[30]

"Research on Harlequin has shaped the arc of my life," reflects Fo. "Harlequin is a mask that represents all of society, with all the vices and maybe all the virtues of being human. But inside this Zanni is, above all, the voice of our passions: hunger, sex, and the spirit of play."

HARLEQUIN:
THE PHALLIC EXHIBITIONIST

By DARIO FO Translated by RON JENKINS

PROLOGUE Now I would like to present to you a piece that comes from the popular tradition of the French "*Fabliaux*" which was appropriated and re-invented by the actors of the commedia dell'arte. The "*Fabliaux*" are typical examples of medieval theatrical narrative, based on obscene allusions. Obscenity in the Middle Ages, and also in the commedia dell'arte, had a liberating function, although it is known that in other social contexts it was also used as a game with its own ends. Just think of the plays of Cardinal Bibbiena, which are the apotheosis of obscenity and the spirit of the libertine, but which have nothing to do with the tone of the piece I'm about to show you, which carries within it an explicit denunciation of 'phallocracy.' Consider the title: "Harlequin: The Phallic Exhibitionist."

Here's the story. Harlequin has to carry out an order from his master, "Il Magnifico" ("The Magnificent One"). "Il Magnifico" is an ironic name. In fact Harlequin's master possesses none of the splendor of the aristocrats of the Italian court in that era. He is a fallen nobleman, pitiful, pompous, and constipated. "Il Magnifico" is in love with a prostitute who is trying to exploit him as much as possible, relieving him of the few coins he still has. The prostitute sets up a rendezvous: they will see each other at her house and finally make love. But "Il Magnifico" fears that he might not be up for the encounter, and might embarrass himself on the level of sexual potency. So he decides to resort to a sorceress who will prepare him a magic potion that will provide him with vigor and endurance. Harlequin is sent to fetch the flask with the miraculous liquid. The sorceress warns him that if "Il Magnifico" drinks more than a spoonful of the highly concentrated potion he risks having his phallus explode. Harlequin meets with the sorceress, and being as impudent as he is, haggles with her until he succeeds in pay-

ing only half of the price that had been established. With the extra money he goes to a tavern where he buys a few flasks of wine that he guzzles down. He sings, laughs, and in his pickled condition also ends up drinking the contents of the magic flask. He is horrified when he realizes what has happened. He feels a great heat building up in his groin. He notices that something superfluous is growing to extreme proportions in an exaggerated manner, so much so that it can no longer be contained within his trousers. His buttons pop off. His belt bursts open. A few women happen to pass by. Harlequin doesn't know how to conceal his extra hump. He spies the fur of a cat hanging out to dry, and puts it on to hide his "extravagance."

A little girl wants to pet the cat. Harlequin chases her away. An aggressive dog arrives and bites the cat. He throws the cat fur into the distance and the dog runs after it. More women show up. How will he hide his "beast?" Harlequin finds some baby blankets hanging on a line. He wraps them around his "extremity" as if it were a baby. He also finds a bonnet for it, but he doesn't know how to distinguish the front of the child from the back, so he pretends to sing it a lullaby. Some girls come by who, enchanted by what they believe to be a baby, try to lift it up in their arms to cradle it. Harlequin tries desperately to avoid them. The girls are insistent. They grab the child, rocking it from side to side. Harlequin is desperate.

(Dario Fo puts on a primordial Harlequin mask and becomes Harlequin who sings happily and then realizes he has swallowed the potion.)

(Singing, as Harlequin) Oh, what a fine wine this is, so sweet and full-bodied that it tickles my intestines and wiggles its way through my testicles all the way down to my cock-a-doo-

dle-doooooooooooo. (*He turns to the audience.*) That's a seventeenth-century Bergamesque song for drunken soloists.

(*Onomatopoeic sounds*) Testozzeroni... testicolicci. Whatsa matter? That's amore. That's a mucho amore. Mucho macho. O che cojones! (*He realizes that he drank from the wrong flask.*) Oh no. Oh no. The potion. Where is it. I drank it. Uhi. Uhi. Uhi.... I don't feel a thing... ohi... I'm getting bigger. It's busting my belt! Keep still, you rascal. (*He mimes his struggle to stop the tremendous growth of his phallus.*) Ohii. I have a hump under my stomach. (*Onomatopoeic sounds*) How can I hide this uncontrollable rogue. Oh. What's this? The skin of a cat. (*He mimes covering his phallus with the fur of the cat.*) Oh look. What a nice little kitty. I like cats. Meow. Yes I'm crazy about little kitties. Oh, what a good kitty cat. Ohiii. (*He sits on a stool and tries to cross his legs, but the size of his phallic appendage prevents him from doing so.*) That's a big kitty cat! (*Onomatopoeic sounds. He mimes the imaginary arrival of a group of women.*) I'm sorry, ma'am, but you can't touch the cat. You either, little girl. It hasn't been domesticated. No dogs allowed. Get out of here. Out. Out. Out. Ouuuuutttt! (*He mimes fending off the attack of a dog.*) Ahia. Oahia.

Ahiaaaa. Whoa. What a bite. That hurts. That's very painful. Dammit! (*He mimes throwing the cat's fur as far away as possible.*) Baby clothes. Ahoa. Ahoa. (*He mimes grabbing a large baby blanket from a phantom clothesline. He mimes wrapping up the baby and turns toward someone who is approaching.*) His mother's gone away. It's always the father who has to take care of the babies. Babies are always with their father. (*He rocks the baby*). Rock-a-bye, baby.... Here's a little blanket for him too... which side is the front and which is the back? (*He sits on the stool. Same business as above.*) Good evening, madam. This is my baby. Yes... no, no. I don't know if it's a boy or a girl. It's probably a boy. Yes, I'm the father. Yes, I'm the mother too. I don't know if he looks like me. What? I'm not rocking him the right way? Why? How are you supposed to do it? You keep your chest still and move only the baby from side to side.... I guess I'm just too attached to this baby. (*He mimes being assaulted by the women, who insist on taking the little child in their arms.*) Let go. You can't do that. Go away. Iah! Iah! Pfah! Oh boia! Dhiiiiiii. My baby exploded. Castration doesn't feel so bad at all!

CHAPTER 7

MONOLOGUE AS DIALOGUE: FRANCIS, THE HOLY FOOL

A MULTIPLICITY OF CONVERSATIONS

Fo is the theatrical equivalent of a medieval miniaturist. His texts are densely packed with rich details that come alive in performance like an illuminated manuscript leaping off the page. The multi-layered visual and linguistic textures of his writing can be viewed most clearly in his monologues, which are actually constructed as webs of overlapping and interlocking dialogues. Although the texts are written for a single voice, they are designed to launch an actor into a multiplicity of simultaneous conversations. When Fo performs his own monologues he projects an illusion of effortless conviviality that downplays the complexity of his intricately structured entertainments, but he is in fact engaging in a series of provocative dialogues that shift direction with the speed and precision of a virtuoso ventriloquist.

Alone on stage, Fo is first of all talking to his audience, in an interactive conversation that is sculpted into his text. Throughout the first months of performing a new work, he constantly rewrites and revises his monologues in response to the reactions of his audience. Fo believes that "a writer has to have an ear,"[1] and he uses his writer's ear to listen to the places in the text where the audience laughs, sighs, gasps, cries, or coughs in distraction. Space for the audience response is built into the rhythmic structure of the writing, so that when the text is performed there is a natural give-and-take

between the actor and the public. This built-in dialogue is heightened by Fo's occasional improvisations inspired by what happens in the theater at any given moment, but more often than not, the audience's participation is so skillfully and invisibly woven into the monologue that lines that seem to be extemporaneous are actually part of the text and are performed the same way every night, like a musical score in which the audience's part is written into the orchestration.

Embedded in Fo's dialogue with his audience is his dialogue with his wife and primary collaborator, Franca Rame, who uses her instinctive theater skills to help Fo edit and revise all of his texts. In each phase of his writing Fo turns to Rame for criticism and assistance. Their dialogue usually takes place offstage, but in the first performances of a monologue Rame often sits on the edge of the stage, serving as Fo's prompter. When she stops him to correct him or suggest a change, she is playing the role of the ideal audience. At these moments the couple is publicly performing the private dialogue of their collaboration, which has been essential to Fo's writing for nearly half a century.

In addition to establishing an immediate dialogue with the audience, Fo's texts are created with the intention of opening a dialogue with history. Many of his plays are based on historical or contemporary documentation of some kind, and he uses his source material to challenge conventional perceptions of well-known events and personalities. After researching the lives of figures like Christopher Columbus, Queen Elizabeth, and Jesus, Fo re-imagines the past in provocative ways that force the audience to re-evaluate the historical images they have come to accept as fact. This dialogue with history is carried out on many levels at once. The historically based characters to whom Fo gives voice speak in the first person, challenging their own popular images, while Fo as narrator provides commentary that contradicts the commonly accepted view of their place in history. Fo also encourages audience members to initiate their own personal debate with historians, who, he suggests, have censored the past to serve their own ends. In his plays with contemporary settings Fo sets up the same kind of dialogue with current events, using newspapers and interviews as sources and encouraging his audiences to evaluate critically the information they receive from the mass media.

A more subtle dialogue transpires between Fo's texts and the visual sources that have inspired them. Trained as an architect and painter, Fo structures his plays in visual terms, which have a profound effect on his narrative strategies and language. Fo often paints his stories as he writes them, drawing each scene in a notebook that resembles a filmmaker's story-board. These sketches attest to the rich visual texture of his language, which corresponds so closely to his drawings that he uses them as visual note cards when he is memorizing and rewriting a new piece. In the process of creating a new work, Fo shifts back and forth between drawing a scenario and writing out the text, so that as he performs, the words of the play are engaged in an ongoing subliminal dialogue with the pictures on which they are based. Sometimes the images come from historical paintings, sometimes from Fo's own drawings, which are part of a yet another visual dialogue that he sets up between himself and the artists of the past who are his models. Often he starts out by imitating a historical artwork, then manipulating the images according to the story he imagines is concealed in the original. "I paint the things that history leaves out," notes Fo. "It is my own form of art restoration."

The dialogue between Fo's visual sources and the language of his plays is inseparable from the dialogue he sets up between his texts and the bodies of the actors who perform them. Fo's words provide a blueprint for the gestural composition of an actor's performance. Language that is so intimately inspired by visual images inevitably evokes physical responses from a sensitive performer. Ideally an actor's body will animate Fo's language with gestures that illuminate and amplify the visual sources that inspired the words in the first place.

Fo's dialogues with his audiences, his historical sources, his visual models, and his body or the bodies of his actors are so compelling that it is possible to overlook the unusual dialogue he establishes with language itself. Fo stretches the boundaries of what words can express by creating texts full of regional dialects, street slang, and onomatopoeic phrases that he invents as it suits his needs. His language play is taken to extremes in pieces that he calls "grammelot." According to Fo, grammelot is a technique of invented language that the medieval *giullari* used to avoid the censorship of the Church and other authorities who did not want to be satirized in public. Speaking in this language of elaborate gibberish also enabled *giullari* to perform throughout Europe for audiences of any native tongue. Grammelot conveys meaning through rhythmically structured phrasing combined with onomatopoeic sounds, expressive gestures, and a handful of actual words. Although Fo's grammelot cannot be written, it provides a key to his use of language in his more formally structured texts. As is made explicit in his grammelot performances, the musical structure of his language is as important to him as its content. To achieve the sound and rhythm necessary for a desired effect Fo will stretch words, sing words, transform words, and invent entirely new words. The end result is a text that makes fun of its own relationship to language. Fo's ongoing dialogue with words seduces the spectator or reader into entering the text's other interrelated dialogues with a freedom that would not be possible with more formally constricted language. The lush comic poetry of Fo's uninhibited wordplay is the lubricant that enables all the other dialogues embedded in his work to co-exist with such ease.

SAINT FRANCIS AND FO'S DIALOGUE WITH THE AUDIENCE

The full richness of Fo's texts can be most easily appreciated when Fo performs them himself. While the visual, historical, social, and gestural elements that are embedded in his multi-layered scripts are all present or implicit in their written form, Fo's acting can serve as a guide to unearthing them. The biggest pitfall for actors, especially in the United States, is to approach the texts as if they were written for performers in the realistic tradition of Stanislavsky and the Actor's Studio, when in fact they were written to be staged in the epic tradition of Bertolt Brecht and the popular entertainments of the Middle

LINGUAGGIO DEI GIULLARI UMBRO

IO SONÇO LU ÇATTO LUPESCO

USERÒ UN DIALETTO SIMILE LOMBARDESCO

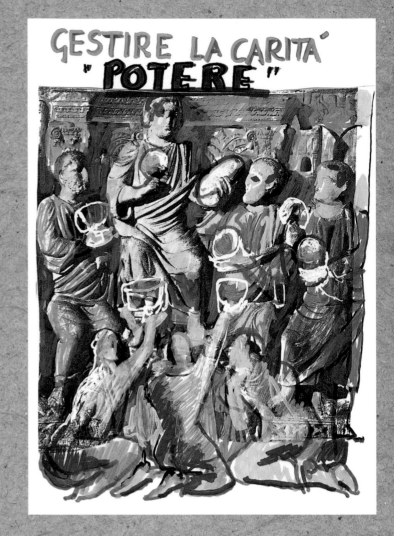

GESTIRE LA CARITÁ "POTERE"

ASSISI

GUBBIO

PERUGIA

TRASIMENO

AREZZO

STANZIANO

SIENA

SOGNO DI INNOCENZO...

COME UN RAGNO OL TEGNE TUTO FERMO

Ages. Readers of the texts can also be deceived by the simplistic label of "political satire," which often accompanies Fo's plays, limiting expectations and inhibiting the provocative associations that the work can evoke when it is encountered without preconceptions. As an antidote to the misconceptions, unfaithful translations, and political controversies that have shaped public opinion of Fo's work for those who have never seen or read it in the original Italian, Fo's performances of his monologues can serve as a theatrical Rosetta stone for decoding the texts as he intended them to be read. Many of those who criticized the awarding of the Nobel Prize to Fo claimed that his virtuosity as an actor had been confused with the value of his writing as literature, without considering that his performance skills might in fact have helped him expand the conventional definition of literature to include a more fully developed relationship with the reader or listener, a relationship that echoes back to the oral literature of the singer-poet Homer at the same time that it looks ahead to the dialogic literary techniques of the contemporary avant-garde.

The world premiere of Fo's monologue about Saint Francis of Assisi provides a key to Fo's theatrical artistry in action. The piece, *Lu Santo Jullare Francesco*, was staged for the first time at the 1999 Festival of Two Worlds in Spoleto, Italy. After giving a free open rehearsal, Fo performed the piece twice for regular audiences on July 8 and 10. These performances were the culmination of several months of writing, drawing, researching, and rehearsing. Fo's process of preparing and presenting his monologue provides insight into his vision of theatrical literature as an art of overlapping dialogues.

The importance of the audience to Fo's process could be seen at many stages, most obviously in his insistence that an open rehearsal be built into the festival's schedule. He wanted to be sure he had the opportunity to test the text in front of an audience and sense their reactions as he shaped the rhythms of the language. Each of the performances in Spoleto was different, because the text was cut and re-edited based on the responses of the previous audience. By the time the last performance was over, the play had a musical shape and structure that seemed to breathe naturally in a give-and-take relationship with the laughter, applause, and silences of the public.

Even before he arrived in Spoleto, Fo demonstrated his allegiance to the audience by listening to Rame read the text aloud as he wrote it. She would come into the drawing-filled studio of their Milan apartment and recite the words of the play

for him scene by scene. It was not a passive reading: Fo would stop her, tell her where to pause, what words to emphasize, like a conductor directing a musician. He was concerned with rhythm, timing, tone, and inflection. In these mini-rehearsals Rame used her long experience with Fo to intuit the music he had written into the text. Fo, meanwhile, became his own audience, listening to Rame as the audience would be listening to him in Spoleto. Rame's expertise at performing the musical score built into the language gave Fo the opportunity to direct himself as if he were performing. While she played the role of Fo, he was free to listen to the text from the perspective of the audience. Using both his ear and the ear of his wife, he changed words to heighten the cadences of the text, thus beginning his dialogue with the public before the public arrived.

This continuing conversation with the public intensified in Spoleto. As Fo performed the text, Rame sat on the edge of the stage prompting him, in effect reversing the roles they had played for each other during the writing process at their home. Now she was the surrogate audience, sensing when he was losing his rhythm and feeding him words at a moment chosen precisely to prod him to pick up his pacing. "Sometimes Dario is just pausing for effect or preparing his next line, and if I prompted him then, it would throw off his rhythm," explains Rame. "I have to wait for an empty pause, and then the prompting helps his momentum." An example occurred at a moment when Rame reminded Fo of the Latin words "*Jogulatores Obloquentes*," a key phrase in Fo's explanation of the attempts made to censor *giullari* by royal decrees in the era of Saint Francis. Fo astutely turned Rame's interruption into an informative aside, explaining that the phrase can be translated as "obstreperous jesters" and that it reflects the scorn with which these performers were viewed by the authorities at a time when Saint Francis provocatively referred to himself as a *giullare*. Fo liked the interruption so much that the next night, when Rame did not prompt him, he went over to the table where she was sitting and asked for her notes, so that he could read the Latin again and repeat the aside. In this way the initially improvised exchange between Fo and Rame became a fixed part of the performance and was included even after Rame had stopped prompting him.

Throughout the evening, of course, Fo was at the same time listening to the reactions of the real audience and adjusting to their signals. The degree of his sensitivity to the public could be ascertained from the timing of his extra-textual improvisations. When he sensed the crowd tiring, he would stop to take a drink of water, then chastise them jokingly for their silence, inviting them to listen to the sound of the water bubbling down his esophagus as it was amplified by his body microphone. The ploy served to focus the audience's attention on the simplicity of an action in the present moment, and renewed their receptivity to the complexities of Saint Francis's story. The teasing also helped to create a sense of intimacy between Fo and the audience, letting them know that he was paying as much attention to them as they were to him.

After each performance Fo's comments indicated the intensity of his attentiveness to the public. The open rehearsal had not been advertised, leading to a sparse attendance that threw off Fo's timing significantly. He complained to the festival representatives that he could not gauge the effectiveness of his text in a half-filled space. The official opening night was sold out, but Fo felt that his usual rapport with the public was inhibited by the presence of the head of the Italian government, Massimo D'Alemo, and his entourage. "It was like performing for an armored tank," quipped Fo after the show, exaggerating his perception of the evening for comic effect. "D'Alemo's bodyguards were all over the place with machine guns. Everybody in the audience who didn't have a gun was looking over their shoulders to see if the person behind them had one. And if they weren't worried about the guns, they were preoccupied with how expensive the tickets were. Even the V.I.P.'s who got complimentary passes were wondering if they would have thought the show was worth a hundred thousand lire if they had had to pay for the ticket themselves." Only after the last performance, when the dynamics between the stage and the audience were smooth, lively, and full of emotion, did Fo feel satisfied. And even then he worried that the public seemed too enthusiastic. "They wanted to applaud all the time," Fo noted. "It would have slowed down the rhythm of the show, so I tried to discourage the clapping whenever I could."

Between shows Fo listened to recordings of the performances, stopping the tape to comment on corrections that he wanted to make for the following evening. Sometimes Rame would listen to the tapes with him in their hotel room, suggesting sections that could be eliminated or changed. "You lost a laugh there," she said after a dead spot on the tape that occurred during a scene in which Francis's fellow monks

distract the guards at the pope's palace by lifting their robes to reveal their buttocks. Fo agreed, and stood up to re-enact the scene, deciding that the gesture of lifting the robes needed to be highlighted with a more visually vivid line in the text. He rewrote the line while re-choreographing the action: stopping next to the bed, he looked over his shoulder and bent down as if mooning the imaginary papal guards. "How would you like to see the two globes of the universe?" he yelled with a grin, delighting in the phrase's bawdy blend of mysticism, astronomy, and slapstick. Franca laughed too, an accurate barometer of the audience's response to the revised scene the following night.

Most of Fo's dialogue with the audience is subliminal. Sometimes he articulates what has transpired between himself and the public in his post-performance discussions with Rame or other collaborators, but more often the results of his conversations with the audience can only be discerned by observing the changes that appear in the text from one evening to the next in the early phases of a new work's creation. The nature of his dialogue with the public is also apparent in the prologues he writes for each of his pieces. Instead of simply launching into a play or monologue, Fo begins by addressing the audience directly, telling them why he has chosen to tell a particular story. In the prologue to *Lu Santo Jullare Francesco*, he confesses that he has spent most of his life misinformed about the character of Saint Francis. He talks of Roberto Rosselini's film *San Francesco, Giullare di Dio,* and of how he had always imagined that it was Rosselini's idea to call Saint Francis a *giullare* when in fact it was Francis who had defined himself in those terms. These personal reminiscences, and references to a popular film, make the audience feel as if they were sitting down with Fo for an intimate after-dinner conversation, an impression Fo strengthens by stopping on occasion to help latecomers find their seats. "Oh, we were waiting for you," he teases. "If you can't find a place, come and sit on the stage. The view's much better from up here."

Fo builds on the intimacy established in the prologue by stopping on occasion to comment on the state of the audience's attentiveness. On the last night in Spoleto he told the crowd that they were much quicker than the opening-night audience, and then he imitated the deftness with which they had laughed at the jokes the others had missed. By the end of the evening there was a palpable bond between Fo and his public, and he cemented it with an epilogue that made reference to the space they had shared for the evening. The Spoleto performances were held in the courtyard of a medieval castle

that had been used until recently as a maximum-security prison. Fo sent the spectators home saying he hoped they would remember not only the magnificent architecture of the castle but also its symbolism as a place where men had treated each other with the kind of cruelty that Saint Francis had worked to eliminate from the world. In this way, Fo extended his ever widening conversation with the audience to include a dialogue with the space they inhabited, the prisoners who had once been incarcerated there, and the saint who had been the subject of his performance. Many of these improvisations would eventually be edited out of the published version of Fo's play, but the presence of a vital two-way exchange between a writer and his public is indelibly etched in Fo's text about Saint Francis. The words that Fo eventually sets down on paper inevitably vibrate with the public responses that first brought them to life onstage.

ST. FRANCIS AND FO'S DIALOGUE WITH HISTORY

It is characteristic of Fo's style that his dialogue with the audience blends seamlessly into his dialogue with history. During the prologue to *Lu Santo Jullare Francesco* Fo takes advantage of his intimate rapport with the public to discuss historical controversies about the life of Saint Francis that might seem overly intellectual in another context. Most significant is his contention that it was Saint Francis himself who referred to his calling as that of a *giullare*, because of his love of paradox and his willingness to use humor and song to communicate ideas during his sermons. This line of argument has a personal resonance for Fo, who, as his Italian audience is well aware, also defines himself as a *giullare*, inspired by the medieval tradition of popular entertainers, satirists, and clowns. Fo presents his initial misconceptions about Francis as a personal confession to the audience: "I considered him the most mythic of saints, a mystic par excellence, a visionary poet, a dreamer with his head in the clouds who traveled around the world detached from everyday realities. But then after I did a little reading and research, especially in the popular tradition, which is often more faithful to the truth than the official sacred texts, I realized I was expressing a conventional and oversimplified view. In truth, Francis was actually an authentic *giullare*."[2]

Luring his audience into a polemical dialogue that pits "official" history against "popular tradition," Fo casually cites his

sources, referring to testimonies written by contemporaries of Saint Francis as well as to a biography by Chiara Frugoni, a historian at the University of Rome. Citing Francis's love of song, Fo imagines the future saint opening his sermons with bawdy popular love-ballads. According to Fo, Francis often used the rhetoric of irony and reversal to make his points. Although none of Francis's sermons have survived, Fo uses contemporary descriptions to imagine what one of them might be like. The speech Fo chooses to reinvent was given in Bologna in 1221, in an attempt to end a war between that city and the neighboring town of Imola. Fo alerts the audience to the fact that he has fabricated the speech using the documentation he was able to collect about Francis's speaking style, so it is clear that his performance is a dialogue between historic facts about a medieval *giullare* and the imagination of a modern-day *giullare*.

When Fo begins to perform his re-creation of Francis's antiwar oration, he uses the classic comic device of pretending to be mistaken about where he is speaking. Fo, as Francis, speaks in the dialect of Naples and asks why everyone in the audience seems to be from Bologna. This is Fo's way of suggesting that Francis used the *giullare's* trick of speaking mixed dialects and "grammelot" to communicate with audiences all over Italy. He then continues the speech by ironically praising the war efforts of the people of Bologna on the behalf of the pope, and denouncing the boredom of a world plagued by peace. The language in the section on war is written with a military bravado that thunders with the rhythms of artillery, cannon fire, and death. The words in the section on peace are sung with the delicate cadences of courtship, picnics, and children's games. Having already been invited by Fo into a dialogue with the historical legacy of Saint Francis, the audience listens to the antiwar speech and is drawn farther into Francis's ironic dialogue with the historical conflicts of his era. At the same time, they cannot help but make connections to the recently ended war between Yugoslavia and NATO, whose humanitarian pretexts were very much on Fo's mind as he wrote his text about Saint Francis. Speaking in the simulated voice of Francis, Fo challenges the medieval papal support of "holy wars," provoking a reconsideration of religion's role in warfare during modern times as well.

Fo's most provocative conceit is to portray Francis as a political revolutionary in a scene that describes his youth in Assisi. Not much is known about Francis's early years, so it is revealing to examine the creative uses Fo makes of his sources as he imagines a formative event in the shaping of

the saint's identity. Frugoni's book on Francis, which was Fo's primary source, contains a few lines about an uprising of working class residents of Assisi against the feudal aristocracy. Fo takes these lines as the premise for a sketch that defines Francis as a champion of the downtrodden, at the same time that it provides the audience with an action-packed episode of comic slapstick.

Frugoni writes that many of Assisi's aristocratic families were murdered or forced to flee to their castles outside the city walls "while their towers and storehouses in Assisi were torn down and set on fire." She wonders whether "the young Francis might have fought on behalf of 'the people' when he was seventeen, learning firsthand—rather than from colored miniatures—about the violence and horror of wounds and mutilations, and seeing the deaths of friends, children, men, and women of his Assisi."[3] Sensing the theatrical possibilities of the historian's speculations, Fo was inspired to write a vivid scene in which Francis participates in the battering of the aristocrats' towers. He heightens the dramatic tension of the episode by conjecturing that Francis's political action would have been opposed by his father, a wealthy merchant who probably depended on the business of aristocrats for his livelihood. During the riot, Fo has Francis volunteer to climb one of the towers as a means of avoiding detection by his father's friends. As part of a group that tries to tear down the structure by pulling on ropes from a nearby bell tower, he loses his footing and ends up dangling in the air on his rope. Fo's farcical fantasy depicts Francis being swung into the bell tower and ending up inside a bell, where he clings to the clapper and becomes a human gong. Rendered slap-happy by the trauma, he is carried home to recuperate, but from that day on he begins seeing angels, talking to animals, and bestowing blessings on all the creatures he meets.

It is typical of Fo that the comic climax of this story coincides with a revolutionary act of defiance. Francis's spiritual awakening is linked to his political awakening, while the zaniness of his experience inside the bell renders his wake-up call unforgettable. There is, of course, no factual basis for believing that Francis was traumatized by a bell, but a close reading of Frugoni's book offers insight into the nature of Fo's imaginative relationship to his historical sources. One of the ways in which Fo makes history palpable is to re-create a past that is alive to the senses. His historical characters live in landscapes full of vivid sights, sounds, smells, and flavors. Frugoni herself has a historian's gift for physical detail, and

describes medieval Assisi as a place where "the violent sounds of the bells drown out the voices and shouts of men marking time in prayer and work."[4] Fo took that simple phrase, "the violent sounds of the bells," and elaborated a comic fantasy that gives physical form to the bells' violent sound at the same time that it defines Francis's character. Although it is based on research, Fo's dialogue with history is more than an intellectual exercise. He draws audiences into an encounter with the past that makes history as tangible to the senses as it is to the mind.

ST. FRANCIS AND FO'S DIALOGUE WITH THE VISUAL ARTS

The sensual immediacy of Fo's language is rooted in his affinity to the visual arts. While researching his plays Fo examines paintings, drawings, and prints as well as verbal documentation. Before he begins writing, or while he is in the process of re-writing, Fo sketches his ideas in drawings so that the text will have a basis in physical form as well as in words. Throughout his creative process Fo is immersed in the visual details of his stories, using his training as an archi-

To lend authenticity to his depiction of Assisi, Fo studied Giotto's famous sequence of frescoes on Francis's life. Fo copied the towers of Assisi from Giotto's designs, but added a significant alteration: while Giotto's towers are still, Fo's are in motion. He paints them falling, in the moment of their destruction by Francis and his fellow revolutionaries. The visual effect suggests the epicenter of an earthquake.... "It's Giotto gone berserk," says Fo.

tect and painter to structure the world of his characters with a designer's precision. "I often draw to clarify my thoughts," explains Fo. "There are certain moments when I'm confused, not about my ideas, but about how to express them. Drawing helps."

The parallels between Fo's writing and painting were apparent in the process through which he created his text on Saint Francis. While he was working on a second draft of the text, struggling to render it in a medieval Umbrian dialect that would approximate the language used by Francis, Fo began to assemble a collage of drawings he had once done on the saint's life. He started with a mural he had painted years before on a wall at his son's home in Umbria, near Assisi. The mural depicted well-known events like Francis's sermon to the birds, and Fo began touching it up, restoring its lines and colors. While he painted in the afternoons, Fo devoted his mornings to studying books of medieval Umbrian prose, and sharpening the syntax of his play. Eventually he had the mural photographed so that he could blow up the images, cut them out, and reassemble them in a new configuration. The collage left lots of space for drawing new images, and he proceeded to paint in the scenes from his play that he had not included in the mural. He was reshaping the pictures in accordance with the way he was re-editing the text.

The central image in Fo's new collage became the scene of Francis swinging from the bell tower as he participated in the uprising against the aristocrats. To lend authenticity to his depiction of Assisi, Fo studied Giotto's famous sequence of frescoes on Francis's life. Fo copied the towers of Assisi from Giotto's designs, but added a significant alteration: while Giotto's towers are still, Fo's are in motion. He paints them falling, in the moment of their destruction by Francis and his fellow revolutionaries. The visual effect suggests the epicenter of an earthquake. The turbulent motion that swirls through the entire collage seems to originate with Francis's act of political defiance. The towers crumble as Francis dan-

gles from a rope, suspended between his earthly obligations and his devotion to heaven. Fo has transformed Giotto's serene and reverential frescoes into a visual manifesto of revolution that seethes with subversive activity in all directions.

"It's Giotto gone berserk," observed Fo as he scanned his finished collage. "The story of Saint Francis has been cleaned up by official historians. This is what was censored out." Seeing his collage as the outline of his play, Fo had chosen to depict the falling of the towers not as an architecturally accurate event, but as a staged disaster. With the eye of a set designer he showed the towers coming apart in neat segments that arc toward the ground. This corresponded to the way he had seen fake buildings fall in the theater, where they are constructed so that they can be destroyed and reconstructed again for the next night's show. Choosing his images selectively from classic paintings, theatrical artifices, historical documents, and his own quirky imagination, Fo assembled a grab bag visual tapestry that one might be tempted to call a postmodern deconstruction of Francis's life were it not for the fact that Fo was applying these techniques to theater long before they came into fashion as academic terms of art criticism. Fo's motivation for creating his visual collage was not theoretical but practical: he designed it as a backdrop for his performance. He gave his image to the stage technicians at the Spoleto Festival, who enlarged it into a seven-meter-high canvas that dominated the stage in the castle courtyard where he performed. Fo's unseen dialogue with his visual sources became evident on stage when he turned to his creation during the performance to point out the details of various episodes to the audience. The scene depicting Francis's death, for instance, was borrowed from a painting by Bosch that satirized the methods of medieval doctors, who tortured their patients more often than they cured them. This was Francis's fate as well.

Before each performance the audience watched Fo touch up his backdrop, adding blood-red paint to the tip of the instrument the doctor is plunging into Francis's eye, or providing a nude portrait of the future saint with realistic genitals, which the technicians had modestly eliminated when they transferred the design to the stage. This visual tinkering occurred at a time when Fo was still tinkering with the language of his text, adding phrases for emphasis, or inserting details in the saint's life that he imagined might have been censored by Church historians.

As Fo performed the story, his quicksilver gestures often echoed the body shapes of the characters behind him on the collage. He had painted figures in moments of action: kneeling, preaching, dancing, fleeing, strutting, reaching, flying, embracing. The language of his narrative captured a parallel range of motion. The words of the story, like the figures in the backdrop, all seemed to be responding to the earthquake of action at the center of Fo's collage.

SAINT FRANCIS AND FO'S DIALOGUE WITH THE ACTOR'S BODY

The most striking element of Fo's painting is its sense of movement. The bodies he draws sometimes seem to defy the laws of gravity and fly through the air, like characters from a canvas by Chagall. Fo sees the world in motion. That is the way he paints it and that is the way he writes about it, driving the action of his texts with language that moves as vibrantly as the bodies in his paintings. The kinetic impulses that fuel Fo's drawings and texts are also intended to animate the bodies of the actors performing his work. Actors discover that if they relax while speaking Fo's texts, the words naturally suggest physical actions that bring the story to life. This dialogue between the actor's body and the language he or she speaks can be vividly observed when Fo performs his own monologues. His supple body give the illusion of being sculpted and re-sculpted by every phrase he utters. Even in his seventies Fo is capable of establishing a dialogue between his body and his words that unfolds with instantaneous precision. His muscles respond with elastic clarity to the language of his texts, as if his synapses made no distinction between words and gesture.

When Fo rehearsed the story of Saint Francis for his Spoleto performances, he sat at a table with Rame surrounded by his drawings of the episodes in the story, which were labeled with key phrases from the text. The drawings of Francis participating in the uprising against the aristocrats were sketched in multiple perspectives, so that he was seen swinging from a rope tied to the outside of the bell tower on the same page in which he was depicted holding onto the clapper inside the bell. As Fo began reciting the text, his hands made tiny gestures that enacted this sequence in miniature. His left index finger twirled like the swinging rope while his right fist tilted back and forth like the bell. "Francis found himself hanging outside the bell tower," muttered Fo, in a muted voice that matched the diminished gestures of his hands but still captured the musical details of the phrase's Italian cadence. "Oh, God, I'm going to get bashed against the Cavrari tower," Fo continued, his hand gestures becoming slightly more frenetic as he shifted from the voice of the narrator to the voice of Francis speaking of the danger in the first person.

A parallel set of physical and vocal transformations occurred when Fo performed the story on stage. Throwing his entire body into the action, Fo pantomimed the story as if he were Francis dangling from the rope, balancing on one leg when the movement intensified. "Francis twisted sideways, kicked the corner of the tower, and barely avoided smashing into it," he narrated with growing alarm, as his body shifted again to give the audience a new visual point of view. Now Fo's upraised arm was making circles over his head to match the carnival imagery of the next line: "he was dancing around the tower as if he were spinning on a carousel."

At this point the cinematic momentum of Fo's gestures had become so compelling that he deviated from his written text and added a new line that created a jump-cut in point of view, as if someone from the crowd below was ironically shouting up to Francis, "Hey, how do you like it up there on the merry-go-round?" It was as if the line had been written by the kinetic force of Fo's body, which was responding to the action-filled images Fo had painted of the story. For the audience the effect was like a split frame in a movie, showing Francis hanging from the rope in a long shot while the camera zooms in for a close-up of a man in the frenzied throng below him. The new line also served to speed up the narrative at a key moment of heightened suspense.

"Around and around on the rope, turning and turning," narrated Fo, his torso enacting Francis's contortions. "Then the carousel started spinning in the opposite direction," he went on, "and the rope got shorter and shorter with every turn." Fo's upraised arm moved in smaller and smaller circles, operating in isolation from his torso as if his body itself had become the split screen and its parts were simultaneously enacting the story from two different points of view. Each physical shift of perspective corresponded to a change in

the text, which gave voice in turn to Francis, the people watching him, and the narrator. "He's going to be crushed," shouted Fo, as the spectator, tilting his head upward to convey the illusion of viewing the action from below. "No," said Fo, as the narrator, creating a tone of contradiction with his voice as his body created a parallel visual surprise by reversing the direction of his gestures. "He slid down the rope and was swung into the arched window of the bell tower where he flew right into the bell itself." At this point Fo tilted from side to side, transforming his entire body into the bell, while his voice enacted a similar metamorphosis. "DONG. DIDONG . . . DORONGDONG." The onomatopoeic sound triggered another visual shift, as Fo crouched in a desperate clinging pose to portray Francis inside the bell. "He grabbed onto the stem of the metal clanger and swung like crazy," said Fo, resuming the neutral pose of the narrator. Now the bell's motion was suggested only by the slow swaying of his head: "DONG. DIDONG . . . DORONGDONG." Finally, relaxing his body, Fo ended the sequence with the verbal equivalent of a camera pulling away to a fade-out. "It was like the festival of the Redemption," he mused, bringing his audience back to the present with an image they had all experienced in their own churches. "Enough bell-ringing to deafen a man born without ears."

By responding physically to the visual cues embedded in his language, Fo gave his audience the impression of having watched a documentary film of Francis's dilemma, complete with changing camera angles and high-speed editing effects. Other actors can accomplish the same illusion by performing actions that match the narrative complexity of the text. When he writes, Fo is speaking to the actor's body. He simply asks that actors listen to his words with their muscles as well as with their minds.

SAINT FRANCIS AND FO'S DIALOGUE WITH LANGUAGE

At the same time that Fo's texts trigger provocative dialogues with his audience, his wife, history, current events, visual arts, and the human body, they are also engaged in a playful relationship with language itself. Using words that are both familiar and strange, Fo teases his public into listening to language with more than ordinary attention. His linguistic approaches differ according to the needs of each piece he writes, but among his strategies are the use of regional dialects, the mixing of dialects to create an imaginary dialect, invented words, onomatopoeic sounds, and musical gibberish. Trained as an architect, Fo takes a

designer's delight in constructing phrases that reshape his listeners' aural landscape.

Fo's most unique and ineffable use of language involves what he calls "grammelot," a rhythmic mélange of verbiage that gives the illusion of being a language without using more than a few actual words. According to Fo, grammelot was used by medieval *giullari* and commedia dell'arte actors to reach out to as wide a public as possible when they performed throughout Europe. It was also useful as a means of avoiding censorship, because it enabled actors to express blasphemous sentiments while claiming afterward that they hadn't really said anything at all, at least not anything that could be repeated or written down.

Fo's account of the first time he used grammelot is typically playful: "When the American soldiers came to Italy during World War II, nobody could understand what they were saying, so I just started making things up whenever I talked to them." Fo re-enacts these meetings with a comical discourse that sounds vaguely like English because of the accent and musical qualities of the phrasing, but contains no recognizable words.

Some of Fo's pieces are performed entirely in grammelot, but sometimes the device is used in a short segment of a more elaborate work. In the part of *Lu Santo Jullare Francesco* where Francis talks to a wolf, Fo uses a modified grammelot to convey the wolf's side of the conversation. The grunts and growls are performed with enough expressiveness to give the audience the illusion that they understand the wolf's intentions, and when Francis urges the creature to speak more clearly, the wolf's inarticulate bellowing evolves into the rudiments of comprehensible speech. "It's a dog's life," the wolf admits, after he has promised Francis to give up his violent ways. In the end it turns out that it is not in the wolf's nature to live with mankind in peaceful domestication, so Francis thanks him for saving his life and advises him to go back to being a wolf. "I was wrong," admits Francis. "Instead of trying to teach animals how to be good creatures, I should have been teaching humans how to be good animals."

As Fo plays with language by giving voice to the wolf's gruffly intelligible speech, he is also altering the language spoken by Francis to give the impression that he is speaking in the forgotten regional dialect of thirteenth-century Umbria. When Francis tries to coax words from the wolf's growling he tells the animal to speak more clearly, but not by using the Italian word "*chiaro*," with its hard "k" sound and its three clearly articulated syllables. He uses "*charro*" instead, a dialect version of the word that slurs the three syllables into two and softens the "k" into "ch." The transformation makes the exchange between Francis and the wolf more intimate than it would be in formal Italian—more like a father trying to get a child to speak its first words. Fo highlights this intimacy by rupturing it with a comic interruption. "Louder" ("*Voce*"), he shouts, in the voice of someone in the crowd that has gathered to watch Francis talk to the wolf, as if it were a performance. The shout, employing the word modern Italian audiences use when they want an actor to speak up, is also an ironic reminder of the fact that the entire dialogue is happening in a theater. Shifting from grammelot to dialect to Italian, Fo plays with frames of history and narrative at the same time that he transcends the language barrier between man and animal.

Fo's use of dialects makes Francis's relationship to the listener or reader more intimate, because a closer attentiveness is required. The fact that he occasionally throws in words that he invents himself to approximate a medieval dialect seduces the audience into still another level of playful readiness; careful attention is required to tell whether he is using a vernacular that is contemporary, historic, or imaginary. Fo's use of these changing language patterns creates the estrangement effect described by Brecht in his definition of epic theater as a form that renders what is familiar into terms that are slightly strange. In this sense Fo is the ideal Brechtian actor, always working to surprise the audience out of their habitual complacency and to intrigue them into an active sense of engagement with what is happening on the stage.

Fo's manipulation of language takes on another level when Francis sings to the wolf in dialect. The song is about a wolf who falls in love with a lamb. In order to make sure the audience will understand the lyrics, Fo has Francis translate them for the wolf before he sings. Freed from the burden of literal

translation, the audience then is able to listen to the free-form way in which Fo heightens the musicality of the language in his song for comic effect. The song becomes an exercise in jazz scatting that ends with the wolf loving the lamb so passionately that he cannot help but devour her.

In performance, the songs, dialects, and grammelot flow easily off the actor's tongue, but the laborious effort that Fo puts into his dialogue with language can be seen when one examines his writing process offstage. For *Lu Santo Jullare Francesco* Fo collected dictionaries and prose collections of thirteenth-century Umbrian dialect. He often spent ten minutes choosing a single word. "*Città*," the Italian word for "city," became the less definitively accented "*cittae.*" When asked why he didn't use another possibility, "*cittade*," Fo replied, "That would sound too self-consciously medieval."

Fo is so deliberate in his attempts to avoid self-conscious literary effects that he sometimes despairs of ever getting the words just right. "This dialect is untranslatable," he laments to Rame after a particularly trying day of rewrites. "Maybe I should just throw this scene away." His wife reassures him in her personal facsimile of medieval Umbrian: "*Cossa disshe, San Franshesco.*" Softening "ch" into "sh," Rame teases her husband as if he had become Saint Francis, using the dialect the way Fo uses it, to make her humor more intimate.

The words come slowly to Fo, but their eccentricities give the language a nonchalant poetic edge that serves the story well. When Francis finally receives official permission from the pope to preach the Gospels he is not just "*ubriaco di gioia*" (drunk with joy) but "*embriaco di jocondia*," a nonexistent phrase that is close enough to Italian to be understood at the same time that its eccentric sound seems to have been born out of the sheer exuberance of the moment it describes. "Droonken with joyestness" might approximate the effect in English.

The longer Fo immersed himself in the medieval

ALTHOUGH THE TEXTS ARE WRITTEN FOR A SINGLE VOICE, THEY ARE DESIGNED TO LAUNCH AN ACTOR INTO A MULTIPLICITY OF SIMULTANEOUS CONVERSATIONS. WHEN FO PERFORMS HIS OWN MONOLOGUES HE PROJECTS AN ILLUSION OF EFFORTLESS CONVIVIALITY THAT DOWNPLAYS THE COMPLEXITY OF HIS INTRICATELY STRUCTURED ENTERTAINMENTS, BUT HE IS IN FACT ENGAGING IN A SERIES OF PROVOCATIVE DIALOGUES THAT SHIFT DIRECTION WITH THE SPEED AND PRECISION OF A VIRTUOSO VENTRILOQUIST.

language of Saint Francis, the more he seemed to enter the medieval world the language evoked. He wrote his text by hand, the old-fashioned way. One evening when he was working in his son's eighteenth-century Umbrian farmhouse, the electricity went out, and Fo continued writing with a candle, scratching out one word at a time like a medieval scribe. When his wife asked why he was writing in the dark, Fo quipped, "It's the rule of the monastery." Later a research assistant arrived to inform him that Francis's antiwar speech in Bologna was given just three days before the city signed a peace treaty with Imola. It was as if a herald had arrived with a news flash from the Middle Ages: Fo incorporated the new information into the text, as evidence that Francis's oration had been persuasive. In Fo's universe language has power. The artfully constructed phrases of a *giullare* can end a war or turn out to be the difference between life and death.

THE GIULLARE IN FLIGHT

In Fo's version of Francis's story the persuasiveness of the saint's preaching is rooted in his virtuosity as a *giullare*. Francis's mastery of language in its most intimate, poetic, and accessible forms gives him the eloquence to communicate with animals as well as men. The saint's famous act of preaching to the birds is transformed by Fo into a poetic ode to freedom, as much a tribute to the art of the *giullare* as it is to the birds he is ostensibly addressing: "Blessed are you birds so close to the Lord that out of love he created you with an exaggerated lightness, fragile but with wings that beat strong enough to lift you into the air to float on the wind. The air of the wind is the creation most close to God, who is as infinite is the air itself. And you blessed birds are launched into the breath of the breezes, the north and west winds that are the breath and spirit of the Lord."

"An exaggerated lightness." The quality Francis attributes to the birds is the same quality that Fo attributes to actors, clowns, and *giullari*: "to be light and never give the impression of being fatigued."[5] When Fo speaks of the lightness of the performer, he is not referring to something that is superficial or easily earned. He is thinking of the *giullari* and clowns who "never give the impression of being fatigued" but are actually exhausted from wrestling with language, history, the visual arts, the human body, and the demands of the audience. At a 1999 conference in Umbria on the art of clowning, which was attended by the American clown and physician Patch Adams, Fo took exception to Adams's notion that someone could simply put on a red nose and call themselves a clown. To Fo, whose conception

of clowning is rooted in the intellectually and acrobatically rigorous art of the medieval *giullare*, Adams's idea was as absurd as putting on a stethoscope and calling oneself a doctor. "A clown can't always be smiling," argued Fo, whose conception of a modern clown mirrors his vision of a medieval *giullare*. "There has to be passion behind the red nose. You have to have anger—anger at the injustice and oppression in the world. And the anger has to be supported by hard work. A clown has to have virtuoso technique, an understanding of the grotesque, and an extraordinary sense of generosity and love of people."[6]

The world already knew that Saint Francis had "an extraordinary sense of generosity and love of people," but the passion and sense of the grotesque were qualities that Fo included in his version of the story to show that the saint was also a human being. And then Fo went a step farther, presenting Francis as "The Holy Fool" ("*Lu Santo Jullare*"), a clown who learned to stand up for his beliefs in social justice by swinging through the air on a rope from an Assisi bell tower. "The greatest clowns," says Fo, "are the ones who know how to walk the high wire and perform double backflips in midair. A clown has to defy the laws of nature. A clown has to fly and make the audience fly with him."

Flight as a metaphor for breaking free from convention is fundamental to all of Fo's work. Propelled by the provocative dialogues inherent in his language, his gestures, his images, his re-invention of the past, and his rapport with the audience, Fo flies in the face of convention every time he writes a new piece or performs an old one. In *Lu Santo Jullare Francesco* he presents Francis as a controversial *giullare* whose shifts of fortune bear an ironic resemblance to those experienced by Fo himself after he received the Nobel Prize and the acclaim that went with it. Francis notices, while speaking to the birds, that the townspeople of Assisi, who pelted him with stones when he began preaching, have gathered in astonishment when they see how successfully he has captivated his feathered listeners. Like a suddenly acclaimed artist who has always aimed high but rarely been taken seriously, he is bemused by the change in the public's attitude. "I guess if you want people to pay attention to you," he remarks, "you have to talk to the birds."

PAGE 67: Drawing of the Holy Crusades, from Fo's notebook for *Francis, The Holy Fool*; PAGE 71: Drawing of St. Francis preaching to the birds, from Fo's notebook for *Francis, The Holy Fool*; PAGES 72–75: From a performance of *Francis, The Holy Fool*, Spoleto, 1999

As Fo performed the story, his quicksilver gestures

ften echoed the body shapes of the characters behind him on the collage: kneeling, preaching, dancing, fleeing, strutting, reaching, flying, embracing. The language of his narrative captured a parallel range of motion.

EXCERPT FROM
FRANCIS, THE HOLY FOOL

From the millennial edition of FRANCIS, THE HOLY FOOL
By DARIO FO Translated by RON JENKINS

(In this scene, Francis joins in a revolt against the aristocrats of Assisi, by helping to tear down the towers in which they store their wealth. This is a monologue in which Fo plays all the characters as well as narrating the story.)

—Pull harder! Pull all together, like this! Come on, that's it! Let go, let go now! Yank it again, it's about to fall…. Watch out! The tower's collapsing. Look out behind you!

—PTUIMB! PTUAMB! Stand clear of the falling rocks and stones! PUM! TUA! PUM! BBBUUU! PTOM! POM! PI!

—*(Mimes that a stone has fallen on his foot)* Ahia! Right on my foot!

—It's down! It's crumbled! Let's get another one!

In this way, on a single morning, they succeeded in knocking down forty towers. Now it was time for the Mangia tower, which was the most formidable of them all: a huge tower that stretched up to the sky. Hurriedly the rebels had started to tie ropes to the top of the tower. Then they went up the stairs

and fastened one cord here, three cords over there, ten on the other side, hundreds and hundreds all around the enormous tower, and they started tugging:

—Ohi! Pull all together! Over here! Now you pull over there! Everyone on the other side let go! Pull, pull with all your weight! *(They struggle. He stops and sighs with disappointment.)* No, it's not moving. It just stands up there like a big erection!

—*(He turns to the members of the public who laugh at the sexual allusion and speaks in his own voice.)* "That's pretty good! You even understand medieval Italian."

(Continues the narrative) A supervisor intervenes:

—We can't pull it down like this because the base is too wide and the tower's too high, so much so that we're pulling the ropes on a vertical line from underneath the spire and we can't get a good enough angle to dislodge it from the ground.

—So what should we do?

—We have to pull it from the side at the same time, transversely. All we need is a bunch of people to go up to the top of the bell tower that's next to Mangia. From there they can throw across about ten cords that we can tie to the big tower. That way we can pull horizontally and vertically at the same time. Understand? All right, who's going up the bell tower?

Francis, and ten other boys, carried a load of hemp up the stairs of the bell tower.

When they reached the highest open arch, they threw the cords to their friends who attached them to the top of the tower they were trying to topple.

To achieve the maximum pulling power Francis and the other young men planted themselves in the open arch with their legs spread apart and their feet pressed against the columns. One of his friends was positioned above him, another below: a tangled knot of legs, columns, feet, and taught ropes.

—Pull on the cords all together! Yank them as hard as you can! You too, down below. Pull! Heave-hoooo... Oih!

Suddenly, without warning, Francis's leg slipped out of the arch... his foot that was pressed against the other column also slipped loose: VROM!

He found himself hurled out of the arch, dangling from his rope, heading like a lightning bolt straight towards the Mangia tower.

—I'm going to smash myself to pieces!

Francis, with a desperate twist of his hips, barely managed to avoid hitting the side of the tower. He kicked the wall as he passed it.

—I'm saved.

Slipping away, still hanging onto the rope, he found himself spinning, rotating around and around the enormous tower.

—Hey, it looks like you're having fun up there on that merry-go-round, aren't you?

With every circle the rope pulled him closer to the tower... it kept getting shorter and shorter.

—Oh, God! I'm going to bash into it again.

Another kick... that sent the merry-go-round spinning in the opposite direction. The rope was unwinding.

—Ehhh! Wider, wider, wider! I'm going back where I came from: to the bell tower, the bells...

VRUHOM! He swung all the way through the arch of the bell tower, and ended up inside the biggest bell! BLUM! He found himself embracing the clanger which was chiming with tremendous thumps against the dome of the bell. BLUM! BLIUM! BLIUM! DON DON!

—My skull is exploding! God, what a brain-banger!

DIN DON! He was reduced to the state of a human bell-clapper! DIN DON! The other bells started chiming as well, ringing out: DIN DON DON DEN DON DIN DON DON...PLAFF!

—My heeeaaad!

When his friends extracted him from the niche, poor Francis was all twisted up. One friend supported his head, while they tried to straighten his legs.

—How are you?

—Fine...

—So now you can go down the stairs by yourself, but watch where you're going, because there are two hundred and fifty steps... so be careful.

He started to descend the stairs, going down slowly, and he tripped: TON TON TON DIN DI TON TON! (*He mimes the tumbling fall*) TROTOTOTON... SLAFF!

He rolled all the way down to the bottom where he was found all twisted up like a ball of rags. They lifted him up and tried to untangle him. One leg was knotted around his neck, another was under his elbow. An arm was dislocated behind his back.

—Give it a yank!

—No, that leg is mine!

In the end they put him back together and got him on his feet. They tried to make him move but he was too stiff. They decided that four of them would lift him up onto their shoulders so that they could carry him home.

That was how his mother saw him:

—Ohooo... my son is deeeaaad! Ihiiiiiiii!

—Mamma... don't shout... twelve bells are throwing a party in my head!

FRANCA RAME:
A HALF CENTURY OF COLLABORATION

FRANCA RAME: *I was born into a family of actors who also were born into a family of actors and puppeteers going back to the seventeenth century, so my relationship to the commedia dell'arte is in my DNA. . . . This is a profession that I would not have chosen and that I do not love. I would have preferred to do anything else in life but this. People laugh. They don't believe me. But it's true. . . . I might have ended up as a union organizer, or maybe I would have become the president of the Republic. That would have made me happy, anything but an actress. But what good does this work do for me? Why did I continue even after I realized it didn't interest me? Because through my work I can advance the causes that I believe in. So when people ask me, "What do you do when you prepare a theatrical text for the stage, for a debut? How do you rehearse?" I would love to give them exceptional responses that could be carved in marble. But the only thing that occurs to me to say is that I memorize the words and then I go onstage. . . . This is my profession. I don't romanticize my methods of working. Now you know everything. That's it.*

DARIO FO: [interrupting] *Can I say something? Everything you have just heard is completely false. It's true that Franca was born into a company of commedia dell'arte actors, and it's true that if she had been born into another family she probably would not have chosen to be an actress, but I have to say that being an actress has become her life, and she is not only an actress of great professional-*

ism, but also (and here you have to give me some credit for knowing a little bit about the theater) Franca is a phenomenon inside the world of theater. She has mastered the techniques of improvisation in a way that no one I have ever met in my life has ever done. It comes naturally to her. She has a tremendous presence, a natural power. But she never performs anything without understanding what she is doing . . . it is her habit to study the process and development of everything that she brings to the stage, by examining and reconstructing a text each time she performs it. Every time she prepares a performance, even for a text she has acted two thousand times, I always see her there studying, putting things in order, re-arranging them, inserting new lines that fit the place and time in which she is performing. . . . That text that you heard Franca perform yesterday [Sex? Don't Mind if I Do!], and that we put down on paper three years ago, underwent such an enormous transformation from the time we developed it six years ago, that when we edited it for publication we had to take the original text and throw it away, because she had changed it so much in the course of the various situations in which she had performed it. This is a sign of her scientific knowledge of the developmental process in theater. The improvisations that Franca performs are something that can only be done with the highest level of knowledge. She didn't tell you that when she was a little girl, in her company was her uncle, whom I knew, and that if they decided to put on a new work, they had in their repertory some-

thing like forty plays and that they could play a different one every night...

FRANCA: *Two or three hundred plays.*

DARIO: *Two hundred, and if they decided because of current events or because of a particular situation to change the program on any given night, they would meet together a half hour before they were scheduled to go onstage and decide amongst themselves: "You play Lucia." "You play the daughter of the Duke." "You play the policeman," etc. And then they would go onstage. So just imagine what kind of memories they had to hold all of those dialogues in their heads.*

What they remembered were the situations. The theater of situations was completely different from the official theater that is normally performed on the stage. . . . They had this extraordinary skill, they had a truly geometric structural understanding of certain phrases, and these phrases would be performed at the moment when they needed to change a situation. They had gestures that they used to indicate to the other actors the transition from one mode of acting to another. They also had prompters. They prompted one another without the audience realizing it. I have found that when I am onstage with Franca, and it happens that I lose track of a line and substitute another in its place, cutting out an enormous portion of the text, sometimes even a half hour of the text, and I wonder how I am going to recover, Franca always finds an effortless solution, inventing a line that becomes a cue to bring us back to the earlier text. This is not just professionalism, this is the result of a mental structure that comes from an entirely different way of conceiving theater. . . . Franca may not love this work, but I tell you that I would be happy to find lots more people in the theater who don't love the theater like Franca.

FRANCA: *I have to say that this old boy of mine loves me very much, because it is true that I have a sense of professionalism...*

DARIO: *A talent.*
I'm not interested in professionalism.

FRANCA: *Whatever. I have that quality, because it doesn't cost me anything and it comes naturally. But I should tell you that when I first met this boy Fo he was very attached to the text, and he followed the lines very closely. . . . When I am acting I am divided into three people. One who thinks about her own affairs and pays attention to what she is saying. At the same time I am watching the lighting and the sound system. Then at the same time I pay attention to the timing of the person onstage with me, and when it is Dario we have a set of signals that we use.*

DARIO: *That comes from her profession.*

FRANCA: *So if Dario gets carried away, there is a precise signal that refers to the diaphragm, which means take it easy, you're too loud. Or there's another to tell him to cut the text shorter [she demonstrates by squeezing her fist]. Or if the sound system isn't picking up the voice well enough you hit the microphone. Or you tap the microphone during a moment of applause to tell the technician that the second lighting instrument on the right has gone out. But let's go back to when Dario was very precise. He wrote a text and then he respected it. I, when I was acting, would think about other things. In 1962 I had a terrible memory lapse. I didn't know who I was, or what play I was acting in, or where I was. I only knew that it all had something to do with a wedding. I was talking about a wedding and I had Dario in front of me and the public was out there, in a theater in Milan, and I had just said something about a wedding. So I began to talk about this wedding and that wedding and the people at our wedding. And Dario was getting pale, truly turning white and sweating, and in the wings the stage manager was giving me a sign to ask "Should I close the curtain?," but I just kept talking and talking and finally I recovered. . . .*

"IT IS NOT THE AMOUNT OF LAUGHTER THAT INTERESTS ME," REFLECTS FRANCA, "IT IS THE QUALITY OF THE LAUGHTER. I AGREE WITH MOLIÈRE, WHO SAID THAT LAUGHTER SHOULD OPEN THE MIND OF THE AUDIENCE SO THAT THE NAILS OF REASON CAN BE HAMMERED IN. I WANT THE AUDIENCE TO GO HOME THINKING, SO I ALWAYS TELL THEM I HOPE THEY LEAVE THE THEATER WITH THEIR HEADS FULL OF NAILS."

Everyone breathed a sigh of relief and the play ended. Dario in that moment discovered what it was to improvise, and I have to say that from that day on he has never stopped.[1]

Franca Rame made her stage debut when she was eight days old, carried onto the stage in the arms of her mother as the infant child in a melodrama called *Genoveffa and the Pirates.* "I didn't have much to say that night,"[2] quips Rame, who soon graduated to playing the baby Jesus and eventually went on to the roles of Juliet and Desdemona in her family's populist adaptations of Shakespeare.

La Famiglia Rame, as her family's troupe was called, had toured throughout Italy for generations, preserving an oral tradition of theatrical expertise that could be traced back to the actors of the commedia dell'arte. Rame credits her family for giving her an instinctive understanding of theatrical dynamics. "I have this radar that lets me see everything that is happening on and off the stage, not just the things that are connected to the role I'm playing. It's a gift that I received in the belly of my mother. That is the tradition of our family."[3]

Fo and Rame met in 1951, when they were working together in a theatrical revue in Milan. When they married, in 1954, Fo said that her family's stage techniques were the dowry she brought to their wedding. Rame's skills in dramaturgy and stagecraft

have been essential to the shaping of his work ever since. When Fo won the Nobel Prize he called her and said "Hello, Mrs. Nobel. We won it together. It's a Nobel for two."[4]

Rame's contributions to Fo's texts go far beyond the simple role of editor and nursemaid often assumed by wives of famous writers. The texts "were written with Franca, not for

CANZONISSIMA
una sfida aperta con i censori
ve la descrivo io su
SETTIMANA RADIO
TV
l'unico giornale che dice la verità sul mondo della TV

Supplemento al N. 46 di Settimana Radio TV

THIS PAGE, TOP: Magazine cover story about the censorship of Fo and Rame's television show, *Canzonissima*, 1962; **THIS PAGE, BOTTOM:** Threatening letter received by Fo and Rame from "a group of Sicilian workers" after a controversial television broadcast of *Canzonissima*; **OPPOSITE, TOP AND MIDDLE:** Newspaper cartoons about *Canzonissima*; **OPPOSITE, BOTTOM:** Newspaper headline about the censorship of *Canzonissima*, 1962

Franca," explains Fo. "As a critic, she has a great theatrical ear. It is a result of her having actually been born onstage, almost physically, and having breathed in unconsciously all aspects of theatrical representation."[5] Rame has a wide-ranging theatrical intelligence that has made her a full partner and collaborator in all of Fo's works. "Night after night," says Fo, explaining how the couple revises their texts during the runs of their performances, "Franca, paying attention to the responses of the audience, which is always our most important collaborator, alters the rhythms and structures of the phrases, quickens some passages, adds or cuts lines, etc. Then after a few months the text is completely transformed in respect to what it was originally."[6]

The instincts that enable Rame successfully to perform such intricate surgery on Fo's plays were inherited from her family. *La Famiglia Rame* relied on improvisational techniques much like those employed by the actors of the commedia dell'arte during the Renaissance. Like all the Harlequins, Pierrots, and Columbinas before them, *La Famiglia Rame* went onstage with a knowledge of the basic scenario they would perform, but they were constantly inventing variations on those scenarios according to the demands of the situation. From her family, Rame learned to see theater as a living organism, born of interaction between the actors, the audience, and their shared circumstances. She developed a mastery of timing and stage rhythms that can only come with years of experience. "My family knew the secret of synthesis," recalls Rame. "They cut their dialogue down to only what was essential. They also made sure that the audience understood what they were saying by using the vernacular dialect of everyday speech."[7]

The popular theater techniques that Rame's family used to build a relationship with their audience are still fundamental to her approach to theater. The contributions she makes to Fo's work have helped him connect more directly to the audience. Where Fo sometimes has a tendency to elaborate passages with more detail than an audience can absorb, Rame's skill at synthesizing his texts helps keep the audience focused. ("Dario is very generous to the audience" is Rame's diplomatic assessment of her husband's tendencies.[8]) She also has a keen ear for the kind of language that will be clear and accessible to an audience, and Fo relies heavily on her advice in word choice and phrasing. Fo also credits Rame with teaching him how to improvise. "The function of improvisation is the most important lesson I've learned about my craft from Franca."[9]

The kind of improvisation Rame advocates is not a digression but a way of personalizing the text and creating intimacy with audiences by making them feel that the performer is responding to the specific circumstances of time and place in which the play is happening. During a 1999 performance of *Sex? Don't Mind if I Do!* Rame discussed the causes of male impotence, citing excessive intelligence as a contributing factor. "I feel sorry for women who are married to Nobel Prize winners," she joked, following the text she and Fo had written before he won the prize. Fo, who was in the audience, left the room in mock embarrassment. "He's only kidding," improvised Franca. "Dario has a very active sex life . . . outside the house!"[10]

Rame's improvisation created a bond of camaraderie with the audience. She had let them know that she wasn't adhering rigidly to a memorized text but was responding to the life of the room in which she was performing. The audience felt included in her performance, and its members would occasionally express that closeness by talking back to her from their chairs. "You are my nourishment," she told the audience. "When I die I want them to write on my tombstone, 'She made us laugh.'" "Don't die, Franca," wailed a girl in the crowd.[11]

Rame's skill for connecting immediately to the concerns of the audience can be traced back to the techniques of her family. "My uncles would research the history of every town we performed in," recalls Rame. "That way they could incorporate local references into their improvisations during the show or in the prologues when they introduced the plays."[12]

Rame structures her monologue, *Sex?*, as a combination confessional and counseling session, recounting stories about her own experiences as a wife, mother, and grandmother that she hopes will inform her audience as well as entertain them. "It is not the amount of laughter that interests me," reflects Franca, "it is the quality of the laughter. I agree with Molière, who said that laughter should open the mind of the audience so that the nails of reason can be hammered in. I want the audience to go home thinking, so I always tell them I hope they leave the theater with their head full of nails."[13]

Once audiences have had a chance to think about the subjects of Rame's performances, they often come back to talk to her about them in person. "For years," says Rame, "I've toured the world with shows on the conditions of women: exploitation in the workplace, sexual exploitation, the family, problems with children, betrayal . . . constricting marriages, open marriages . . . her getting old and knowing it . . . him getting old and not

knowing it! And as the years went by, my dressing room slowly turned into a therapist's office. I'm like a magnet: men, women, young people, very young people, come to me with their problems, ask me advice, write me letters. They tell me stories they wouldn't tell in the confession booth at church."[14]

Sex? draws in its audience with an engaging tapestry of personal stories, comic fables, medical information, historical anecdotes, and politically charged current events. Rame wrote the text in collaboration with Fo, and his influence can be seen in the visual elements of her performance. The monologue was originally performed in front of a huge canvas backdrop painted by Fo to represent a mythical Garden of Eden with a fantastical display of phallic candles. Rame's delicate gestures bring her stories to life with a comic eroticism that is never crude—at times, in fact, it is almost childlike in its innocence. Describing her first encounter with the male sex organ Rame draws a phallus in the air that recalls the graffiti she had seen on walls as a child. "I was looking at it without understanding," she explains, while drawing two circles in the air under the phallus. "It looked to me like some kind of deep sea diving

suit with a helmet . . . with two wheels underneath. And I asked myself, 'What kind of bicycle is that?'"[15]

Rame's words and gestures fill the stage with images that evoke all dimensions of sexuality, from Eve's enraptured description of lovemaking with Adam to the politics of rape. She tells the story of her embarrassment as a young student nurse assisting a doctor with the insertion of a catheter into a male teenage patient's penis. (The doctor transferred her to the pediatric ward, so she could "get used to them gradually."[16]) Rame also describes her prudish mother, who never acknowledged the existence of her daughter's private parts, refusing even to give them a name. ("The behind she called 'the rear end,' and what was in front she called 'the rear end in the front.'"[17]) The comic climax of the play is a re-enactment of an aerobics-like class in which the teacher is giving lessons to a gymnasium full of women on how to fake an orgasm. In a delirious montage of pantomimed embraces, exaggerated sighs, and rhythmic moaning, Rame plays the part of the teacher, her students, and their imaginary partners, giving audiences the impression of watching an American self-help clinic gone crazy. (Rame swears to have seen it all on a U.S. videotape.)

WHEN FO WON THE NOBEL PRIZE HE CALLED RAME AND SAID "HELLO, MRS. NOBEL. WE WON IT TOGETHER. IT'S A NOBEL FOR TWO."

PRIMARIA COMPAGNIA ITALIANA
DI GRANDI SPETTACOLI MARIONETTISTICI

FAMIGLIA RAME

PROGRAMMA

OPERE

APPOSITA RIDUZIONE

Roberto il Diavolo - Loengrin - Favorita -
Traviata - Trovatore - Ernani - Rigoletto -
Lucia - Forza del Destino - Norma -
Ballo in Maschera - Sonambula -
Barbiere di Siviglia - Otello - Faust - ecc.

Spettacoli Popolari

Guerino Meschino - Giovanna D'arco
Figli di Nessuno - Solferino e S. Martino
Diluvio Universale - Promessi Sposi
Fornaretto di Venezia - Giro del Mondo
- Genoveffa - Napoleone -
Conte di Monte Cristo - I Piombi -
Maino della Spinetta - Gasparoni
Mastrilli - Musolino ecc.

Apparati Elettrici - Gran messa in scena -
estiario apposito - Balli e riviste - Commedie buffe
- Farse giocate da Gianduia e Sandrone

NRIM MERAVIGLIE & C. MILANO

Audience responses continue to be lively during the orgasm section of the play. When Rame informs the public that they can check to see whether their partner is really having an orgasm by looking for enlarged pupils and curled toes, someone shouts out that he can't see those body parts. "Why not? Do you make love wearing socks and an umbrella?," asks Franca. "Take them off and make yourself comfortable."[18]

From bemused innocence to jaded fakery, Rame's theatrical survey of sexual identity epitomizes the epic style of physical comedy that she and Fo have perfected over their half century together on the stage. The final segment of the performance, however, takes her into theatrical territory that is markedly different from anything attempted by Fo. It is a brutally dramatic monologue about a rape, told from the first-person perspective of the woman experiencing the assault. Unlike Fo, who possesses a comic genius that is rooted in tragedy but does not play tragic roles, Rame can shift swiftly from comedy to heartwrenching characterizations of genuine emotional depth. Sitting in a chair, almost motionless, never raising her voice, Rame takes the audience into the mind of a woman whose body is under siege. The virtuosity of the piece is in its understatement. Rame employs her family's principles of dramatic synthesis with surprising restraint. Her minimalist approach leaves the audience shattered. People have fainted during the performance. And though Rame never mentions it onstage, a good portion of the audience is aware that she is performing a true account of her own experience.[19]

In 1973 Rame was kidnapped outside her home by right-wing political terrorists who raped her in a van and left her bruised and bloodied on the street. The attack was intended as punishment for the outspoken left-wing political views that infused the satirical theater she performed with her husband. Rame's courageous performance of the rape monologue is a powerful statement of a woman's refusal to submit to the victimization of sexual violence, at the same time that it is an act of defiance in the face of political intimidation. The pathetic bestiality of her assailants is revealed by the simple dignity with which she portrays their crime.

In her office in Milan, Rame explains the circumstances surrounding her kidnapping with remarkable calm. She re-

PAGE 84: Drawings from Fo's notes for his Nobel Prize acceptance speech; THIS PAGE AND OPPOSITE: From a performance of *Elizabeth: Almost by Chance a Woman*

enacts the event as she narrates. "I walked out of the house and turned the corner," says Rame, turning the corner around her desk. "Then I felt something in my back." Rame sticks her finger into her own back

A gun, a finger, a piece of wood. I don't know what it was. I was right across the street from the headquarters of the Christian Democrat Party, where there were police in front of the door who didn't do anything to help me....

Being investigated by the police was worse than being raped. They spread the story that I had made up the whole thing. That I had cut myself with razors. It had taken me days to go to them. The day I came home I was a sperm factory, but I was too embarrassed to tell anyone, not even my husband.

Twenty-five years later it comes out in the newspapers that in the midst of another trial there were five pages of testimony in which one of the subjects said he had been with Christian Democrat Party leaders who had ordered the kidnapping. He said when they heard about it, they made a toast to celebrate.

Dario wrote a letter to the president of the Republic. Two weeks went by with no answer, and then we had dinner with a

urged the women to focus on communicating the truth of the event through the clarity of their movement. At the beginning of the monologue the character describes a knee being pressed against her back by a man holding her down. Rame stops the actress at that point and advises her to "take it slowly, deliberately. It's not a story of past facts. It's as if you're living it yourself, now. And make sure that you're giving weight to the words. Think of what it is that you are saying. Always remember the position in which you're being held. Being held in that position gives a certain tone and pitch to your voice."[21] In Rame's subtle dramaturgy the actress is directed to move only imperceptibly, but to convey the impact of her physical contortion through the nuances of her vocal tone. It is a style that eschews melodrama, opting instead for a delicacy that creates a thought-provoking and intimate rapport with the audience.

Not all of Rame's theater is so directly autobiographical. She is capable of connecting to her audience in a deeply personal way even when her characters are based on other people's stories. In the 1970s, Rame and Fo conducted seminars, workshops, and public discussions that eventually led them to write a collection of monologues about women's issues based

minister. The next day the postmaster general arrived at our house saying he was sorry for having taken so long to deliver the letter. He brought an apology from the president.

Still acting out the story, Rame stands with an imaginary letter in her hand, in silent mockery of the postmaster and the president. After a long silence she says, "Do you think when the president of the Republic sends a letter, he goes out and puts it into a mailbox where it can get lost?"[20] Her wry question temporarily turns the nightmare into a moment of horrific farce. It is clear that Rame has exorcised her demons by performing the piece about the rape hundreds of times onstage. The unflinching honesty of her account is another of the many elements that helps Rame connect so closely to her audiences.

Onstage and off, the urgency of Rame's stories is heightened by the underplayed precision of her gestures. In a workshop in London in 1983, Rame coached young student actresses who were rehearsing English translations of "The Rape". She discouraged the use of tears or any form of sentimentality. She

on true stories of women who had been mistreated by men. Rame performed the fictionalized pieces under the name *Tutta casa letto e chiesa*, a title that could be translated "It's all about home, bed, and church"—the three places where men typically expected to find their wives. The monologues formed a collective critique of a culture in which abortion was banned by the state and birth control was banned by the church.

Rame introduced the performance with a prologue that cut to the core of sexual stereotypes by mocking the phallus, declaring that it would be a central character in her monologues. "It's like a little tail," she jokes." The devil has it in the back. Men have it in front."[22]

To help free society from the stifling influence of the phallus, Rame offers a series of comic sketches that show women breaking out of their traditional subservient roles. Her heroines are working mothers and housewives. One of the characters gets so fed up with nursing a bed-bound, lecherous relative, fielding obscene phone calls, and being locked in her apartment by a jealous husband that she ends

TEATRO IMPERO - BRINDISI
TEATRO PUBBLICO PUGLIESE
Comune di Brindisi - Ass. alla Cultura
—— ETI · GTA / AGIS ——
MERCOLEDI 18 MARZO 1987 - ore 21,00
GIOVEDI 19 MARZO 1987 - ore 20,00

Le prenotazioni inizieranno da SABATO 14 MARZO 1987 - ore 16,00

SPETTACOLO IN ABBONAMENTO I SERATA (INIZIO ore 21,00)
II SERATA (INIZIO ore 20,00)

PREZZI:

	I SERATA		II SERATA
I Posto	L. 15.000	I Posto	L. 14.000
II Posto	L. 12.000	II Posto	L. 11.000
III Posto	L. 10.000	III Posto	L. 9.000
III Posto Rid.	L. 8.000	III Posto Rid.	L. 7.000

NON SARA' CONSENTITO L'INGRESSO DOPO L'INIZIO DELLO SPETTACOLO

FRANCA RAME

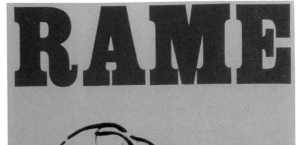

in
COPPIA
APERTA

di FRANCA RAME e DARIO FO

con

GIORGIO BIAVATI

up confronting the men in her life with a shotgun.[23] In another monologue a mother tells her daughter an ironic bedtime story about a little girl who is enslaved in a sterile, abusive marriage with an engineer until she is rescued by a magic rag doll that comes to life, tells her dirty jokes, and makes the husband pregnant by inserting itself into his rectum. The husband is unable to bear the pain of childbirth; his belly gets bigger and bigger until he explodes, leaving only the laughing dolly in his place. "Now you're free," the rag doll tells the girl. "You're in control of your body, your choices, your self."[24] The story concludes when the girl meets a group of other young women who realize that they have all lived through the same sequence of events. "We all have the same story to tell," they say, echoing the response of Rame's audiences, who often tell her that they see themselves and their life dilemmas in her stories.

At the end of *Tutta casa* Rame risks what she calls the *salto mortale* (fatal leap). Circus acrobats use the term to describe their most dangerous stunts. Rame uses it to describe the leap from comedy to tragedy. Sometimes she concludes her performance with "The Rape". Other times she re-enacts the ancient Greek story of Medea, in a version she and Fo adapted from Southern Italian folk legends. Rame's portrayal turns Medea into a recognizable modern woman who is victimized by her husband's abuse. With a portrayal of fierce pride that draws on her family's tradition of making the classics accessible, Rame performs the monologue in a Central Italian dialect that renders Medea's story more intimate. She also makes the choice to start the monologue as a one-woman chorus, speaking in the voices of the women of Corinth trying to understand what Medea has done. When Rame begins to speak in the voice of Medea, she is talking to a group of women in a confessional tone, and she accomplishes the almost impossible feat of creating sympathy for a woman who has murdered her children— an act that is seen as an inevitable consequence of the brutality to which she and other women are forced to submit in a ruthless society ruled by men.

"The writers who created the myth of Medea were men," explains Rame. "Even the actor who played the part in Greece was a man. My version tells the story from Medea's point of view as a woman." Rame reasons that Medea had no choice but to murder her children. Her husband, Jason, was preparing to marry a younger woman, which would have resulted in Medea's enslavement in the palace as a cast-off second wife." Whenever Medea tried to assert herself, everyone told her that she had to remain silent for the good of her children," says Rame. "In Medea's culture, children were the yoke that society put around women's necks to make it easier to oppress them."[25] Rame believes that this dilemma is still familiar to women in modern Mediterranean cultures, where the Church discourages them from divorcing husbands who have taken mistresses, forcing them to accept the role of second-class wife for the children's sake.

Another figure from the past whom Rame has made recognizable to modern women is Queen Elizabeth I of England. When Fo wrote the first version of his play about the sixteenth-century monarch, Rame declared it unworkable and urged him to rewrite the central character. The result was *Elizabeth: Almost by Chance a Woman*, a tragicomic portrait of a queen with the heart of a woman who is forced to wield power like a man. In the play, Elizabeth believes that Shakespeare has written Hamlet as a transvestite parody of her indecisive policies. The theme of sexual identity and power reversal is heightened by Fo's role (played in drag) as the queen's comic maidservant, who administers secret beauty treatments to ease her mistress's insecurities. At the same time that the queen submits to leech-sucking as a method of weight reduction, and to bee stings as a breast-enlargement technique, she battles fiercely against the conspiracies of men who are jealous of her power. Confronting kidnapping plots and assassination attempts, Elizabeth makes political pronouncements that echo the clichés of modern Italian politicians, and also of Ronald Reagan, who was in office at the time of the play's premiere, in 1985.

In performances of the play, Rame (playing Elizabeth) and Fo occasionally toy with the boundaries between past and present that are written into the script by partially slipping out of character and improvising dialogue in which the arguments between the queen and her servant resemble arguments between the husband-and-wife team that has created the work. At one point, as Elizabeth changes her gown behind a screen, Fo jokes that the people in the balcony are getting a view of her underwear. When Rame senses her husband's improvisation going on too long, she chastises both Fo and his character. "Stay in your place and try to be quiet," she admonishes, as the monarch, "because now I'm the queen, and for once, at last, you are the servant. So shut up. Is that clear?"[26] Fo responds with a mock threat to assert his authorial authority: "Dario Fo wrote this play, and he wouldn't like to see you treating me like this," he quips. "One word from me and he'll cross out 'Queen' next to your lines and write in 'the maid.'" Fo then steps completely out of character to address the audience directly. "She's really been immersing herself in the role. At home she answers the telephone: 'Hello, this is the queen speaking.'"[27] The self-parody that Fo and Rame slip into their play recalls the techniques used by Rame's theatrical family to create a bond with audiences. In this case spectators see the bickering of a modern couple overlapping with the squabbling of a sixteenth-century servant and her mistress. The distant past is made more immediate and the complex tapestry of social, literary, and political themes becomes more accessible to the contemporary audience.

On another level the improvised banter (some of which eventually becomes fixed into a form that is repeated every night) is emblematic of the creative partnership that Fo and Rame have evolved over their half century of collaboration. Rame plays the role of the beleaguered editor, reining in the excesses of Fo's over-enthusiastic stage impulses. Fo, in turn, plays the role of the writer with a wounded ego, while he is actually responding happily to Rame's suggestion with an improvised speech that weaves them both into an epic tapestry of sexual politics that transcends the barriers of traditional theater. Instead of a period play that would fit easily into the category of tragedy or comedy, the couple have created a unique theatrical event that fuses contemporary political satire, historical costume drama, parody of new-age medicine, old-fashioned melodrama, transvestite farce, Brechtian social critique, postmodern celebrity gossip, and the resurrection of traditional commedia dell'arte, with Fo playing his usual Harlequin role in drag.

The complexity of Fo's and Rame's theatrical teamwork is also revealed in their shared moments of physical comedy. When Fo, as the maidservant, begins recounting the plot of Hamlet, Rame, as Elizabeth, tries to stop him, insulted by what she perceives to be Shakespeare's satiric portrait of herself and her family. Silenced by the queen, Fo begins pantomiming the action with his hands, and when she grabs his hands he continues to enact the story by gesticulating with one foot in the air. This slapstick physical duet becomes a vivid visual metaphor for censorship. The queen's authority is used to silence a powerless underling who refuses to submit and continues speaking with his body even after his words have been taken away. Every attempt to suppress the servant's expression is met with a wacky form of physical resistance. The scene is comical on the surface, but the serious issue of censorship emerges clearly in the aftermath of the laughter. Fo and Rame have fought battles against censorship repeatedly throughout their careers. In 1962 they were fired from Italy's most popular television show, *Canzonissima*, after refusing to alter the political content of their scripts. In the 1970s Fo was barred from state-controlled television stations for performing religious satire that the Vatican deemed offensive. In the early 1980s Fo and Rame were repeatedly denied visas to enter the United States under the McLaren Act, which is used by the State Department to bar entry to foreigners perceived as a threat to national security. In 1983 Fo was briefly jailed in Sardinia for refusing to alter his scripts in compliance with the government censorship office, and Rame's kidnapping was of course an extreme attempt at censorship through violent intimidation. In this context the physical comedy of the seemingly lighthearted routine in *Elizabeth* can be read as an allegory linking the personal struggles of Fo and Rame to the decades of political turmoil through which they and their audiences have lived. The physical suppression of speech and the visceral need to speak out against oppression were expressed with precision in the couple's slapstick *pas de deux*.

THIS PAGE AND OPPOSITE: Franca Rame in a performance of *It's All About Bed, Home, and Church*

IN HER OFFICE IN MILAN, RAME EXPLAINS THE CIRCUMSTANCES SURROUNDING HER KIDNAPPING WITH REMARKABLE CALM. SHE RE-ENACTS THE EVENT AS SHE NARRATES. "I WALKED OUT OF THE HOUSE AND TURNED THE CORNER," SAYS RAME, TURNING THE CORNER AROUND HER DESK. "THEN I FELT SOMETHING IN MY BACK." RAME STICKS HER FINGER INTO HER OWN BACK. "A GUN, A FINGER, A PIECE OF WOOD. I DON'T KNOW WHAT IT WAS."

The theater of Fo and Rame has always had a subtext of subversion, drawing audiences into a co-conspiracy against the social forces that suppress information. The satirical portrayal of the queen's secret police in *Elizabeth* was meant to parallel secret actions taken by Italian security agents and politicians in the famous kidnapping case of Prime Minister Aldo Moro. *Mistero Buffo* tells Bible stories from the apocryphal Gospels, which the Vatican chooses to ignore. *Accidental Death of an Anarchist* makes use of trial transcripts that were left out of media accounts of a police-brutality trial in Milan. Rame's monologues about sexuality, abortion, and gender politics give a public airing to issues not often discussed on the Italian stage. The ongoing connection to real events in even Fo's and Rame's most outrageous farces creates an unusually powerful bond between the couple and their audiences.

The most extraordinary manifestation of that bond occurred in the 1970s when thousands of people joined Fo and Rame in the occupation of a cluster of buildings in Milan that had been condemned by the municipal government. The couple performed regularly in the gardens of the abandoned buildings, encouraging neighborhood groups to turn the space into a community center. When city council members from the conservative Christian Democrat Party (DC) finally had fences erected to prevent the squatters from completing their renovations of the dilapidated ruins, Fo drew pictures of rodents on leaflets that read, "The rats thank the DC." The occupation of the Palazzina Liberty, Fo has said, "was one of the most important performances we ever produced."[28]

Rame has always been the driving force behind the couple's political activism. She is the one who organizes events that reflect their joint commitments to theatrical artistry and social causes. She spends hours a day on correspondence and phone calls that raise money for numerous charities, most recently the Nobel Committee for the Handicapped, which she founded with the money from Fo's Nobel Prize to support the needs of disabled children around the world.

The most ambitious spectacle Rame has engineered since the occupation of Palazzina Liberty in the 1970s took place in December 1999. Called the "Train of Memories," it was an event that brought Fo and Rame into a collaborative performance with thousands of political activists demonstrating against political violence. Worried that Italy's youngest generations are not being told the truth about the terrorism and murders that have scarred the country's recent past,

Rame rented an entire train to carry demonstrators from Brescia to Milan to Bologna to Florence to Rome. Hundreds of art students from the Brera academy and other schools worked under Fo's supervision to paint huge banners memorializing the victims of murders perpetrated by right-wing terrorists and the Mafia in Italy over the past three decades. The banners depicted these crimes in the action-packed style of Fo's drawings. The 1992 assassination of the crusading anti-Mafia judge Paolo Borsellino, for instance, was memorialized in an expressionistic collage of body parts flying through a disjointed space. The 1969 bombing at the Piazza Fontana in Milan was commemorated with life-size puppets on sticks that demonstrators waved in the air to simulate the deadly results of the explosion. In each of the cities visited by the train, hundreds of wooden cut-out silhouettes, painted by Fo to represent faceless corpses, were given names in processions to remember the victims. A ten-piece brass band accompanied the marches.

The only one of the giant banners that was designed by Fo himself was a 200-square-foot pastel collage depicting Rame's 1973 kidnapping. Painted in the style of the frescoes Fo studied in art school, it shows the crime from three different perspectives simultaneously. In the foreground Rame's struggling body is lifted into a van by five thugs. Across the street a policeman turns his back. Floating above the street scene are seven soldiers with wine glasses in their outstretched arms. "Army officers make a toast," reads the caption underneath.

The "Train of Memories" can be viewed as a giant visual recapitulation of Fo's and Rame's career. Their plays have always been reminders of the violence beneath society's surface. A banner commemorating the death of a man—Giuseppe Pinelli—at the hands of the police tells the same story that Fo and Rame turned into a farce in *Accidental Death of an Anarchist*. A painting of Aldo Moro recalls the satire on the government's response to the politician's kidnapping found in their 1981 play *About Face*. Even when the real-life antecedents of their plays were less obvious, the couple has always striven to throw light on the causes of political violence. The giant banners and puppets are modern reincarnations of devices used by the medieval *giullari*, who satirized social hypocrisy in Italy's town squares, and by Rame's ancestors, who toured the country performing stories tailored to the history of each town they visited. With the "Train of Memories" Rame and Fo, always striving to create a connection to their audiences, found a way to recruit the audience fully into the theatrical action

BANDITI FASCISTI
HANNO SEQUESTRATO
LA COMPAGNA FRANCA RAME

Nel tardo pomeriggio di venerdì sera, la compagna Franca Rame del Collettivo Teatrale "la Comune" è stata aggredita e sequestrata da cinque individui mascherati, in pieno centro. Costretta—con una pistola puntata alla schiena—a salire su un furgone, è stata ripetutamente picchiata e quindi scaricata dopo qualche migliaio di metri. La compagna ha riportato numerose lesioni e contusioni al volto e in tutto il corpo.

Il sequestro della compagna Franca Rame, eseguito da banditi fascisti, cade proprio nei giorni in cui la questura tenta in ogni modo di bloccare l'attività del Collettivo Teatrale. Perchè? Perchè i compagni della Comune con i loro spettacoli portano avanti concretamente un discorso di aperta denuncia dello sfruttamento e della dittatura borghese, in pieno appoggio alle lotte della classe operaia, e—in questi giorni in particolare—alle lotte dei metalmeccanici dell'Alfa Romeo. Questo non è tollerabile per i padroni. E allora si comprende il significato della repressione sistematica contro questi compagni: prima le intimidazioni e i ricatti contro i proprietari dei locali in cui i compagni della Comune svolgono la loro attività; poi l'incriminazione del manifesto dello spettacolo "Pum, Pum! Chi è? La polizia!" per iniziativa personale del procuratore della repubblica Viola; contemporaneamente, l'inchiesta promossa dal magistrato reazionario Sossi contro l'attività di "soccorso rosso" svolta dalla Comune nelle carceri del regime per sostenere i compagni colpiti dalla repressione antipopolare. Infine, ieri sera, l'operazione "esemplare" con cui si è voluto "dare una lezione" (punitiva) alla compagna Franca Rame, volendo colpire in lei non solo la Comune ma tutto il movimento di lotta, proprio mentre gli arresti, le denunce, le sospensioni, le serrate, le aggressioni fasciste contro gli operai e le avanguardie di fabbrica si stanno moltiplicando.

Il clima in cui tutto questo avviene è creato dal governo Andreotti, al servizio dei padroni, per inginocchiare la classe operaia; in questo clima, i fascisti vengono apertamente agevolati nelle loro imprese banditesche dai vari strumenti dello stato (polizia, magistratura, stampa, ecc).

Contro questo piano di attacco antipopolare si deve formare il più ampio schieramento, che veda unite le forze progressiste e rivoluzionarie del nostro paese, escludendo ogni possibilità di alleanza con chi (come la DC) alimenta i fascisti.

Il sequestro e il pestaggio della compagna Franca Rame rientra in questo momento dello scontro di classe. Lasciare impunita questa grave provocazione significa lasciare spazio all'azione dei fascisti, mandati e pagati dai padroni di sempre mascherati da "democratici". Significa lasciare spazio a tutte le leggi liberticide del programma Andreotti, prima fra tutte il fermo di polizia. Rispondiamo con una vasta mobilitazione di massa, militante. La forza delle masse popolari, sotto la direzione della classe operaia, può mandare in pezzi qualsiasi manovra imbastita sulla violenza ormai scoperta dei padroni. Facciamo pagare caro ai padroni e al loro potere questo nuovo atto criminale e antipopolare.

- collettivo teatrale «la Comune»
- circolo «la Comune»

MARTEDI 13 ORE 21 AL PALALIDO
MANIFESTAZIONE POPOLARE

ADERISCONO:

ASSOCIAZIONE NAZIONALE PARTIGIANI
ASSOCIAZIONE EX-DEPORTATI POLITICI
FEDERAZIONE ITALIANA ASSOCIAZIONE
  PARTIGIANI (Comitato Regionale Lombardo)
PARTITO SOCIALISTA DI UNITA' PROLETARIA
C.O.G.I.D.A.S.
LEGA DELLE DONNE COMUNISTE ITALIANE
COMITATO GIORNALISTI PER LA LOTTA
  CONTRO LA REPRESSIONE E PER LA LIBERTA'
SEZIONE LOMBARDA DEL SINDACATO SCRITTORI
MOVIMENTO STUDENTESCO MILANESE
ASSEMBLEE AUTONOME
COLLETTIVI POLITICI OPERAI
COMITATI UNITARI DI BASE
UNIONE INQUILINI
GRUPPO GRAMSCI

LOTTA CONTINUA
IL MANIFESTO
ORGANIZZAZIONE COMUNISTA AVANGUARDIA OPERAIA
ORGANIZZAZIONE COMUNISTA (m-l)
PARTITO COMUNISTA (marxista-leninista) ITALIANO
POTERE OPERAIO
RIVOLUZIONE COMUNISTA
VIVA IL COMUNISMO
COLLETTIVO AUTONOMO ARCHITETTURA
COLLETTIVO AUTONOMO BOCCONI
COMITATO DI LOTTA D'INGEGNERIA
COMITATO VIETNAM
RE NUDO
COMITATO ANTIFASCISTA MILITANTE ZONA LAMBRATE
COMITATO ANTIMPERIALISTA ANTIFASCISTA ROMANA-VIGENTINA
COMITATO AUTONOMO DI QUARTO OGGIARO

with performances that re-enacted events in the piazzas and on the street corners where they had actually happened. The intertwining of Fo and Rame's life experience with their plays and the recent history of their country was achieved through parades of gigantic artworks that echoed the grotesque Rabelaisian stories Fo learned on the shores of Lake Maggiore and the populist epics that Rame's family staged when she was a child. "The tapestries are beautiful," said Rame during the event.

If you don't see them in person, you can't imagine their impact. They tell the story of all the massacres and all the victims, from the deaths at the Piazza Fontana to Pinelli, Ilaria Alpi, Aldo Moro and his body guards, Fausto Zibecchi and Serantini. . . . It will be a revelation for many young people who will learn the names of the children who were also killed, like Varelli and Franceschi. We try to give out information at each stop. We're on the go from morning to night. . . . Dario gets up at eight in the morning and works with the kids until night time. . . . I've been very sick, and I'm trying to keep up with my other obligations. I'm working for the handicapped and I'm putting our entire archives onto the computer. And then there's the money from the Nobel Prize. I can't tell you how many organizations have asked us for support and we have to find out who they are and what they need. I told Dario, 'The next time I get an idea like this, just drug me.'[29]

The same political commitment that Rame displays in organizing large-scale events like the "Train of Memories" appears in her more intimate interactions with the public. In June of 1999, she was contacted by the American lawyer representing Sylvia Baraldini, an Italian political activist associated with the Black Panther party who had spent over twenty years in a Connecticut prison for a murder she did not commit. Viewed in Italy as a "political prisoner," Baraldini was eventually extradited to her native country on the special request of the Italian government, but when Rame met with Baraldini's lawyer, the case seemed hopeless. Rame agreed to help organize a letter-writing campaign to support the case, but she took another step typical of her dedication to causes she supports: understanding the suffering of the prisoner's relatives in Italy, Rame invited Baraldini's sister to her home in Milan. There she offered to give a benefit performance to call attention to Baraldini's plight. One of the monologues she proposed to perform was written by Rame and Fo in the voice of another political prisoner from the 1970s, Ulrike Meinhof, of Germany's Baader/Meinhof group of political activists. The monologue describes the psychological torture endured by a prisoner who has no hope of leaving her cell, and Rame read it to Baraldini's sister as a gesture of solidarity. There were only five people in Rame's living room for the impromptu reading, which was understated, almost whispered, but the force of the words reduced Rame's audience to tears.

Solitary confinement. What an elegant euphemism
for being buried in a coffin of silence.

Silence and white.

White cell. White walls. White shutters,
white enamel on the door, the table, the chair, the bed, not to mention the toilet.

The neon light is white, always on, night and day.

But which is day and which is night?

How can I tell?

Through the window there is always
the same white light, natural but fake, as fake as the window and the weather that they have denied me, painting it over in white.

Silence.

From outside there is not a sound, a noise,
a voice. . . . In the corridor there are no steps, no door opening or closing. . . . Nothing.

Everything is silence and white.

Silence in my brain, white like the ceiling.

White is my voice that tries to speak. White
is the saliva that coagulates in the pockets of my mouth.

Silence is white in my eyes, in my stomach,
in my belly that fills me with emptiness....

I have to resist.... You are not going to drive me mad.[30]

At first Baraldini's sister was rendered speechless by Rame's performance. Finally she said, "That's what is happening to Sylvia,"[31] sad but grateful that someone understood Baraldini's dilemma clearly enough to articulate her pain. Rame's ability to give voice to the dark side of female experience is the flip side of her genius for comedy. Both her comic and her tragic performances are rooted in a compassionate generosity that makes audiences feel as if Rame had invited them all into her living room for a heart-to-heart confrontation with the truth.

PAGE 93: Political poster from the exhibition *The Life and Art of Dario Fo and Franca Rame*, 2000; OPPOSITE: Franca Rame in a performance of *It's All About Bed, Home, and Church*

THE INTERTWINING OF FO AND RAME'S LIFE EXPERIENCE WITH THEIR PLAYS AND THE RECENT HISTORY OF THEIR COUNTRY WAS ACHIEVED THROUGH PARADES OF GIGANTIC ART-WORKS THAT ECHOED THE GROTESQUE STORIES FO LEARNED ON THE SHORES OF LAKE MAGGIORE AND THE POP-ULIST EPICS THAT RAME'S FAMILY STAGED WHEN SHE WAS A CHILD.

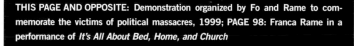

THIS PAGE AND OPPOSITE: Demonstration organized by Fo and Rame to commemorate the victims of political massacres, 1999; PAGE 98: Franca Rame in a performance of *It's All About Bed, Home, and Church*

THE RAPE

By FRANCA RAME **Translated by RON JENKINS**

(At the center of the stage is an actress seated on a chair with her arms behind the back of the chair indicating the position she is describing. To act this piece it is necessary for the actress to be dressed in pants.)

A radio is playing... at first I don't notice it... only after a while do I realize that someone is singing.

Yes, it's a radio. Light music: sky, stars, hearts, love... love...

There is a knee, just one, pressed against my back, as if the man holding me from behind has the other one on the ground. He holds my hands in his, tightly, twisting them. Especially the left one.

I don't know why, but I find myself thinking that he might be left-handed.

I don't understand what's happening to me. I feel the paralysis of someone who's losing her mind, needs her voice... her words. I become aware of things, with an incredible slowness.

God, what confusion!

How did I get in this van? Did I lift my legs one after the other, pushed by them from behind, or did they carry me?

I don't know.

My heart, beating so hard against my ribs that it keeps me from thinking... the pain in my left hand is becoming unbearable. Why are they twisting it so tightly? I'm not trying to move.

I'm frozen.

Now, the one behind me doesn't have his knee in my back anymore... he's sitting down comfortably... holding me between his open legs... squeezing... the way they used to hold children when they wanted to pull their tonsils out.

That's the only image that comes to my mind.

Why are they squeezing me so hard? I don't move. I don't scream. I have no voice.

The radio is playing, not very loud.

Why music? Why did they turn it down? Maybe it's because I'm not screaming.

Besides the one holding me from behind, there are three others.

I see them: there's not much light... not much space... maybe that's why they're keeping me crouched down.

I sense that they are calm. Secure. What are they doing? They're lighting a cigarette.

Smoking? Now?
Why are they holding me like this and smoking?

Something's going to happen, I can feel it... I breathe deeply... twice, three times. It doesn't work. I'm still afraid.

Now one of them is coming towards me. One sits down on my right. The other on my left. I see the red of the cigarette.

They're breathing heavily.

They're very close.

Yes, something's going to happen. I can feel it.

The one behind me tightens all his muscles... I feel him surrounding my body. He's not using more strength, he's just tensing his muscles, like he's getting ready to hold me tighter.

The one on his knees moves between my legs, spreading them apart.

It is a precise movement that he seems to have planned out with the one holding me from behind, because he suddenly puts his feet on top of mine to stop me from moving.

I have my pants on.

Why are they opening my legs with my pants on?

I feel worse than if I were naked.

I'm distracted from this sensation by something that I can't make out... heat... slight at first... then it gets stronger... finally it becomes unbearable... on my left breast.

A burning pain.

The cigarette.

The cigarette... burning through my sweater to my skin.

That's why they were smoking.

I find myself wondering what a person can do under these circumstances. I don't succeed in doing anything. I don't speak. I don't cry.... I feel like I've been projected outside myself, pressed up against a window, forced to watch something horrible.

The one sitting on my right lights the cigarette, takes two puffs and passes it to the one between my legs.

They consume it quickly.

The stench of burning wool seems to disturb all four of them: they slit open my sweater with a blade, lengthways down the front... they cut my bra too... they slice my skin too, superficially. The medical report says the cut was twenty centimeters long.

The one between my legs takes my breasts in his hands.
I feel his coldness on the burns.

Now they open the fly of my pants and all of them do the work of undressing me: leaving one shoe on... and a pant leg.

The one behind me is getting excited.
I feel him pressing against my back.

Now... one of them... enters inside me.

I feel like throwing up.

I have to stay calm, calm.

I concentrate on the words of the song. My heart is splitting. I don't want to recover from my confusion.

"Move, bitch. Make me come!"
I don't understand any words. I don't know any language.

Another cigarette.

"Move, bitch, make me come."
I am stone.

Now... it's the second one's turn. His thrusts are more decisive.
I feel enormous pain.

"Move, bitch, make me come!"

The blade that he used to cut my sweater passes a few times across my face. I can't feel if it is cutting me or not.

"Move, bitch. Make me come."

The blood flows from my cheeks to my ears.
It's the third one's turn. It's horrible to feel these disgusting beasts finding pleasure inside me.

"I'm dying," I manage to say. "I have a heart condition."

They believe me. They don't believe me. They argue.
"Let her out." "No." "Yes." One of them is slapped.

They press a cigarette against my neck... here... hard enough to put it out.
At this point I think I finally fainted.

I feel them moving me.

The one who held me from behind with precise movements. He does the dressing. I am of no use. He whines like a baby that he's the only one who hasn't made love... pardon me... the only one who hasn't opened his pants. But I sense his hurry, his fear. He doesn't know what to do with my torn sweater, so he sticks two pieces of it in my pants, and the van stops long enough to let me out... and it leaves.

I hold the jacket closed with my hand to cover my breasts. It's almost dark. Where am I. In a park.

I feel sick... in the sense that I'm going to faint... not just from the physical pain all over my body, but from the disgust... the humiliation... the anger... the thousand spits in my brain... the sperm I feel dripping out of me.

I rest my head against a tree. Even my hair hurts. Yes, they pulled on it to hold my head still.

I pass my hand across my face. It's full of blood.

I raise the collar of the jacket and leave.

I walk... I don't know for how long.

Without realizing it, I find myself in front of the police station.

I lean against the wall of a building across the street and stand there watching the entrance for I don't know how long... the people who go in... and out... the policemen...

I think of what I'll go through if I go in there now... I hear their questions... I see their faces... their half-smiles...

I think... and then I think again.

And then I decide...
I'm going home... I'm going home...
I'll report them... tomorrow.

A SCANDAL OF EPIC PROPORTIONS: MISTERO BUFFO

FRANCO ZEFIRELLI: *I have no difficulty in declaring that Fo is one of the great phenomena of the Italian theater and that his performances are almost always brilliant. And I am also aware that the scurrilous quality of his theater comes from its roots in our theatrical history, for instance Plautus and the commedia dell'arte. . . . And now we come to the point. In my opinion, this type of scurrilous theater should not be presented to mass television audiences who are not prepared for it. I regret that this work of Fo's* (Mistero Buffo), *because of its large audience, is becoming a pretext for a political controversy that will end up harming the work and its author, given the ridiculous comparisons that have been made between* Mistero Buffo *and* Jesus *[Zeffirelli's television series on the life of Christ]. . . . We cannot force the provocations of Fo into the homes of people who have nothing to do with these arguments. . . the idea of broadcasting* Jesus *on channel one and* Mistero *on channel two [In April 1977] was a questionable choice. People coming out of the religious reverie that, for better or worse,* Jesus *could have put them into, find themselves immersed in a climate of violent de-sanctification. I wanted above all to create a mood of pacification, of love. My* Jesus *was intended to enter the lives of people without disturbing them. . . . It doesn't seem right to me to subject the Gospels to satire. . . .*

DARIO FO: *I accuse Zeffirelli of having cut out of his program the greatest moment of the Gospel tradition, not to mention the most popular, which is the episode on the wedding at Cana. Zeffirelli has censored the moment of joy, the great festival of a community, which is rooted in a very important fact: the union, also sexual, of two young people. This "cut" is in opposition to the popular tradition of reading the Gospels as the return of springtime. The great ritual of resurrection is already there in that episode, in the transformation of water into wine, in the almost Dionysian pleasure of love. To remove this aspect is to follow the catechism and to support the vision of the ecclesiastic powers of the church, and to ignore above all the more culturally elevated point of view found in the great popular tradition.*

ZEFIRELLI: *I reject this counter-reformist etiquette that Fo is trying to saddle on me. When Fo makes a "life of Christ" he emphasizes pagan joy, and that doesn't seem to me to be the central message of Christianity. . . . I am worried about a public that is not accustomed to these kinds of shocks. . . . I would like to conclude by encouraging people to read the Sermon on the Mount, which is a testament to communal life and reciprocal tolerance. . . . What does this have to say when applied to the situation we are discussing? It reminds us that as Christians we don't have to be afraid of anything and we have to accept all challenges. And if anyone finds Dario Fo's performance repugnant, all they have to do is turn off the television or change the channel.*

FO: *I will conclude by reminding Zeffirelli, and others, of a phrase from the screenplay of* Jesus *by [Carl] Dreyer. The film is never shown, as we all know. One of the disciples of Christ says: "As long as Jesus spoke only to the sages and wise men in the synagogues, no one attacked him, but when he went up onto the mountaintop so that his voice could be heard as far away as possible, and thousands finally could hear him (and I emphasize finally), the authorities began to understand that this was a man to be eliminated as soon as possible."* [1]

The 1977 television broadcast of *Mistero Buffo* stirred up controversy throughout Italy. Fo and Rame's one-person re-enactments of Bible stories and church history were denounced in the Vatican newspaper, *L'Osservatore*, as "the most blasphemous program ever broadcast in the history of world television." [2] Fo responded to this criticism with gracious irony: "That is the best compliment the Vatican could have paid me." [3]

Some sources reported that the Vatican considered threatening to break off diplomatic ties with Italy if the state-controlled television station broadcast the second installment of the program. This strategy was rejected, but the Church exerted its political influence with the leaders of the ruling Christian Democratic Party and managed to keep Fo off the national airwaves for the next seven years, a banishment that seemed to be measured in Biblical proportions. A rebroadcast of the series that had been scheduled for 1982 was canceled, and a television executive who was a Christian Democrat called Fo "an ideological swindler, a liar, Jacques Tati's mongoloid brother, the true expression of the arrogance of television's power." [4]

After they were barred from television, Fo and Rame continued performing *Mistero Buffo* on stage in Italy and throughout the world. Demand for the performance was so strong that they sometimes staged it in outdoor sports arenas to over thirty thousand spectators at a time. The 1986 American tour of *Mistero Buffo* played to standing-room audiences and excellent reviews in New York, New Haven, Washington, D.C., Baltimore, and Cambridge. The couple estimates that the work has been seen by over forty million people worldwide.

Mistero Buffo is the quintessential creation of the Fo/Rame collaboration. The techniques employed in it are key to understanding the theatrical imagination that animates all their work. It is particularly important as an expression of Fo's attempts to reinvent the techniques of the medieval *giullari* for a modern audience. "When I began a long time ago to research the history and origins of the theater," says Fo, "I realized that most of the early texts were based on religious stories, and that it was impossible to revive the theater of the *giullari* without coming to terms with Christianity, its protagonists, and its temporal power. So, little by little, I put together over the years this play that has as its protagonists Christ, the apostles, and the Madonna, and that deals with saints, miracles, and the Gospels." [5]

THE WEDDING AT CANA

Fo's debate with Franco Zeffirelli over the "scurrilous nature" of *Mistero Buffo* was representative of the scandal that surrounded the play's broadcast. It also echoed a scene from the play in which an angel and a drunkard argue over the correct way to tell the story of Jesus turning water into

PAGES 100–101: Fo Performing *Mistero Buffo* at Palazzina Liberty in 1974; OPPOSITE: Fo's rendering of a satirical portrait of Pope Boniface VIII from a fourteenth-century codex that inspired a sketch about the pope in *Mistero Buffo*

wine during the wedding at Cana. Like Zeffirelli, the angel promotes a conventional view of the Gospels and is scandalized by any suggestion that Christ's miracle might be linked to a Dionysian love of pleasure. Like Fo, the drunkard humanizes Christ by emphasizing his connection to the peasants and their celebrations of fertility, springtime, and wine-fueled revelry. The drunkard, who has attended the wedding, rhapsodizes over the wine's sweet fragrance, quoting Christ as saying, "Drink, people! Be happy! Get drunk! Don't wait! Enjoy yourselves!"[6] In the debate, Fo criticized Zeffirelli for leaving this episode out of his filmed life of Christ, arguing that its exclusion promoted the Church's repressive doctrine of urging people to suffer silently in life and wait to enjoy themselves until they get to Heaven. For Fo this stands in contrast to the popular peasant tradition that celebrates Christ's Resurrection as a continuation of pagan rituals of rebirth that emphasize earthly pleasures.

In the prologue that introduces the "The Wedding at Cana," Fo refers to the visual arts to make his point that popular tradition has long linked the figure of Christ to the pagan divinities of Dionysus and Bacchus, the Greek and Roman gods of fertility. Showing his audience a slide of a nineteenth-century engraving called "Palm Sunday," which depicts a Sicilian religious festival, Fo notes that it "depicts three different moments of time in the same situation: the entrance of Christ into Jerusalem—you see, he's the one under the palm branches, surrounded by revelers; Bacchus; and finally the descent of Dionysus into hell. Dionysus is a Greek divinity whose origins can be traced back to Thessalonica fifteen centuries before the birth of Christ. They say he was so enamored of mankind that when a demon kidnapped springtime, to enjoy her all to himself in hell, Dionysus sacrificed himself for humanity by going down to hell on the back of a donkey. He paid with his life so that men could

enjoy the spring again. And fifteen centuries later Christ is a god who comes onto the earth to try to give springtime back to man. Springtime is a metaphor for dignity. . . . And in the middle is Bacchus, the god of happiness, of drunkenness even, of letting yourself go so that you can be happy."[7]

It is significant that Fo's inspiration comes from an engraving that juxtaposes three cultures into a single image. Regardless of its literal accuracy, this visualization of history resembles the epic vision of narrative that is embedded in all Fo's writing: he conflates time, merges characters, and blurs the boundaries between history, fiction, anthropology, politics, religion, and slapstick. In *Mistero Buffo,* Fo accomplishes all this alone onstage (he and Rame never appear together in the piece), playing a succession of disparate roles with disarming simplicity. "When I stand here, I'm the angel," he tells the audience at the conclusion of his prologue. "When I stand over there, I'm the drunk. You'll follow it because you're used to watching the news on television."[8] Fo's performance of "The Wedding at Cana" endows the nineteenth-century engraving of Palm Sunday with the immediacy of a contemporary newsreel.

When Fo first performed *Mistero Buffo*, in Milan in 1969, he introduced the monologues by showing slides of artwork ranging from medieval depictions of performing *giullari* to satirical drawings of the popes. Eventually Fo eliminated the slides, but he continued introducing each piece with a prologue that placed it in historical context. Essentially Fo became the slide show himself, using his voice and gestures to communicate the meanings and forms of the images that had inspired his writing. As years went by, he synthesized the presentation even farther and eventually stopped mentioning the artwork, but his performance of "The Wedding at Cana" continues to embody the spirit of Bacchus, Dionysus, Christ, and the revelers surrounding them in the Palm Sunday engraving.

Two other slides that were initially included in the prologue to this scene depicted a close-up of an angel from a fresco by Cimabue and a medieval sketch of a drunkard. The contrasting attitudes of these two images are mirrored in Fo's body language as he depicts the two central characters in his monologue. When he plays the angel he raises his arm in front of his upright body, letting his wrist drop to the same angle used by Cimabue to give the cherub an air of nonchalant tranquillity. The angel's near regal detachment is contrasted to the visceral movements of Fo's drunkard, whose slouching postures echo the quirky angles of the souse depicted in the eleventh-century fresco. The drunkard's body throbs with every word he speaks; the angel barely moves, and is annoyed when the drunk keeps interrupting her prim and proper version of the wedding story from which all references to wine have been excised.

"Be quiet, you big drunk," the angel blurts out in a strangled shout, "Don't speak."[9] Repressing her exasperation and maintaining a facade of calm, she becomes a comic emblem of censorship, silencing her own feelings at the same time that she muzzles the drunk and attempts to stifle the truth of what happened at the wedding. "I don't want to hear about that drunkenness," she shouts, losing her composure every time the drunk starts talking.[10] She won't let him move a finger, because when he moves, his body makes too much noise. Thinking is also prohibited, because the drunkard's alcohol-soaked brain is also very noisy. By the end, even breathing is forbidden, and the angel threatens to kick her adversary if he doesn't comply.

The drunkard retaliates by pulling out a few of the angel's feathers and threatening to completely deplume her. "I'll pluck you like a chicken," he growls. "Every feather, one by one . . . from your ass too . . . from the rear. Come here, you oversized hen. Come here."[11] The angel flees in terror and the drunk is free to tell his story without interference. It is a bacchanalian tale that depicts Jesus's miracle in vivid detail. The drunk is enraptured as he retraces the path of Christ's wine down his esophagus and into his belly. Then he pantomimes the fragrant aroma returning up his gullet through his nostrils, and wafting in the air so enticingly that a man passing by on horseback is inebriated just by its smell. "*Jesus*" the rider shouts, "*sei di/vino,*" which means both "you are divine" and "you are of wine."[12] The pun is a delicious culmination of the story's Dionysian flavor. Fo embodies both Jesus and the wine, using his gestures to visualize the path of the miraculous liquid through the body of one of Jesus's lowly followers. The scene is a comic inversion of holy communion, foreshadowing the drinking of wine as Christ's blood at the same time that it conjures up pagan visions of the wine gods Dionysus and Bacchus. These densely textured associations are achieved without didactic explication. The sketch itself is

structured in the form of a classic circus routine known as the interruption gag, where the austere white-faced clown is frustrated by the ever more annoying interruptions of the goofy august clown. It is the same pattern one finds in the films of Laurel and Hardy or Abbott and Costello, and is immediately accessible to all audiences.

One reason the dialogue between the angel and the drunkard functions so effectively as both slapstick and theological debate is the context in which Fo presents it. The audience may not have heard the argument between Fo and Zeffirelli, but most spectators and readers are familiar with the basic issues that separate Fo's populist interpretation of the Gospels from the doctrine endorsed by the Vatican. By exploring these issues more fully in the comic provocations of his prologue, Fo invites the public into the debate before his story begins, encouraging them to look at the narrative from a multiplicity of viewpoints. When the angel appears, for instance, the audience recalls not only the fresco of Cimabue's angel, but also a Renaissance painting of Jesus at the wedding in Cana that Fo has discussed in his prologue to the story. The painting is by Veronese and Fo acts it out as he describes it, imitating in turn the drunken peasants and their noble patrons, who are shown occupying two different tables. Fo also notes that the painting depicts Christ as one of the aristocrats, removed from the rowdy crowd. "He stays close to the proprietors of the palace with a very aristocratic attitude. He has long fingers, long feet, very fine robes, double-sided . . . as if they were from Scotland . . . almost cashmere." Here, Fo teases his audience with references to contemporary tokens of wealth to make it clear that this is a story with modern implications. "He holds a beautiful goblet . . . wine isn't good enough for him . . . he drinks whiskey!" [13]

Continuing to mock the depiction of Christ as a figure detached from the pain of the world, Fo then refers to a painting by Piero della Francesca. Noting that the painting has recently been stolen from a museum in Urbino and then almost immediately returned to it, he wonders what has happened, and imagines a scene in which a disgruntled thief and an art collector complain about the quality of the work and send it back. Jumping from the present into the world of the painting, Fo imitates the position in which Piero shows Christ: "Very well composed," says Fo, "with his hip tilted. Little clothing, but well covered. Beautiful buttocks. Nicely defined muscles. He's in this position. Note the position." Fo assumes the soft curves of the body shape to show how inappropriate it is for a man being whipped. His hands are joined at the wrists above his head, in a pose of sublime relaxation. Then Fo leaps into the role of the torturer flaying Jesus. A second later he resumes the tranquil pose of Christ, who sighs languidly, "Are you done yet?" Labeling this figure as "completely absent, alienated from suffering, joy, and sadness," Fo rejects the vision of Jesus as "lost in the world of ideas, above it all, almost Platonic." He is preparing his audience for the Jesus who will be presented by the drunkard in *Mistero Buffo* as "full of joy, exuberant, someone who, when he is introduced to friends, is the first to have a drink and start singing." [14]

Fo performs the prologue's physical and vocal transformations over the course of a few minutes, taking the audience with startling velocity from ancient Palestine, to medieval Europe, to Renaissance Italy, to heaven, and back to modern times. He even takes time to impersonate the audience in the theater,

OPPOSITE: Cimabue fresco that Fo used as a model for his portrayal of an angel in "The Wedding at Cana" in *Mistero Buffo*

enacting the squabbling between a husband and wife who disagree on the politics of his show. "Why did we come here?" says the husband. "You knew these people would be a little to the left," says the wife. "I just came to be exasperated," the man concludes. This improvised diversion grew out of Fo's response to the isolated laugh of a spectator during the television taping of *Mistero Buffo*. Fo later stepped out of character to say he expected Christ's diatribe against the rich to be deleted from the broadcast, and launched into an impersonation of a future television viewer muttering about Fo's audience marching around with red flags and little red books by Chairman Mao.

Fo's polyphonic technique renders his stories far more complex and absorbing than the sum of their plots. By shifting voices swiftly, from Jesus to the drunkard to the Madonna to minor figures in forgotten paintings, to angels to scholars to modern politicians to audience members to himself as narrator, Fo activates the public's participation in the ongoing reshaping of the story from each new perspective. Spectators have to leap back and forth between centuries and viewpoints, deciding which side they are on and whom they believe. The confrontation between the drunk and the angel is only one of the many shifting dialogues woven into the performance. By the time these two appear they are sharing the stage with an epic cast drawn from different time periods, each individual triggering a new internal dialogue with the action of the play.

Taking yet another leap through time and theology, Fo muses on the absurdity of presenting Christ as an aristocrat when the Bible provides evidence of Jesus' scorn for the rich. Becoming Christ, Fo yells that it will be harder for a rich man to enter heaven than it would be for a camel to pass through the eye of a needle. Assuming this pronouncement might be a response to overcrowded conditions in heaven, Fo envisions a paradise as crowded as a rush-hour trolley car. He demonstrates the way heaven's residents would have to walk to avoid being poked in the eye by angel wings while they kick tiny cherubim out from under their feet. Next he imagines all the rich people in Palestine trying to squeeze their camels through the eyes of needles. At one point he even becomes a camel, whose hump has been flattened out in the process—"This," he says, "is how the first horse was created." He then hurls himself into a depiction of rich people leading their children in flattening exercises that will enable them to pass through the eye of a needle. They end up walking like Egyptian hieroglyphs, or figures on a Greek vase. Fo demonstrates their two-dimensional movements in

a style that parodies Vaslav Nijinsky's famous bas-relief-like choreography for *The Afternoon of a Faun.*

At this point Fo has turned himself into a living hieroglyph. The link between his body and the wall drawings of antiquity becomes part of his comedy. The audience is reminded that all of Fo's texts require the actor to play the role of a human pictograph. His body, or the body of any actor who plays his roles, enters into a dialogue with the spoken text and communicates coded messages to the audience that resonate with multiple meanings. The comic hieroglyph of the rich Palestinian, for instance, in conjuring up associations with Greek vases, is also intended to recall Fo's discussion of Dionysus, who often appears on such vases, and who also appears with Christ in the Sicilian engraving of Palm Sunday that Fo introduced in his prologue. Fo's hieroglyph also provides a precise visual metaphor for the state of detachment from worldly affairs that is satirized in his version of "The Wedding at Cana." The surreal body shape assumed by Fo epitomizes the aloofness depicted in the Renaissance painting of Christ and the Cimabue fresco of the angel. And finally Fo makes a connection to current events by demonstrating the similarity of his hieroglyphic walk to the real-life walk of a modern Italian politician named Ugo LaMalfa, who also acts as if wealth had placed him above the concerns of his working-class constituents.

No spectator will absorb all these associations at once, but by the end of the piece the viewer's head will be swimming with ideas triggered by images of body shapes and gestures, which linger in the memory as vividly as Fo's words. The way Fo pronounces the word "Ugo," for instance, has a pinched nasal condescension that echoes the manner in which he has distorted his facial grimaces to match his flattened-out hieroglyphic walk. The image of snooty condescension conveyed by his face and body is embedded in the haughty tones with which Fo endows the two syllables of the politician's name when he wrinkles his nose and says "Ewe-go." Fo jokes that LaMalfa changed his name because he could not pronounce the one he was born with through the pursed lips of his flat face.

A similarly dense constellation of ideas is linked to many of the other images in Fo's visual style of writing and performance. The drunkard, ending his account of "The Wedding at Cana," denies that his story is blasphemous, and asserts that if God had taught Adam how to make wine, he would have resisted the temptation of the snake, and we would all still be living in Paradise. This claim is followed by a revisionist version of the story of the Original Sin, in which the drunk plays the part of Adam while his left arm plays the part of the snake slithering up his body and telling him to eat the apple. Instead Adam throws the apple on the ground and takes up a glass of wine. Pouring a few drops on the ground, he makes a toast: "To God, to you, to me, to the earth. Hallelujah."[14] His libation recalls the pagan rituals suggested in the Palm Sunday engraving with which Fo has opened his prologue. The toast is accompanied by a sequence of gestures in which Fo raises his glass to the left, to the right, above his head, and then out to the audience. It is almost as if he were forming a cross in the air: his offering to the earth recalls the pagan rituals of Dionysus and Bacchus, antiquity's gods of wine; his reaching out toward the public is a gesture of inclusiveness, linking the present life of the audience to the timeless world of the Gospels; his gesture toward the heavens and his final "Hallelujah" evoke a celebratory sense of spirituality. Taken together, these movements that end Fo's story form a gestural hieroglyph of compassion, fertility, and reverence for life that humanizes Christ at the same time that it brings Fo's inebriated narrator one drink closer to the angels.

THE PASSION OF MARY AT THE CROSS

Mistero Buffo continues to humanize the figures of the Bible with its depiction of the Madonna. In "The Wedding at Cana" the drunk argues that wine cannot be a sin because Jesus offered it to his mother at the wedding. In "The Resurrection of Lazarus" Fo presents Lazarus as a relative deeply mourned by the Madonna, proposing that Jesus performed the miracle "so that he could once again see a smile on the face of his mother."[15]

In the monologue entitled "The Passion of Mary at the Cross" Franca Rame plays the part of the Madonna. Depicting Mary as a mother pained by the sight of her son's suffering on the cross, Rame adds a dimension of raw emotion to the play's populist Gospel stories. Her Mary is no saint; she blasphemes against the angel Gabriel and tries to bribe the soldiers to let her climb up and wipe the blood from Christ's mouth. Like Fo, Rame shifts roles swiftly, turning her back to the audience and spreading her arms in a Crucifixion pose to speak in the voice of Christ reassuring his mother that he needs no help. She also gives voice to the bystanders, who try to spare Mary the sight of her son "twisted like the roots of an olive tree gnawed at by ants,"[16] and to the guards, who advise Mary that it is better to let her son die quickly than to comfort him and prolong his pain. The situation between the mother and her dying son becomes real and immediate. The Madonna is seen as a human being, not an icon.

"IN MY RESEARCH ON MEDIEVAL TEXTS I ENCOUNTERED, TOO OFTEN TO IGNORE, THIS FIGURE OF CHRIST TRANSFORMED BY THE PEOPLE INTO A KIND OF HERO IN OPPOSITION TO AUTHORITY, AND TO THE HIERARCHY OF THE CHURCH.... HE WAS MORE HUMAN AND ALWAYS ON THE SIDE OF THE WEAKEST. HE HAD IN HIM A PAGAN, ALMOST DIONYSIAN JOY FOR LOVE, FEASTING, BEAUTY, AND EARTHLY THINGS."

The most startling element of the piece is Mary's anger. As envisioned by Rame, Mary rages against the angel Gabriel when he tries to comfort her—she calls him a charlatan and a fraud for failing to warn her that bearing the child of God would end with her watching her son die a hideous death. Berating him with the fierceness of a woman unjustly wronged, she provokes her audience to imagine an element of the Passion story they may never have considered: the exploitation of a woman by a man whose angelic life in heaven renders him incapable of fully understanding the emotional implications of what he has done. "Turn around and spread your wings, Gabriel," shouts Mary in contempt,

> Go back to your joyous heaven, which has nothing in common with this wretched earth, this anguished world. Go, so you don't dirty your finely colored wings. . . . Don't you see the mud and blood and cow dung, that it's all a big sewer? Go, so you don't dirty your ears with the desperate shouts and cries and begging that rises up from all directions. Go, so you won't cloud your eyes with the sight of sores, scabs, and buboes, and of flies and worms coming out of butchered corpses. You're not used to these things because in Heaven there's no noise, no crying, no war, no prison, no hanged men, no raped women. There is no hunger, no famine, no sweat-soaked workers, no babies without smiles, no mothers without hope, no one paying for their sins with pain. Go, Gabriel, go! [17]

Borrowed from a popular tradition of Passion plays that was familiar to Rame's family of traveling players, this interpretation of Mary's disenchantment reinforces *Mistero Buffo's* vision of the Gospels as a story of earthy passion. Gabriel is criticized in the same terms Fo has used in his prologue to condemn the Renaissance and medieval paintings that depict Christ as an aloof aristocrat. Rame's fiery performance becomes a hieroglyph of a mother's devotion, a searing portrait that takes the Madonna off the pedestal of conventional religious art and makes her pain as immediate as the suffering of one's next-door neighbor. The emotional truth of Rame's grief-stricken performance establishes *Mistero Buffo* as a play conceived with reverence for Christ's story. At the core of its buffoonery, satire, and irony is a deep respect for the misery of a mother and her persecuted son. It re-interprets the Gospels as a challenge to the hardships of an unjust world.

THE RESURRECTION OF LAZARUS

What separates an epic clown from an ordinary actor is the quantity of paradoxes that the clown knows how to express through his body, through his voice, through his comic violence. —Dario Fo [18]

Fo found his inspiration for "The Resurrection of Lazarus" on the wall of a cemetery in Pisa, where a fresco had faded away to reveal a fragment of the artist's preliminary sketch. "Lazarus wasn't even in it," notes Fo. "Its focus was concentrated on a crowd of spectators, as if they were at the theater, expressing through gestures their astonishment at the miracle." What intrigued Fo the most, however, was a small detail. "One of the characters was reaching into the purse of a spectator standing near him. He was taking advantage of their astonishment, of their amazement, of the miracle, to steal their money." [19]

Fo builds his version of the Lazarus story around the comic paradox he found painted on the cemetery wall: while the public's attention is turned to heavenly miracles, there will always be someone ready to bring them back to earth by picking their pockets. Beginning with this premise, Fo decided to portray the miracle of Lazarus's resurrection from the point of view of the crowd that came to watch it and the swindlers who try to profit from it. Fo plays over fifteen different roles in the course of his monologue, including the cemetery guardian who sells tickets to the miracle, a fish vendor, and gamblers taking odds on the likelihood that Jesus will succeed. There is also a man renting chairs so that people can watch the miracle without fear of fainting from shock and hitting their heads on a tombstone. Any such fatal accidents would be permanent, reminds the huckster in his singsong pitch, because "the saint only performs one miracle a day." [20]

THIS PAGE: Sketch of a drunkard that Fo used as a model for "The Wedding at Cana" in *Mistero Buffo*; OPPOSITE: "Palm Sunday," a nineteenth-century engraving of a Sicilian festival that inspired Fo's prologue for *Mistero Buffo*

Shifting from one character to another, Fo uses his voice and body to create a cinematic montage that turns the scene of the resurrection into a carnival fairground where onlookers scramble to get a view of the miracle. The arrival of the apostles is greeted with shouts of recognition: "Hey, Mark," yells an excited spectator, proposing that the saint join him for a drink after the miracle. Another viewer complains that he is tired of standing around waiting for the resurrection to begin: "They should have a timetable for these miracles, and stick to it." [21]

When Lazarus actually rises from his tomb, a bystander recounts his shaky first steps with the suspenseful tones of a prize-fight announcer at ringside wondering if a woozy boxer will make it to the next round: "He's rising. He's rising. He's up on his feet. He's falling. He's falling. He's going down. He's going down. He's up. He's down. He's moving forward. He's coming out of the grave like a dog coming out of water. He's shaking himself off. The worms are flying everywhere." [22] At this point Fo uses a film-editing technique to give the audience the illusion that they are watching someone being sprayed by the worms that Lazarus shakes off his partially decomposed body: having pantomimed the action of Lazarus shaking himself "like a dog coming out of water," he shifts position to become an onlooker picking the worms off his chest. "This passage is clear," Fo has written in a post-performance analysis. "One, two, three, I get into position and suddenly reverse the images, or should I say our movie camera changes position. From there it returns to there: a reverse angle shot in respect to the narrator." [23]

Beginning with a drawing that he re-imagines in the form of a film director's storyboard, Fo has written the monologue as a kind of medieval screenplay, articulating his technique in cinematic terms but performing the piece alone onstage as he imagines it would have been performed by a *giullare* in the Middle Ages. He explains how he moves from a close-up to a wide-angle shot by having the character change the tone of his voice during a crowd scene: "At this instant the situation changes. . . . I made it clear that there were people moving around me . . . other spectators who were crowded together and pressing up against my shoulder. Then someone pushes. Note that up until this point the frame of your [the audience's] viewing lens was limited to my face. Then when I pretend to lose my balance the image is enlarged to include the entire stage. I force a change in point of view."[24] Even though there is only one actor onstage, Fo orchestrates the action like a film director handling a cast of hundreds, using a camera to guide the eye of the public to the crucial details of the scene. "If I lower my voice and shrink my gestures, I force you to pay attention and concentrate harder," says Fo. "I almost oblige you to stretch your neck to catch what I have miniaturized. But watch what happens when I execute a big gesture, stretching out my arms. . . . I move toward you, turn around and exclaim, 'Who's pushing? Idiot, there's an open grave up here.' Then I make you imagine that the stage space is full of people pushing all around me. . . . The tone of annoyance is not raised just to indicate that the character is afraid of being pushed into the open grave. The main goal is to make it clear to the audience that the character is talking not only to people close to him but to the crowd that is all around him."[25]

By deftly playing with the focal point of the spectator's attention, Fo builds a relationship with the audience that makes them active partners in shaping the narration. Following his theatrical jump-cuts requires the public to keep thinking about the ideas and moral implications being raised by the changing points of view. This level of audience involvement is an important element in the epic style of theater championed by Bertolt Brecht. Fo is the most successful contemporary practitioner of Brecht's legacy, and refers often to the principles of epic performance. "Raising and lowering the voice dilates the stage space and physically involves the audience, so that they are transformed into a chorus participating with me onstage. This is the key of epic representation, involving the audience and always keeping them off-balance. The spectator has to be put in the position of being a public witness, conscious of his role, not sprawled out on his seat, passively digesting what he sees."[26]

"Lazarus," like all of Fo's monologues, was conceived in cinematic terms and written in a language that evokes the gestural equivalent of ever-shifting camera angles. The short phrases, fragmented syntax, and paradoxical juxtapositions are intended to activate the metaphoric movie camera that Fo imagines in the eyes of every spectator: "The actor,

the director, has to succeed in changing the audience's point of view whenever there is a need. We are accustomed, often without realizing it, to executing incredible zoom effects, focusing on a particular detail, or enlarging the wide panorama of the frame, or stretching things out, or highlighting the shadings of color from the chiaroscuro of the background. In fact we have in our brains a camera that no technical engineer could equal."[27]

The final passage in "The Resurrection of Lazarus" is representative of Fo's cinematic writing technique at its most concise. It depicts the moment Fo found painted on the cemetery wall in Pisa, the moment when the crowd realizes that the miracle of the resurrection is actually taking place before their eyes. "Bravo, Jesus," shouts one of the spectators. "My purse" yells another in alarm. "I've been robbed. Thief!" The instant of the miracle coincides with the instant of the crime, and the body of the actor becomes a visual metaphor for that paradox by virtue of the three words he repeats as the scene ends. Saying "Bravo, Jesus," demands that the actor assume a position of reverential awe. A second later his body shifts to a shape of angry frustration as he shouts "Thief," in an attempt to stop the pickpocket's escape. "Bravo, Jesus," and "Thief!" are repeated three times, pulling the actor's body into two opposing directions as if he were playing both sides of a reverse camera angle in rapid succession.[28] The physical paradox enacted by the actor's muscles parallels the paradox that animates the entire story: pure faith is juxtaposed against crass exploitation. The pickpocketing

...FO HAS TURNED HIMSELF INTO A LIVING HIEROGLYPH. THE LINK BETWEEN HIS BODY AND THE WALL DRAWINGS OF ANTIQUITY BECOMES PART OF HIS COMEDY. THE AUDIENCE IS REMINDED THAT ALL OF FO'S TEXTS REQUIRE THE ACTOR TO PLAY THE ROLE OF A HUMAN PICTOGRAPH.

is seen as a sleight-of-hand deception on a par with the profiteering of those who have exploited Christ's miracle as if he were a magician in a carnival sideshow. The parallels to modern-day religious charlatans and television evangelists are obvious, as Fo leaves his audience with the image of a man torn between the sincerity of his beliefs and the realization that his pocket has been picked. The repetition of the two phrases is deceptively simple, but the scenario they express is a complex evocation of paradox in motion.

THE BIRTH OF THE GIULLARE

I am not as interested in politics as I am in justice. What I hope to do is involve the audience in a sense of moral indignation against injustice, not with the theatrical equivalent of political pamphlets, but with entertainments that have a sense of elegance. —Dario Fo [29]

In Fo's cinematic vision of theater, the soundtrack is just as important as the camera angles. His texts unfold in rhythmic speech patterns that shrewdly heighten the themes of his stories. A recurring dynamic in Fo's narrative technique is the tension between freedom and oppression. In many of his stories Fo orchestrates the comic climaxes so that they coincide with the victim's liberation, creating a situation in which laughter arises from the defeat of tyranny.

The links between Fo's performance rhythms and his sense of moral indignation emerge clearly in the segment from *Mistero Buffo* entitled "The Birth of the *Giullare*." It recounts the miracle that gave the first *giullare* his talent for storytelling. Fo begins the piece as a traveling player trying to gather a crowd in an open-air piazza. His body whirls though space with the irrepressible energy of a child at a fairground, and he shouts out to his audience in an intoxicating nonstop stream of mixed Italian dialects. Once he wins people's attention, he suddenly stops the cascade of movements and sound, creating a moment of still and intimate eye contact with the public. "I was not always a *giullare*," he tells them in a confessional tone. "I used to be a peasant, a farmer. But I will tell you how it happened that I became a *giullare*" [30]

In a series of flashbacks Fo now re-enacts the unfair humiliations that the peasant has endured at the hands of corrupt landowners, priests, and government bureaucrats. Playing all the characters, Fo vividly conveys the peasant's growing sense of frustration in each new encounter with authority. The priest tries to cheat him out of his land with an oppressive litany of religious double-talk, which Fo builds to

an intolerable rhythmic intensity climaxing in the peasant's long-awaited moment of revenge: a good old-fashioned slapstick kick in the buttocks. The same basic pattern of oppression, frustration, rage, and liberation is repeated in the peasant's encounter with a local notary, but when the landowner and his soldiers rape the peasant's wife, the tone of the piece shifts to a blacker mood of resignation and despair.

As the grief-stricken peasant prepares to hang himself, he is stopped by a gaunt beggar who asks for a drink of water. It turns out to be Jesus, who praises the man for resisting the tyranny of the powerful and counsels him to share his story with others to inspire them to do the same. The peasant argues that his tongue is twisted, his mind is slow, and he has no facility with language. In response, Jesus kisses the peasant on the lips, miraculously giving him the gift of telling stories that will move his audiences to laughter and understanding.

Fo performs the moment of the miracle with an exhilarating sense of musicality. As the peasant is transformed by the kiss into a *giullare*, words spring loose from his mouth like water bursting from a fountain that has been blocked up for years. His arms flow expressively through the air like unbound windmills. The triumph of freedom over tyranny is palpable in each sound and movement. As he viciously satirizes the landowner with a tongue that now has the power to cut like a knife, it slowly becomes apparent that the piece is ending where it had begun. The *giullare* is again shouting for the public's attention in the piazza, but now his actions resonate with indignation and the memory of the injustices he has suffered. In "The Birth of the *Giullare*" as in all of Fo's work, the cadences of the comedy echo the rhythms of revolt.

POPE BONIFACE VIII

Now we come to Boniface the Eighth, the pope in the era of Dante. Dante knew him well. He hated him so much that he sent him to hell (in the Inferno) even before he died. —Dario Fo [31]

In telling the story of the medieval Pope Boniface, Fo uses all the epic theatrical techniques at his disposal, including the creation of a compelling soundtrack, in which the pope sings Gregorian chants, and a modern-day prologue that introduces the story with a portrait of Pope John Paul II. Boniface is seen from a variety of viewpoints, and Fo has compared his narrative strategy of multiple perspectives to the techniques of a sculptor, saying that he circles the story the way a sculptor circles an unfinished statue, examining the way the lights and shadows form when viewed from different directions. [32]

Fo's circling of his stories often begins with a drawing. In one of the first outlines he wrote for *Mistero Buffo* there is a passage that reads, "Boniface sits on a monk. Christ at his feet."[33] This describes a satirical drawing Fo had copied from an early-fourteenth-century codex in which Pope Boniface is expressing his disdain for the dissident beliefs of Segalello da Parma by using the monk as a chair. Segalello belonged to a religious order that believed the Church should renounce its earthly possessions and that its representatives should follow Christ's example by living in poverty. The drawing led Fo to create a story about Pope Boniface that stresses the contradiction between the Church's wealth and Christ's poverty.

At the beginning of the piece, Fo communicates this contradiction through the style of the pope's singing. Preparing for a public procession, Boniface sings a Gregorian chant with the aid of choirboys who help him dress in his finest robes and jewels. Although the solemn rhythms and lofty words of the chant summon up images of spirituality, the pope interrupts the song at irregular intervals to polish his jewels and adjust his luxurious vestments. At one point he pauses for a few beats to clean a mirror with his breath. Then, after admiring himself, the pope resumes the chant with renewed fervor. The rupture of the religious rhythm corresponds perfectly with the collapse of the pope's pious facade.

Boniface's suppression of dissent, which the medieval drawing had shown through the image of the pope sitting on the monk, is expressed by Fo in a recurring comic gesture. Each time the choirboys fail to assist him properly, Fo's pope threatens to hang them by their tongues from the church door—a punishment Boniface is actually said to have imposed on dissident monks. Smiling through gritted teeth, the pope makes his threat with a sly pantomime that begins with the gesture of hammering a nail and ends with the evocation of a body swinging in the breeze as it hangs suspended by its tongue. "Better watch out," warns the pope, with a barely suppressed rage that suggests the choirboys will end up squirming in the wind if they don't follow his orders more efficiently.[34] The nail through the tongue is a stark emblem of censorship, and Fo achieves a gruesomely comic effect by repeating it several times in the course of the story, each time with smaller and smaller gestures until it becomes an ironic visual shorthand for the absolute power of the pope, a slapstick hieroglyph of oppression.

The story ends when the pope's procession meets Christ, who is dressed in rags. Boniface is so self-absorbed that he

doesn't at first recognize the gaunt and bearded figure, even when the choirboys tell him who it is. When he realizes who is in front of him, he tries to cover up his blunder by blaming the choirboys: "Oh, *that* Jesus," he exclaims. "Jesus Christ! He's got two names. Why don't you use them?"[35]

Fearing that Christ's own renunciation of worldly possessions will make him skeptical of a pontiff dressed in gold and silk, Boniface quickly sheds his robes and jewels and orders the choirboys to cover him with mud. Jesus sees through the charade and gives the pontiff a kick in the tailbone, a blow, according to Fo, that is the origin of the coccyx's Italian nickname as the "sacred bone." Even more humiliating for Boniface is Christ's assertion that he never authorized Saint Peter to establish a papacy in the first place. The pope reacts to the news of his illegitimacy with hysterical silent laughter.[36]

In his prologue to the story, Fo calls the meeting of Jesus and Pope Boniface "a typical anachronism of the Middle Ages." It is the kind of juxtaposition Fo attributes to the medieval *giullari*, who depicted the pope's actions from Christ's viewpoint to highlight his destructive impact on the present , just as Dante did by writing him into the *Inferno*. Fo adds his own anachronistic elements by juxtaposing the tale of the medieval pope with a story about the 1983 assassination attempt made on the life of Karol Wojtyla, the current Pope John Paul II. Surprisingly, Fo turns the episode into a comic montage, using his cinematic technique to make the audience feel as if they were watching a documentary newsreel of the event. Fo becomes a crowd waiting for the pope's arrival at the airport. He also becomes the pope's airplane, breaking through the clouds with an oversized papal skull cap on its cockpit, as well as an onlooker, who believes the pope himself is flying and has to be reminded, "No that's not him. The Pope's inside. . . . The pope doesn't have little windows."[37]

The theme of censorship appears in the prologue when Fo describes the pope tripping down the stairs from the plane to the runway. "No one knows how to go down stairs more quickly than the pope," says Fo, using the flapping of his hands to create a close-up of the pope's feet fluttering down a staircase. "The only problem was, he didn't see the last ten steps." Fo then shows how the fall is censored by the television cameras transmitting the event on a delayed broadcast: he shows the pope beginning to go down the steps, then depicts the pope dusting himself off after a jump cut in the tape that eliminates the fall completely.[38]

Fo's re-enactment of modern media censorship in the prologue echoes the graphic tongue-piercing threat of censorship that is at the heart of his portrait of Boniface. The audience is reminded that the medieval story has modern resonance, a resonance made even more immediate by the fact that the play they are watching was actually censored by the Vatican, whose newspaper accused it of "encouraging the complete disintegration of Italian society."[39] Fo added the modern version of the prologue to *Mistero Buffo* after the play had been banned, under Vatican pressure, from the national television stations, which were controlled by the Christian Democratic Party. The prologue re-inforces the prismatic nature of the performance, encouraging audiences to re-evaluate the relationship between politics and religion from multiple perspectives, ranging from television broadcasts of the pope to the threat of a nail through the tongue.

THE QUINTESSENTIAL GIULLARE

If there is a single work that embodies the essence of Fo and Rame's theatrical artistry, it is *Mistero Buffo*. Their masterpiece, the play provides a key to

the techniques that animate all their theater. Every monologue is infused with the rhythmic drive of a jazz improvisation, the immediacy of a newspaper headline, and the epic scope of a historical novel. Like all their work, *Mistero Buffo* elicits a multiplicity of overlapping dialogues: between the actor and the audience; between the text and the body of the actor; between conventional visions of the Bible and provocative reinterpretations of the Gospels; between the visual sources of the play and the text they inspired; and between standard uses of language and the invented dialect with which the stories are told. The literal meaning of *Mistero Buffo* is "comic mystery play." The mystery plays were sacred representations performed in the Middle Ages. Going back to those medieval source materials, Fo created a virtuosic work that established him as a modern-day *giullare*. He has continued to perform *Mistero Buffo* throughout his career, and returns to its biblical themes in numerous other works, including a collection of monologues entitled *The Peasants' Bible* (1996). Always respectful of the populist versions of Christ's story, Fo chose to tell it the way he imagined it had been preserved through the oral tradition of the medieval *giullari,* and through the paintings and frescoes of their contemporaries.

In my research on medieval texts I encountered, too often to ignore, this figure of Christ transformed by the people into a kind of hero in opposition to authority, and to the hierarchy of the Church, which had always tried to monopolize him and keep him distant from the people. It should be remembered that until well after the year 1000 people were prohibited from reading the Gospels, and that their translation into the vernacular took place very late. Yet the people did not accept their exclusion and had given life to a vast number of apocryphal gospels, from which a different Christ emerged. He was more human and always on the side of the weakest. He had in him a pagan, almost Dionysian joy for love, feasting, beauty, and earthly things. And at the same time he was full of hatred and violence toward hypocritical priests, the aristocracy who wanted to dominate the weak, and a triumphant church and its temporal power. This is probably not the historical Christ, but it is the Christ who was created by the vast culture of the popular tradition. —Dario Fo[40]

IN TELLING THE STORY OF THE MEDIEVAL POPE BONIFACE, FO USES ALL THE EPIC THEATRICAL TECHNIQUES AT HIS DISPOSAL... BONIFACE IS SEEN FROM A VARIETY OF VIEWPOINTS, AND FO HAS COMPARED HIS NARRATIVE STRATEGY OF MULTIPLE PERSPECTIVES TO THE TECHNIQUES OF A SCULPTOR, SAYING THAT HE CIRCLES THE STORY THE WAY A SCULPTOR CIRCLES AN UNFINISHED STATUE, EXAMINING THE WAY THE

THE RESURRECTION OF LAZARUS

A monologue from the millennial edition of MISTERO BUFFO
BY DARIO FO Translated by RON JENKINS

PROLOGUE Now we come to the miracle of Lazarus.

This text is a "battle horse," demanding extraordinary physical and vocal agility, because the giullare finds himself playing the roles of something like fifteen or sixteen characters consecutively, without indicating the changes by shifting his position or body shape. He doesn't even alter his voice, but simply changes his attitude. Consequently this is one of the texts that forces the actor to improvise a little, adapting himself to the rhythm of the laughter, the tempo, and the silences of the audience. Actually, it is a scenario that requires constant improvisation. The central theme of the text is found in its satire of everything that constitutes the "mystical moment," focusing on the exhibition of what people usually refer to as a "miracle." The satire is directed against the exhibition of the miraculous, of magic, of witchcraft, which is prevalent in many religions, including Catholicism: particularly the idea of exhibiting the miracle as a supernatural event, with the goal of demonstrating indisputably that it has been performed by God: whereas, in the original accounts of the miracle, it was interpreted as a sign of the love and connection that existed between the divine and the human.

Here the miracle is recounted from the point of view of the faithful who come from the lower rungs of society: everything is seen and presented as if it were a spectacle in which "the divine son of man" exhibits himself as a great prestidigitator, a magician, someone who can do extraordinary things with great theatricality. No one pays attention to the intentions behind the act.

In a sinopia from the cemetery in Pisa there is a depiction of the resurrection of Lazarus. (A sinopia is a preliminary sketch that precedes the execution of a fresco; during the restoration of this fresco the well-preserved preliminary sketch had been uncovered). Lazarus does not even appear in it: the attention is focused, as it will be in the piece that I am about to perform for you, on a crowd of astonished people, who express through gestures, their amazement at the miracle. One can also see a person in the crowd who takes advantage of the tension generated by the event. He slips his hand into the purse of a spectator, who is pre-occupied with following the resurrection, and relieves him of a few coins.

(The scene begins with conversation between the first visitor and the caretaker of the cemetery)

(*In the role of the visitor*) Excuse me. Is this the cemetery, the holy graveyard, where they're going to perform the resurrection of Lazarus, the one who was buried four days ago? And now a great holy man is coming, a witch doctor.... I think his name is Jesus... 'Son of God' is his nickname... and the corpse is going to jump up with his eyes rolling in his head and everyone shouting: "He's alive! He's alive!"... and then we'll all go drinking and get divinely drunk. Is this the place?

(In the role of the cemetery caretaker) Yes, two shekels if you want to see the miracle!

(Returning to the role of the visitor) You want me to give you two shekels? Why?

(Returning to the role of the cemetery caretaker) Because I'm the caretaker of this cemetery and I've got to be compensated for all the trouble and damages you all are going to cause me.... You people come in here and you stomp on the shrubbery... you trample all over the graves... you sit on the crosses... twist the arms off them... and then you even steal the candles! (He takes a breath.)

Two shekels, otherwise you can go to some other cemetery! I'd like to see if you can find another holy man as good as ours, who with just a wave of his hands can bring the dead sprouting up out of the ground like mushrooms. Move along, move along! You too, lady, two shekels! Half a shekel for the baby. I don't care if he doesn't understand a thing. When he grows up you'll tell him: "What a shame you were too thick headed and dumb to understand what was going on, and not only that, just at the moment of the miracle, you peed all over me." *(He turns to an imaginary boy who's trying to sneak into the cemetery by climbing over the wall.)* Get out of here! Off that wall! Trouble maker, riff raff! Wise-guy... wants to come in and see the miracle for free.

(In the role of the first visitor) Gosh, there's so many graves! What a big cemetery! Look at all the crosses. *(He turns directly to the audience.)* I came here early on purpose to get a good place, because I like to be up front... I like to have a good view of the open grave... because some of these holy witch doctors will try to pull a fast one on you: they put a dead man on top, a live one underneath, they make all these holy gestures and.... TRAC-CHETE!, they pull the old switcheroo: "He's alive! He's alive!" I

want to see it up close! The last time I was here early in the morning; I spent half the day waiting around... but they performed the miracle over on the other side so I ended up standing there like a dope without seeing a thing. But this time I'm going to get it right, and here is Lazarus.... Look at all the people coming! *(Scans the people around him)* Hey! You like miracles, don't you? You don't have anything better to do, huh? *(Mimes getting shoved and losing his equilibrium)* Stop pushing! We have an open grave, here! I'll fall in, and then the holy man will come and say: "Alive! Alive!" And me, I'm already alive! *(Points to the distance)* They're even coming down from the mountains!... Hey mountain boys, you never saw a miracle before, did you? *(Comments ironically)* Foreigners! *(With gestures he indicates the presence of a short man.)* Hey, shorty, stop pushing! Shorty, stop pushing! I don't care if you're too short to see anything. Short people and cripples have to come at dawn to get a good spot. *(Comments ironically)* Ha, ha, ha... you think you're in heaven where the little people will be first and the big people will be last? Ha, ha, ha! *(He turns to another character)* Oh, lady, don't push! I don't care if you're a woman. In the face of death we're all equal!

(Directly to the audience) I don't just come here for the miracles. I come for the laughs. *(Shouting in the distance)* Well, is the holy man going to show up, or what? Isn't there someone who knows where his house is who can go and call him... to let him know that we're all ready for him here... that we can't stand around all day waiting for miracles.... We've got other things to do!... They should make a timetable for these miracles! And stick to it! *(To himself)* Is he coming?... *(To the others)* He's not coming!

(Creating the illusion that a man renting chairs is offering his wares to the crowd in a loud voice) Chairs! Who wants chairs? Ladies! Rent yourself a chair! Two shekels a chair! Get yourself a seat, because it's very dangerous to watch a miracle while you're standing up. Because as soon as the holy man shows up and waves his arms Lazarus is going to rise up on his feet... with his eyes rolling in his head.... And you'll be so terrified that you'll

fall over backwards with a big thump and smash your head on a rock.... TACCHETE! Stone cold dead! *(Turns to the audience)* And the holy man only performs one miracle a day! So step right up and rent a chair! Two shekels!

(Suggesting the end of that scene he returns to the role of the first visitor) Shorty, you got a chair, huh? To make yourself taller! Good for you! I'll help you climb up! Opla! Now you're a big shorty! Don't lean on my shoulder... or I'll give you a good shove... knock you into the open tomb, slam down the cover, and sit myself on top of it. *(Mimes knocking from the inside of the tomb)* TON TON: silence! TON TON: eternity!...

(Turns to those around him) Is this saint going to show up or isn't he? He's not coming! We can't keep waiting here like this... it's getting dark! We'll have to light little candles. The saint will get here, go to the wrong grave, and resurrect somebody else's corpse.... Then Lazarus' mother will show up, crying her eyes out... and he'll have to kill the corpse he just resurrected!

That wouldn't make a very nice impression... not in front of all the foreigners.

(Suddenly he mimes the entrance of a fried fish vendor.) Ohhhhooh! Sardines, here! Nice sweet fried sardines... two shekels... Get yourself a handful! So delicious... they bring the dead back to life!

(In the role of a visitor) Hey, sardine man, why don't you give a few to Lazarus to wake up his stomach!

(Another visitor) Be quiet! Blasphemer!

(In the role of the first visitor) Look at all the people coming... look, look, all the apostles! They're lined up behind the holy man... that apostle over there... that's Peter, with the long beard and all the curls... and that other one with the bald head and the curly beard, that's Paul... and that one... *(shouting out a festive greeting)* Maaaark!... *(Changing tone: turning proudly to the people around him)* I know him! He lives next door to my house... *(He waves his arms in a highly visible greeting and uses gestures to invite the saint out for a drink after the miracle.)* Look. That's Jesus... the little one... he's so young... look, he doesn't even have a beard... he's so sweet... he looks like a little boy. I imagined him much heftier, with a huge head of hair... buckshot ears *(points to his ears)*, a giant coxcomb, tremendous teeth, and great big hands, so that when he makes the sign of the benediction: PAA!... he smacks the faithful to pieces! But he's no bigger than a child!...

(A voice from the crowd) Jeesuuuus! Do that miracle again with the multiplication of the bread and the fishes that was so delicious... God, what a feast that was!

(Another character) Don't you ever think of anything but food!?

(Responding to the one who just spoke) It's natural! Here we are standing around the cemetery... and the excitement of waiting for the miracle gets my stomach so worked up that I'm hungry enough to eat God himself!

(One of the visitors) Quiet, quiet! Jesus just gave the word for everybody to get down on their knees! All the holy men are on their knees praying... so are the others... we should get down on our knees too, otherwise the miracle won't work!

(Another visitor) I won't do it. I won't do it! I don't care! I'm not a believer and I'm not getting down on my knees!

(Another visitor) You'll get hit with a lightning bolt that will cripple your leg. *(He mimes walking with a limp)* Then you'll go to Jesus: "Jesus, can you do that miracle for me, the one..." Nothing doing! Another lightning bolt... TRAK!, there goes your arm too! *(He mimes a paralyzed arm.)*

(Another character) Quiet, quiet, he's given the order to lift the stone off the grave. *(One of the bystanders shouts orders and supervises the raising of the stone)* Come on! All together! Lift

that boulder! Watch out for your toes!

(A spectator holding his nose) Woooah, what a stench! That stinks! What do they have in there... a putrefied cat?

(Another visitor) No, no, it's him, it's Lazarus, look what a state he's in!

(Another visitor) Ohia, he's almost rotted away... all those worms are coming out of his eyes... Ah, that's disgusting!

(Another visitor) They're playing a joke on him.

(Another visitor) On who?

(Another visitor) On him, on Jesus! They told him the guy had only been buried four days... but it looks like he's been down under for at least a month! He'll never pull off this miracle...

(Another spectator) Why?

(In response) Because this corpse is too ripe.

(Another visitor) I think he'll do it anyway, because this holy man is so great that even if there were nothing left in the grave but four putrid decomposing bones, all he'd have to do was lift his eyes up to heaven... two words to his Father, and before you know it those bones would be full of flesh, and muscles, and VUUUMMMMMMM!, he'd jump right up out of there like a rabbit!

(Another character) Cut the crap!

(Another visitor) What crap?! Why don't we bet on it? Four will get you five if he pulls it off!

(Another visitor) Seven will get you ten if he can't do it! I'm taking all bets! (He turns to the imaginary spectators with the tone of a bookmaker taking odds.) Three, four, two... eight says he can do it... seven says he can't....

(Another visitor, disgusted) Stop it! Shame on you! The holy man's still praying, and they're taking bets! Blasphemy! You should be ashamed of yourselves... (Suddenly) I bet you five shekels he can do it!

(Another voice) Quiet! The holy man pointed to the corpse and commanded: "Rise up, Lazarus!"

(Another character) Ha, ha! All that's going to rise up are the worms crawling around in his belly.

(Another spectator) Quiet, you blasphemer!

(Another character, dumbfounded) He's moving! God bless him, he's moving! He's alive! (Mimes the movement of Lazarus who rises up, wobbling) Lazarus is sitting up, he's rising, he's on his feet... he's falling, falling, falling... he's going down, he's going down, he's coming up! He's shaking himself off like a dog shaking off water... worms are flying all over the place! (He mimes disgust as he cleans off the worms that have been shaken onto his face and body.) Miserable wretch! Take it easy with those worms!

(Another visitor falling onto his knees) It's a miracle!

He's alive! He's been resurrected! Wooah, look at that: he's laughing, he's crying.

(The characters in turn marvel at the miracle.)

(Another visitor, now on his knees) Amazing Son of God, I had no idea you were this miraculous! (Subsequently, he turns quickly to the bookmaker.) I won. You owe me seven shekels! (To Jesus) It's amazing! Bravo, Jesus, bravo!... (Suddenly he pats his belly and his hips.) My purse?.... Thief! Bravo Jesus! (Turns toward the distance.) Thief! Thief! Jesus, bravo! (He exits running, repeatedly turning his head back and forth between Jesus and the distance.) Thieeeeeef!.... Jesus! Bravo Jesus! Thieeeef! Bravo Jesus! Thieeeeef! Bravoooo Jesus!

TOTALITÀ SCENICA

LEVITAZIO
MEC

ART RESTORATION: LEONARDO'S LAST SUPPER

C H A P T E R 5

Do you see that statue? When I was in art school at Brera we used to call it "What a Nice Ass!" Leonardo is up on the pedestal surrounded by his students. But look where his eyes are focused: he's gazing down approvingly at the buttocks of his favorite disciple. That's why we called it "What a Nice Ass!" It's what we imagined Leonardo was thinking at the time —Dario Fo, commenting on the statue of Leonardo da Vinci in Piazza della Scala, Milan[1]

Dario Fo has a gift for bringing art to life. When he sees a statue, he hears it thinking. When he goes into a church, he imagines the struggles of the architects and artisans who built it. When he looks at a painting, he reconstructs the swirl of historical conflicts that led to its creation. For Fo there is no such thing as a still life. Every work of art teems with actions on the verge of unfolding and with words waiting to be spoken aloud. Fo is capable of approaching even the most familiar art and pointing out a detail that makes viewers see it from a new perspective. He uses the same approach in his plays, taking well-known figures from history or current events and making his audience see them in a fresh light. In museums as well as in theaters, Fo uses humor to make the familiar strange, encouraging his audience to do a double-take and look again more closely at things they might be taking for granted.

ARTIFICIO DEL LEVITARE

To celebrate the unveiling of Leonardo's newly restored *Last Supper*, in 1999, the municipality of Milan invited Fo to give a nationally televised lecture on the painting. His discourse on Leonardo's masterpiece provides a unique glimpse into his larger vision of the arts. Ostensibly, Fo was discussing the restoration of a single faded fresco, but his ideas had wider implications. For Fo, art restoration involves the restoration not only of color and form but of an artwork's social context, as well as of its power to draw viewers into a dialogue with history, language, visual landscapes, human anatomy, and each other. Fo's lecture gradually turned into a performance that evoked these multiple dialogues in the present tense, at the same time that it unearthed them in the career of Leonardo.

Fo chose to give his talk in a theatrical setting: the porticoed courtyard of the Brera academy, where he had been a student in the 1940s. While acknowledging the audience's applause at the opening of his lecture, Fo looked at the statues of famous artists that surrounded him and quipped, "I thought for a second that the statues were clapping too."[2] He commented on how familiar the columns seemed to him, for he had spent eight years of his youth as a student at Brera. These remarks served to draw Fo's audience into a shared awareness of their immediate environment and its historical resonance.

Fo's personal past blended into his present as he introduced his wife, Franca Rame, who, he said, "has agreed after forty-six years of partnership to do me the honor of turning the pages as I speak."[3] The pages he alluded to contained not written words but drawings that he had made to visualize the concepts he wanted to cover in his speech. As Rame turned the pages at an antique wooden lectern, a television cameraman behind her shoulder projected these visual notes onto a giant screen over Fo's head, for the benefit of the hundreds of people who had crammed into the courtyard to watch the lecture in person. Several million more people would watch it on television a few days later.

The television program presents a visual montage to accompany Fo's lecture: the camera cuts from Fo to his drawings to the audience to the porticoes to the statues to Leonardo's fresco in a nearby church. Fo's drawings for the broadcast also appear as a montage of jump cuts, close-ups, establishing shots, and dissolves. They depict scenes from Leonardo's life and times, as well as highlighting details that Fo has extracted from Leonardo's artworks. There is Gutenberg's printing press, invented in 1452, the year of Leonardo's birth. There is a fifteenth-century pope whose armies waged war throughout Europe. There is the fifteenth-century playwright and actor Ruzzante, who, like Leonardo, was an illegitimate child, and was denied the benefits of a formal university education. Then there are fragments of Leonardo's studies for paintings like *The Adoration of the Magi* and designs for his mechanical inventions. Finally there are Fo's renderings of *The Last Supper*, each sketch focusing on a different element of Leonardo's technique.

Sometimes Fo discusses the subjects depicted in his drawings. At other times he acts them out with his body, or uses them as an inspiration for digressions on topics like the war in Yugoslavia (current at the time of the lecture) and the windmills along the canals of fifteenth-century Milan. The text of the lecture becomes a springboard for a performance in which Fo uses his body and his drawings to make connections between Leonardo, Renaissance history, the Machiavellian roots of modern war, and the immediate sensory experience of the audience in the Brera courtyard. Fo also teases the cameramen who hover around him with jokes that create a link between the live audience and the future audience that will watch the show on television. He blurs the boundaries between past and present, painting and theater, politics and art, the painted body and the performing body, the electronic performance and the live performance, the spoken word and the visual image, the epic and the intimate. In doing so he creates an uncategorizable event encompassing all these contradictions with a disarming sense of informality that draws the audience effortlessly into the performance.

Although Fo's onstage presence appears casual, his preparation is prodigious. His architectural training gives him a sense of space and design that he applies to every detail of the televised performance, from the angles of his gestures to the placement of the stage in relationship to the architectural elements around it. "I have never worked with an artist who is so precise about the mise-en-scene of the camera," says Felice Cappa, the television director of the Leonardo lectures. "He knows exactly where he wants to stand and what parts of the setting will become the background in the shots of him performing, as well as what parts of the setting will become the background for the reaction shots of the audience. His movements on stage seem spontaneous, but he is constantly calculating camera angles and lighting effects, and taking them into account with every step he takes."[4]

Fo is as deliberate in his layering of texts, drawings, and gestures as he is in coordinating the montage of the cameras that film him. An example of his collage technique can be

PAGES 120–129: Drawings from Fo's notes for his lecture on Leonardo, Milan, 1999

seen in the way he conducts his ongoing dialogue with history. The first image projected on the screen over Fo's head is the Gutenberg press. Fo does not just tell us that it was invented in the year of Leonardo's birth; he envisions the machine as a weapon in the historical battle against censorship, reminding his audience that the Church opposed the mass production of Bibles written in the vernacular, preferring that the sacred text be available only in Latin, so that the power of interpreting its meaning would rest with the clergy and other educated members of the elite. This leads Fo to a discussion of the holy wars started by the Church, which led to Renaissance Italy's nickname as "the land of death." The label appears on the screen over one of Fo's drawings of soldiers and corpses.

The theme of Church censorship emerges again later, when Fo describes how sixteenth-century monks destroyed part of *The Last Supper* by building a doorway in the wall on which it was painted. The top of the arched doorway cut into the fresco, eliminating the feet of the apostles under the table. Fo cites this as an example of arrogance on the part of Church officials: had they been humble enough to bend down when entering the room, they could have made a shorter doorway that would not have destroyed the bottom of the painting. For Fo the absurd pride of the sixteenth-century monks is matched by the modern Italian bureaucrats who refused to restore the lower part of Leonardo's fresco, arguing that the four-hundred-year-old hole created by the monk's doorway is now itself regarded as a historic monument that cannot be destroyed. This "historic hole," which few visitors to *The Last Supper* ever stop to consider, is seen by Fo as a battleground of political forces from the fifteenth, sixteenth, and twentieth centuries. His visual imagination transforms the empty space into a metaphor for the intersection of arrogance, absurdity, and censorship.

While making epic connections between historical eras, Fo sometimes focuses on surprisingly intimate details. Issues of arrogance and social status also emerge in the lecture's discussion of the strained relationship between Leonardo and his father. As a bastard child with no legal rights to his father's wealth, Leonardo watched his stepbrothers become partners in his father's business while he was disenfranchised. Showing a drawing of the brothers lined up in a row for their inheritance, Fo speaks ironically of Leonardo's love for his father, comparing it to the feelings of another illegitimate child of that era, Ruzzante, who said, "Oh how I wish I could return to the embracing womb of my mother, and then go back even farther to find myself melted into the sperm of my father, and then back farther still into my father's balls, so I could keep on busting them whenever I wanted."[5] Fo speculates that Leonardo never manifested even this degree of "filial love" for his father.[6]

At the same time that Fo is inviting the audience to reconsider their image of the historical Leonardo, he is luring them into a playful dialogue with language. The quotation from Ruzzante is in an archaic Italian dialect, but Fo asks the

audience not to worry about the language barrier: "If you don't understand it," he counsels, "laugh anyway, so you won't make a bad impression. Then I'll translate the entire passage for you, but don't laugh at the translation or people will know you didn't understand it the first time."[7] By calling attention to his manipulation of language Fo encourages the audience to think about the nature of translation, and gets them to laugh twice at the same passage, chastising them for laughing during the dialect version and throwing off his rhythm. They also laugh at the onomatopoeic qualities of Fo's voice, and at the gestures he uses to communicate the contrast between luxuriating in the womb of the mother and busting the balls of the father. Stopping his performance to comment on the laughter patterns of the audience, Fo establishes an intimate give-and-take relationship with the

BY MAKING LEONARDO'S ARTWORK A GATEWAY INTO HIS PSYCHE, FO PRESENTS A METHOD OF ANALYSIS THAT COULD BE JUST AS FRUITFULLY APPLIED TO THE OUTPUT OF HIS OWN VISUAL IMAGINATION.

crowd that is based on his understanding of the musical qualities of Ruzzante's dialect.

Fo moves on to explain that Leonardo also knew how to create a relationship with an audience. He discusses the theatrical machines Leonardo invented for entertainments at the castle of the Duke of Milan, and the startling effect they had on the audience: "In the art of staging spectacles with magical scenic effects, Leonardo was truly a genius," says Fo. "His famous mechanical lion terrorized the audience. The lion was activated

by a mechanism made of multiple clockworks that created more than twenty different movements."[8] Fo sees a link between the witty ingenuity of Leonardo's theatrical devices and the satirical qualities embedded in many of his paintings. Having located these humorous touches with the detective work of an art historian, Fo has made drawings that heighten the details he finds in Leonardo's work. "In the preliminary sketches for *The Adoration of the Magi*," notes Fo, "we find an element that has almost gone unnoticed: there in the sky are the angels who blow on long horns to announce the birth of the Savior to the shepherds.

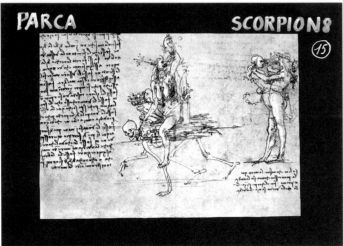

In the background on the left there is a prankster angel honking and blaring with great vehemence into the ear of another angel who is stunned into a state of dumbfounded wobbling."[9] Fo accompanies this comment with his own drawing of the clown angel, based on Leonardo's original. His visual sleuthing reveals the comic spirit woven into the background of *The Adoration*.

In another preliminary study for the same painting Fo discovers a scene in which soldiers on horseback "stab each other in a whirlwind of spears and swords, while women flee shouting in terror." Fo attributes significance to the placement of the battle

scene in the background of a painting that depicts the Madonna and her child receiving gifts from the three wise men. "The allegory is clear," reasons Fo. "The human race continues to commit butchery, murder, and violence against women, remaining deaf to the announcement of the angel who shouts 'Peace to all men of good will,' and oblivious to the fact that taking place a few steps away on the world stage is one of the most extraordinary events in the history of mankind."[10]

Fo sees Leonardo's painting of the Magi as a theatrical re-enactment of history, full of ironic commentary on the state of the world. It is a point of view that Fo developed as an art student, and might have inspired his own ironic commentary in his play *The First Miracle of Baby Jesus* (1978). Fo opens that monologue with a scene in which the three wise men engage in racist speech and behavior on their way to see the newborn Christ. The long passage devoted to their journey may also owe something to the Brera collection's many paintings of the Nativity that prominently depict an endless landscape of hills and deserts around the manger where Christ was born. These paintings, which Fo studied regularly as a student, suggest the expansive countryside that the wise men had to cross to reach the manger. Fo's version of the Nativity story animates that barren landscape with a parody of the wise men's racist behavior, the verbal equivalent of the visual irony he finds in Leonardo's rendering of the same scene.

Fo finds another kind of sly satire underlying Leonardo's inventions of war machines when he notices that a drawing of an extra-long cannon is labeled "The Phallus of the King." Leonardo's invention of the cluster bomb leads Fo to suggest that bombs found in the Adriatic Sea during the war in Yugoslavia might not have been dropped by the Americans, as the Italian newspapers claimed, but were left over from the days of Leonardo. Fo exhibits carefully rendered drawings of Leonardo's inventions to accompany his ironic commentary.

Fo also re-creates Leonardo's anatomical drawings, using them to speculate that Leonardo may have been an atheist but must have had a profound sense of the miraculousness of the human body. "It is enough to read his random writings in the various notebooks to realize how extraordinarily moved he was by his investigations into the mysteries of creation, and how he was possessed by an almost mystical exaltation as he discovered the ingenious mechanisms of the human body."[11] It is obvious from passages like these that Fo feels a great affinity with Leonardo, and attributes many of his own beliefs to the

Renaissance artist. He himself has a deep fascination with the human body, expressed in the multitude of leaping, dancing, fighting, and flying shapes he gives to the figures in his drawings. Like Leonardo, he also designs stage sets, satirizes political and religious authorities, and has a pagan appreciation of the world's wonders that shapes his approach to religion. As he does in his theatrical portraits of historical icons like Saint Francis and Columbus, Fo exaggerates some of the qualities of his subject in this lecture, but in doing so he draws attention to elements of Leonardo's genius that more detached observers could easily overlook. For example, only a physical actor who is also a playwright, director, and painter would be likely to possess the combination of sensitivities necessary to appreciate the subtle movement patterns that are choreographed into a work like *The Last Supper.*

When Fo finally gets around to discussing the details of the newly restored painting, his analysis is revelatory, particularly in regard to the actions suggested by the postures of the apostles at the table. "Some critics," says Fo,

have noted the positioning of the apostles in groups of three, and see this as a reference to cabalistic numerology or an allusion to the Holy Trinity. Personally I am not drawn to these theories, and would rather focus on how, beginning from the left side, there is an almost wavelike movement that creates a pattern of stretched and broken arches, turning arabesques on themselves. Waves rise and fall, moving past the figure of Christ, who remains immobile as if ensconced in a pyramid, while to his right the gestures of the hands form waves, climb up, and reverse themselves on the shoulder of the prophet. The gesture of Philip, who is standing, is connected to the peak of the wave set into motion by the extended gesture of Matthew, next to Simon, which encompasses the suspended gesture of the last apostle. To highlight the almost musical rhythm of the undulating structure created by Jesus' followers there is a long sequence of vertical shadings that follows their shoulders. . . . If there were a kind of zoom lens camera following the gestures of only the hands, moving from the observer's left, we would have the sensation of participating in a pantomime where the gestures designed a dance. It is the first apostle (still starting from the left) who starts the pantomime by slapping both his hands down on the table [in front of the apostle Andrew] who lifts his hands with the palms out toward the public in a gesture of fear. Suddenly there appears a hand holding a knife—it is Peter, who is continuing the movement toward John. Peter rests his left hand on the shoulder of John, who points toward Jesus with the hand he has opened on the table. Judas is isolated in the foreground, a lump of stone that sticks out of the wave and is removed from the gestures of the other followers.[12]

Fo sees the painting as a dramatic performance rather than a static work of art. He continues to describe the figures' movements in great detail, focusing on the undulations of the ensemble rather than concentrating on the gestures of any single apostle. As he rhythmically delineates the motion in words, and refers to the drawings he has made, Fo actually dances out the pantomime of the apostle's hands, becoming each figure in turn as he glides across the stage and creates the illusion of the gestural wave he is describing. The stage effect draws delighted applause from the audience as they watch Leonardo's painting come to life in the convergence of Fo's drawings, gestures, and words, whose lilting musicality propels the overall swell of the movements. Fo is not only dancing the painting, he is singing it. The moment captures the essence of his theatrical technique. The music of his language animates his gestures, which are in turn a corporal expression of his drawings.

Fo's techniques and observations are motivated by more than aesthetics. Like the link between gesture, painting, and music in his own work, Fo's interpretations of these elements in Leonardo's work have a dimension of social conscience that emphasizes collective rather than individual effort. He believes it is important to avoid isolating individual apostles in the painting and instead to experience the music and movement in *The Last Supper* as though the figures were part of a chorus: "Leonardo calls our attention to the choral nature of the event, forcing us to see it from a wider lens so that we understand the entire expanse of the action. In short, *The Last Supper* in the Church of Santa Maria delle Grazie is not an exhibition of musicians and singers on a stage, each one with his own aria or solo number. What we are participating in is a real and genuine choral concert following a polyphonic score that has a rich orchestration, with its arias, high points, counterpoints, and bass rhythms, but where every sound is part of the whole."[13]

In Fo's analysis, choral structure is so integral to the painting's identity that it democratically includes the spectator as part of the chorus. Fo has calculated that the perspective lines in the painting are constructed so that "the vanishing point is in the right eye of Jesus."[14] This creates the illusion that the painting's viewers are being lifted up toward that level as they approach the artwork. The unusually sharp inclines in the painting's composition "accentuate the spectator's sensation of being lifted off the ground, almost suspended in the action of the painting."[15] Fo imagines that Leonardo created a scenario in which the viewer is invited to sit at the table with Jesus while being lifted through the air in flight. To demonstrate the effect, a series of Fo's illustrations depict the levitation of the spectator, hovering in the air above the apostles' table. These drawings, of course, also reflect Fo's vision of the audience's relation to his own performances, including the one he is giving about Leonardo. Fo always makes a point of breaking down the fourth wall of the proscenium stage and including the public in the performance. He discusses his theatrical techniques with the audience as he employs them, stripping away as much pretense as possible from the theatrical encounter so that his relationship with the audience can be unmediated and direct. Sometimes Fo literally does invite the audience up onto the stage with him, and his professional experience in the theater enables him to envision Leonardo making a similar effort to reach out to an audience. One of his drawings depicts Leonardo painting *The Last Supper* on a scaffold that elevates him to the level of Jesus's right eye, the

AS HE RHYTHMICALLY DELINEATES THE MOTION IN WORDS, AND REFERS TO THE DRAWINGS HE HAS MADE, FO ACTUALLY DANCES OUT THE PANTOMIME OF THE APOSTLE'S HANDS, BECOMING EACH FIGURE IN TURN AS HE GLIDES ACROSS THE STAGE AND CREATES THE ILLUSION OF THE GESTURAL WAVE HE IS DESCRIBING. THE STAGE EFFECT DRAWS DELIGHTED APPLAUSE FROM THE AUDIENCE AS THEY WATCH LEONARDO'S PAINTING COME TO LIFE IN THE CONVERGENCE OF FO'S DRAWINGS, GESTURES, AND WORDS...

that keeps us flying low and short-sighted, and finally succeed in putting on wings . . . that will launch us into the lofty and spirited trajectory of real flyers, and not that of wobbly turkeys."[16]

Throughout Fo's career his drawings have featured figures in flight, an idiosyncrasy he attributes to the human need for freedom. The intricate detail with which he re-imagines the artwork and inventions of Leonardo is evidence of his ongoing attempt to investigate the historical tension between repression and freedom throughout the ages. He presents Leonardo struggling to free himself from the stigma of discrimination, from the ravages of wars in which he himself was implicated, and from the religious hypocrisies of his era. These are all issues with which Fo continues to grapple, in all his performances and in the drawings that inspire them. Without saying so directly, Fo's lecture on Leonardo makes it clear that he sees the Renaissance artist as a kindred spirit. The techniques of satire, music, gesture, chorality, and audience participation that Fo delineates so meticulously in Leonardo's paintings are

same point to which spectators will eventually be raised by the play of perspective he is building into the composition. This drawing imagines a link between Leonardo and the spectator who will view his work five hundred years later, a bond that requires seeing eye to eye.

The illusion of levitation is linked to one of Leonardo's (and Fo's) deepest fascinations, the dream of flight. Fo presents his renderings of Leonardo's flying machines with the interesting speculation that the inventor actually used them himself. "I am convinced," says Fo, "that here in Milan or on the hilly inclines of Brianza, Leonardo has flown." Fo sees Leonardo's fearless testing of his own inventions as an inspiration for the future. "I predict that even in conditions like those under which we now live, in a Milan of harsh problems and creative stagnation, not to mention the endemic constipation in the generation of ideas, courage, and generosity, we will succeed in ridding ourselves of the baggage

techniques that he himself attempts regularly to transfer from the canvas to the stage. By making Leonardo's artwork a gateway into his psyche, Fo presents a method of analysis that could be just as fruitfully applied to the output of his own visual imagination. The links between painting technique and stage technique that are suggested by Fo's analysis of *The Last Supper* are present in his own work as strongly as they are in Leonardo's. Fo's talk on the restoration of a single painting is in fact a manifesto on the restoration of all art to a state that embraces the links between history, music, gesture, painting, and the audience. When he pictures the viewer hovering comically in the air above Leonardo's painting, he is offering a fanciful vision of an art form in which the audience is uplifted, a metaphor for the lofty potential of all arts to free their spectators from prejudice, injustice, and warfare, as well as from gravity in all senses of the word.

PAGE 133: Jacopo Tintoretto, "The finding of the body of St. Mark", 1562–1566

FO'S TRIBUTE TO TINTORETTO

Excerpt from a lecture by DARIO FO
Translated by Ron Jenkins

The following lecture was given by Dario Fo in Milan on December 1999 at the Brera Pinoteca in front of Tintoretto's painting *Il ritrovamento del corpo di San Marco* [The discovery of the body of Saint Mark].[1]

TINTORETTO To begin with, "Tintoretto" was a nickname inherited from his father, who was a dyer. His real name was Jacopo Robusti, but he jokingly adopted this nickname, which he always used with great pride when signing his works.

Tintoretto was passionate about the theater, and had many friends among the theatrical artists of his time. In that epoch of great ferment in the theater, which flowed into the commedia dell'arte, there were extraordinary writers, incredible actors, and above all they were beginning to produce plays with significant scenic designs. And Tintoretto's theatrical friends taught him how to design stage sets.

In fact, if you look carefully at this painting you will see that it is a set design. You should know that Tintoretto had in his house a huge room, a theater where he produced the scene in its entirety. He used wax puppets which were easy to model and color, and whose positions could easily be changed.

Furthermore, Tintoretto had begun painting frescoes when he was a workshop student. When I learned this, it struck me deeply, because I studied the art of painting frescoes for four years here at Brera. And when I came to see this painting—knowing he had been a fresco artist—I also understood the velocity with which he expressed himself. In fact the materials with which one paints a fresco dry out with a startling velocity. After four or five hours you can't paint anymore. You can't have second thoughts or you have to do the whole piece over again.

One of the fundamental characteristics of Tintoretto was the velocity with which he worked. In fact when commissions were offered for new works, the other painters came to the committees with outline sketches; he came with a finished canvas. There were some who advised him to paint more slowly so that he could do a better job. They didn't understand that his talent resided in his passion, in his speed, in the force with which he produced his works, which was the same talent required in both the art of the fresco and in set design.

It is known that he painted many of his canvases while standing over them, like set designers do: he stretched out the canvas over a wooden frame on the floor, then he nailed it on, and took a thin pole to which he attached his paintbrush (Fo re-enacts the technique by which one paints with a pole). Resting the pole against the back of his arm he is able to make a straight line with the paintbrush and increase the speed with which he paints. You have no idea what it is like to paint vertically with big brushes, with someone assisting you, and above all with the colors rolling around on containers with wheels underneath: so they move around while you continue to work. A helper throws you the colors, a little bit of this, a little bit of that, you take the colors as they come, sometimes changing brushes with each one. I employed this technique here at Brera and it helped me to produce many of the set designs that I have painted since then.

So the velocity with which Tintoretto painted, the clarity, the precision, are all due to his mastery of these two professions, on the one hand fresco painting and on the other hand set designing.

THE CANVAS This canvas depicts the moment in which the body of Saint Mark was discovered in Alexandria, which was an Islamic city, but where there was also a Greek Coptic Church which stored tombs on its upper levels, as was the custom in churches of the Orient. Two Venetian merchants went to Alexandria and paid a handsome sum to the Coptic bishop so that they could go in and get the body of this saint, who was viewed in Venice as being nearly divine. They went in to empty out some of the tombs. You see that there are servants taking down the cadavers. They've already taken one down and said, "No, it's not this one," and left it there. At a certain point a transparent corpse appears, radiating the light of the saint for whom they are searching, who, standing next to his own cadaver, says: "But where are you looking? Can't you see that I'm right here?"

Then there is a character who seems to have entered almost by chance, a man who is participating in the search, but who is possessed by demons. And when the spirit of the saint rises up to declare that he is present, this man loses his mind and throws himself onto a woman, while someone else tries to restrain him.... So there are two levels: one part is ironic and grotesque, while the other is tragic. It is a theatrical action. You can almost hear the sounds: "Hey, here I am... but why are you looking... grab him, hold him back..." (Fo acts out the scene that is unfolding on the canvas.) It is an action that lasts only a few seconds.

This extraordinary painter said something marvelous: "I work quickly because the things I am depicting last only a few minutes. I have to paint them immediately or they will finish. The room will empty out and no one will be left."

His velocity and his rhythm can be felt in his style of painting. The tempo, the voices, the pandemonium, the reverberations... he enables you to imagine the reverberations that are present in the situation. All of this went beyond the limited canonical practices to which painters of this era were expected to conform.

For example *The Discovery of the Body of Saint Mark* was commissioned by the character on his knees in the center of the canvas who donated it to a brotherhood of monks. The monks gave the painting back to him because they could not accept the brutality of its execution, the elements of the grotesque inserted into the tragedy of the scene, or the way in which the magic of the discovery was presented without anything that could be termed "mystification".... Take note of the fact that nothing is flying. Everyone has their feet on the ground. Even the ghost of the saint is present, solid, and weighty....

THE PERSPECTIVE OF THE LIGHT You see how the sense of perspective is all directed to the left: the vanishing point is at the hand of the saint's ghost. All the vanishing lines, in other words all the lines that create the sense of perspective come together at that point. This is also contrary to the canonical practices of the time. How! The principal character is the saint, or rather his cadaver and his ghost. And look where they are: in the corner, not in the center... off center, like the sense of perspective.

Then there's the light. In this canvas the principle source of light is offstage. It starts on the far right and catches the back of this woman—you see—then it falls directly onto the man on his knees trying to restrain the maniac who is not illuminated. It glances off the man who commissioned the painting while it gives full illumination to the saint himself on the ground and his apparition.

Now I have had the good fortune to have had [Giorgio] Strehler [late director of Milan's Picolo Teatro] as my lighting teacher.

And one of the fundamental principles in theater is that there always has to be backlighting, in other words, a light that comes from behind, from underneath, or from above. And do you see what Tintoretto does to create this light. He opens up a kind of picture-window that illuminates everything above it through its reflection, and at the same time illuminates the backs of the principle characters with its counter-reflection. And the primary light does not consist of just a single source, but is projected from two positions, one part crossing the stage from the right, and then another part that streams upward to the left.

This is a manifestation of the grand theory of shadows, which searches for ways to give figures their volume by means of light alone. But this painter was born about fifty years before the period in the sixteenth century when artists began to paint with light, reflections, and counter-reflections, creating extraordinary effects with darkness and blackness... This gives you an idea of the importance of this canvas.

THE HISTORICAL CONTEXT You see why it is important to understand what is behind a work of art. I believe it is the only way to read it. We cannot overlook the things that were happening in the times that this painter—and all the other painters whose works are exhibited in this room—depicted the stories of the saints, the stories of the martyrs, the stories of Christ, and so forth.

Behind all of this was incredible conflict. There were the bloodiest of wars. It was a moment in which even the pope went into battle. There was the sacking of Rome, and many other cities were subjected to endless destruction. In a ten-year period there were thousands of deaths, there were the Turks, there was repression, condemnation, and people were burnt alive. All the most important actors in Italy were chased out of the country, because they staged satirical and grotesque plays that were not acceptable to the Church. This diaspora turned out to be fortunate for the Italian theater and for theater all over Europe, because these Italian actors were so successful that they became catalysts for enormous social and cultural changes that were extraordinary and inimitable. And when we speak of the richness of the Italian artistic heritage, I think it is useful to remember that these artists generated a truly vital discourse not just because they were talented, but because they understood how to revitalize the issues of their times. Doubt is the first and fundamental element of conscience. Doubt is necessary for overturning old ideas, sensations, emotions, and for re-examining them in the light of reason.

This historical moment was precisely the time that gave birth to the age of reason, and it is important that even in the midst of wars, massacres, destruction, and the lack of justice, there were these artists, in great numbers, an army of them, who continued to bring enlightenment to all of Europe.

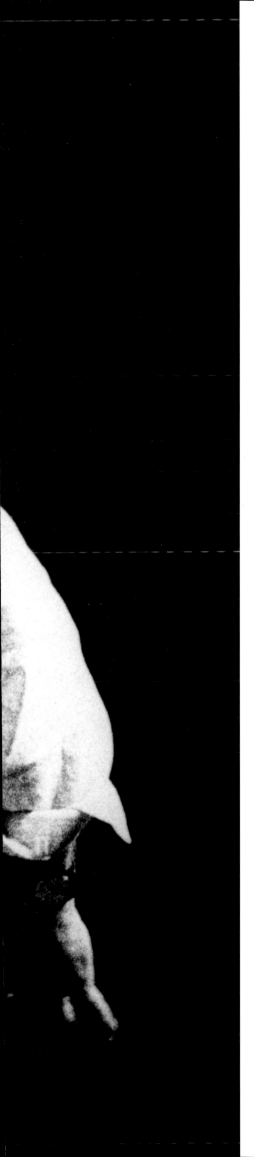

THE GEOMETRY OF JAZZ:
OBSCENE FABLES, TIGER STORIES, AND APOCRYPHAL MIRACLES

C H A P T E R 6

Improvisation in our tradition, which is the commedia dell'arte, is like the blues—you have to fit it into sixteen lines. The blues is improvised in sixteen lines, or in multiples of four lines—you can't do it with an uneven tempo.

I also improvise in a sixteen-line structure. When I invent an action, you can count it out, and you'll see that it fits into that rhythm. If I insert a new gesture, a discovery for achieving a particular effect, I have to take out something else. I can't add a line with impunity.[1]

Stage tempo is a concept that is general but very important, because it is the fundamental rhythm in which the play or the "piece" is performed. It is a tempo that serves as a point of reference, like in music, where at the beginning of a piece you have a signature beat of 3/4 or 4/4 time. Of course the rhythm can be changed: you can stretch it out or speed it up, or even distort it on purpose, occasionally changing the structure and internal rhythms of the speeches and the dialogue. The fundamental tempo is determined by, among other factors, one thing in particular: the audience. It is the audience that defines the rhythm of a performance, but you have to know how to listen: every house, for instance, has its own way of laughing that reveals a tempo of listening and understanding on which you can model the performance.—Dario Fo[2]

Fo's performances have the rhythmic drive of jazz improvisation. This musical pulse is written into the texts of his plays, and is inseparable from his words and images. Like a filmmaker who establishes the rhythm of a movie in the editing room, Fo finds the heartbeat of his plays in the sequencing of the pictures he imagines when he first creates the action of a scene. "Sometimes I find myself designing a sequence of images before I write," explains Fo, "and this sequence gives me a general rhythm, an overarching rhythm. . . . I do it because I need to predetermine a particular narrative drive."[3]

The narrative drive of Fo's work is also determined by his instinctive understanding of the audience's response to the words and images he presents onstage. Fo changes the tempo of his scenes in response to the needs of an audience—the need to laugh, to sustain tension, to relax. "The public is my guarantor, my support, my questioner," says Fo. "They give me my tempo and rhythms."[4]

It is Fo's sensitivity to the audience that leads to the constant re-writings of his texts during the period of their performances. He adjusts, cuts, adapts, and improvises throughout the run of a play until he is satisfied with the music of the text, and with the way it blends into the music of the audience's responses. And because Fo has internalized the reactions of thousands of audiences throughout the course of his career, he does not have to wait until a play is performed in front of an audience to incorporate the public's responses into the cadences of the script. The spectator's part of the duet is in his mind as he writes, so the rhythmic structure of every phrase has space built in for the audience's laughter, sighs, and gasps. "The advantage of an author who acts," claims Fo, "is that he hears the voice and the responses of the audience at the same moment that he is writing the first words on paper."[5]

This audience rapport gives the relationship between Fo's texts and his spectators the quality of breathing. The actor exhales the words while the audience inhales them. Then the actor has the opportunity to reciprocate by inhaling the reactions of the audience, because Fo has left space for them in the pauses between the lines. This is of course something a good actor can do with any text, but Fo's texts are particularly amenable to the impulses of the audience, because Fo writes them with an actor's instincts. "The tempo of breathing," notes Fo, "comes from the necessity to listen to the reaction of the public. To be able to do this you have to interrupt the flow of the performance with a pause that allows you to observe the tension of the room."[6]

THE FIRST MIRACLE OF BABY JESUS

The musical qualities of Fo's work are evident in all his plays, but they can be observed most clearly in his monologues. He frames the story in *The First Miracle of Baby Jesus* (1978) with the journey to Bethlehem of the three Magi, the wise kings who travel for days across the desert to bring gifts to the newborn child of Mary and Joseph. One king sings of his journey in a jaunty jazz-like riff, "Oh, it's swell, it's swell, it's swell / To be riding a camel / Once I jump, twice I jump / Up and down on the camel's hump." His singing annoys the oldest king, who is riding a horse. "That's enough!," he shouts. "I can't take it anymore. For four days and nights you've been singing about how swell it is to ride your camel." The singing king replies with words that stick to the beat of his camel song: "Of course I've got to sing / That's what gives my camel swing/ If I lose the music's beat / Then my camel falls asleep. . . ." The king on the camel refuses to give up the rhythm that sustains him. The words to the song are goofy, almost childlike, as if they had been squeezed into the metric structure of the jazzy tune (also written by Fo) on the spur of the moment. He joyfully clings to his defiant beat as he continues singing about how wonderful it will be to follow the stars to Bethlehem: "The comet keeps us out of danger / Till we get down to see the manger. . . . The Madonna will be sighing / And the baby will be crying / And Joseph will be swaying / And the angels will be praying / And the donkeys will be braying."[7]

Indefatigable, the king on the camel infuses every word he speaks with a bebop rhythm that infuriates his companion, but keeps the narrative drive of the story moving comically forward. The music is connected to the narrative not only by the king's words but by the gestures he makes to accompany each line, acting out snapshot visions of Mary cradling her baby, the proud father Joseph, the flying angels, and the indifferent donkey. His song goes on to describe the difference between riding a horse at a gallop and riding a camel at a trot, explaining that the camel needs the music to keep from getting his legs tangled up and falling on his rider. All these images are presented in a fast-moving sequence of gestures that match the song's rapid tempo.

The music, words, and gestures are deceptively simple, but their cumulative momentum provides a thematically sophisticated introduction to Fo's fable.

THE NARRATIVE DRIVE OF FO'S WORK IS ALSO DETERMINED BY HIS INSTINCTIVE UNDERSTANDING OF THE AUDIENCE'S RESPONSE TO THE WORDS AND IMAGES HE PRESENTS ONSTAGE. FO CHANGES THE TEMPO OF HIS SCENES IN RESPONSE TO THE NEEDS OF AN AUDIENCE— THE NEED TO LAUGH, TO SUSTAIN TENSION TO RELAX. "THE PUBLIC IS MY GUARANTOR, MY SUPPORT, MY QUESTIONER SAYS FO. "THEY GIVE ME MY TEMPO AND RHYTHMS."

Every time the song is interrupted by the older king, Fo is using the rupture of a musical form to demonstrate how the imagination can be stifled by intolerance. This is also a theme of the larger story, which is further developed when a spoiled rich boy smashes the imaginative toys that the baby Jesus has sculpted out of clay. In Fo's version of the story, based on the apocryphal Gospels, the holy child is presented as an immigrant who is taunted by the other children for being "Palestinian." This theme of racism is also established in the framing story of the three wise kings, because the one who sings on the camel is black and the one who tries to stop his song is white. The metaphor of their musical conflict epitomizes the oppressive nature of their relationship.

Fo's depiction of baby Jesus's first miracle also employs a musical structure. After the holy child has been rejected by the other children for being foreign, he amuses himself by fashioning birds out of clay and breathing on them in a miraculous way that brings them to life and makes them fly. The other children are enchanted, and ask Jesus to breathe on their own clay creations to make them fly as well. Each clay bird has its own childish defect: one is shaped like a loaf of bread with five legs and a head on top of it. Another looks like a sausage with fifteen legs and twelve wings. There is a cake with wings all around its circumference. And there is also a clay cat, which Jesus initially refuses to breath on, but he relents when the child who sculpted it screams, "If you could make that big fat turd over there fly, you can make my cat fly too."[8]

Fo uses different gestures and sound effects to demonstrate the flight pattern of each of the children's lopsided creations, evoking an aerial ballet of unbalanced twirlings to the music of oddly syncopated tunes. The flying carnival is brought to an abrupt end by the child of the richest landowner in town, who smashes all of the clay figures because he hasn't been invited to play. As in the opening sequence, the oppressive injustice of intolerance is shown through the comic interruption of an action sequence that has a vividly musical form. The stifling of freedom is suggested by the stifling of song.

The devastation caused by the rich child's intolerance is later portrayed in a subtler musical form: Fo imagines a conversation between the sobbing baby Jesus and his heavenly father, who appears in the clouds and chastises his son for calling him from the other side of the universe over this trivial matter. "I flew so fast that I made holes in the clouds, trampled a dozen cherubs, and threw the Holy Trinity so far out of whack that it will take me an eternity to restore it to order."[9]

Jesus complains to his father in high-pitched gasps that he blurts out between tears. The dry heaving of his breath cuts off the flow of his story with the same pitiless indifference displayed by the child who smashed his toys. This time Fo has composed a music of thwarted feelings that echoes the music of thwarted flight in his earlier scene.

The musical motif of freedom and repression returns in a reprise at the end of the story, when Fo imagines the wise kings riding off into the distance. "That's enough!"[10] the old king is still shouting, while the black king continues to sing the song that gives him the momentum to survive. By this time their argument has become so familiar that Fo does not need to re-introduce the characters with literal gestures. The sound of their musical conflict is enough to summon their images in the audience's mind. To create the illusion that the kings are getting farther and farther away, Fo repeats the song and the interruption several times, each time in a softer voice that becomes fainter and fainter, conjuring up the essence of a timeless human dilemma with nothing more than a rhythmic whisper and a wave of his hand.

These examples are among the most striking uses of music in the monologue, but on a less obvious level, every line that Fo writes is conceived with a sensitivity to the overall musicality of the performance. Even the prologues that introduce his monologues are part of his strategy to orchestrate a satisfying musical structure for his work. "The introductions function to put the audience at ease," says Fo. "It allows them to let off steam and forget the ritual mechanisms of the theater to the point that they can merge into the world of the actors and the tempo of the play."[11] Fo uses these introductions to draw the audience into the cadences of his comedy, understanding that the rhythms of the play are inseparable from its meaning. In the prologue to The First Miracle of Baby Jesus, for instance, he emphasizes the theme of censorship, explaining that the source of his monologue is a story from the apocryphal Gospels that have been left out of the official version of the Bible. Wondering why no one ever talks about Jesus' life as a child, he creates an atmosphere of complicity with the audience, making them share his indignation that they have been denied the pleasures of listening to these tales. Fo is attempting to create a mood that will make it easy for the audience to identify with the characters they are about to encounter, who experience censorship and repression in the course of the story. Fo's introduction is like a musical overture that familiarizes the audience with a central motif that will appear in different forms throughout the monologue.

The motif of censorship appears repeatedly in Fo's plays, and the struggle to find freedom from oppression provides most of his work with its central tension. This recurring theme enables him to create musical structures in his narratives where the tension created by oppression builds to a climax in which the victims of the oppression finally break free. This moment usually coincides with a comic punch line or slapstick sight gag—the laughter is part of the release. In *The First Miracle of Baby Jesus*, for example, a comic climax occurs when God asks his crying son what punishment the child suggests for the boy who destroyed his friends' toys. Suddenly the tension that has reduced Jesus to sobbing is lifted, and he beams with pleasure: "Kill him,"[12] he bursts out with a smile, and suddenly the burden he has been suffering is lifted. His long halting phrases and laborious breathing patterns vanish in an instant of laughter. It is a moment of comic liberation, and the tone of every word and gesture that follows is lighter, more fluid, and free. In this scene as in many others, the cadences of Fo's comedy are shaped by the rhythms of defiance.

THE TUMULT OF BOLOGNA

The same pattern occurs in *The Tumult of Bologna*, another story Fo claims to have rescued from the censored annals of history. "Historians are constipated,"[13] claims Fo, in his prologue to a tale in which the citizens of eleventh-century Bologna suffer under the repressive regime of the pope, whose representatives have conscripted the city's able-bodied men into military service and sacrificed them in a futile war. Constipation is a fitting metaphor for this particular story, because the desperate citizens of Bologna decide that the only weapons that will be effective against their oppressors are cow dung and human manure. Having abandoned the soldiers of Bologna to their deaths, the French contingent of the pope's army has commandeered the city's castle and barricaded itself inside the gates with all the food and wine from the municipal storehouse. In the city outside, the people of Bologna are starving, but

the castle is impregnable by conventional weapons of siege. The soldiers of the pope shout down taunting insults from the parapets of the castle walls, and the people are humiliated. But the arrogant cadences of the soldiers' voices are silenced when their victims come up with the idea of using catapults to launch loads of feces over the castle walls.

The turning point in the story's rhythm comes in a wordless segment in which a once boastful soldier slowly removes his helmet and wipes dung from his face in mute astonishment. From then on the mournful tone and pace of the story change, as the people of Bologna band together to collect excrement to hurl at their enemies. Farmers donate the dung of their cows, citizens compete to out-do each other in contributing to the cause, and the battle becomes a tourist attraction.

And the families of those who produced lots of shit were given great respect and applauded.
  'Congratulations comrades!'
  'These are our patriots!'
  Foreigners who came down from the mountains to watch the spectacle were stopped.
  'What do you want.'
  'We want to see them throw shit at the Papal delegates.
  'You can't come in unless you bring some shit.'
People came from as far as Ferrara…
  'Do you need any help?'
  'Yes, shit.'
  The same with people from Modena.
  'Give us a hand with some shit.'[14]

As the battle continues the pulse of Fo's language echoes the thrusts of attacking soldiers and the sudden release of catapults. The unrelenting cadence throbs with the irreversible momentum of an ambush. "I try to make the rhythms of the language allude to the rhythms of the violence,"[15] says Fo, who gradually builds the tempo of the battle into a carnival frenzy where missiles of manure "splash in the air like fireworks." The homegrown battle efforts are coordinated by a band that heightens the tempo of the dung-throwing with a pounding drum beat. Fo creates a jazz-like riff to accompany the battle, and repeats it in variations as different groups take

wild and raucous concatenation of sounds and gestures to communicate the mother's portrayal of Faina's illicit relationship with her daughter. Volpassa's movements and sound effects make it clear she is talking about sex, even though few actual words are spoken. The musicality of her tirade is acknowledged by Fo in the first words of the narration that follows: "Don Faina understood the scales of her song."[20]

In the wedding scene Fo uses musical images to capture the essence of each character in the story as they dance. Don Faina dances lightly, with a lecherous smile, anticipating his upcoming rendezvous with the bride. Volpassa thunders across the dance floor with callous disregard for everyone in her path. Alessia spins and twirls herself into near oblivion. And the shepherd is totally immobilized, unable to participate in the dance because he has never before worn shoes, and the laces are so tight that his feet are paralyzed. By showing how each of these figures responds to the wedding music, Fo gives us a vivid gestural picture of their relationship to love.

Ultimately, though, it is the dance of the newlyweds' bodies in bed that conveys the most poetic musical portrait of love. Their torsos rise and fall in unison, not in the act of love but simply in their sleeping side by side. "That is what love really is," sighs the shepherd. "Breathing together."[21]

With a body part as its central character, *The Butterfly-Mouse* highlights the relationship between Fo's text and his body, and it is clear that the monologue's music grows out of the dialogue between word and gesture. As is true in all of Fo's monologues, his body undergoes repeated transformations, and each new corporal metamorphosis calls for a change in the rhythm of the text. When the bodies of the couple breathe together, the music of the story slows down to a whispered pace. When Volpassa chastises the priest with lewd accusations about his sexual conduct, the rhythms rise to the crescendo of an out-of-control orgy. And when the scene shifts to the wedding dance, the different relationships that all Fo's characters have to their bodies are reflected in musical movements that reveal their inner natures.

THE STORY OF THE TIGER

In a monologue called *The Story of the Tiger*, the physicality of Fo's language and performance are heightened even farther by the fact that the actor is required to inhabit the minds and bodies of animals as well as men. There are meaningful rhythms in the roars of the animals, as well as in the groans of the human protagonist, a wounded Chinese soldier who seeks refuge in a cave that turns out to be the lair of a mother tiger and her cub. In recounting how the tiger adopts the soldier into her family, Fo moves back and forth between the role of the soldier who narrates the story and the tigers he is describing. Fo has self-consciously created a cinematic structure in which the rhythmic tension comes from the use of point and counterpoint in these shifting perspectives.

"We have one point of view that is direct," states Fo in a post-performance analysis of the play,

and another that is seen from the reverse angle. In the first case I am talking about myself in first person, and I see the tiger and the cub over there, so that the visual angle of the public's imagination coincides with my own and is pointed in the direction that I indicate. The spectator is carried over my shoulder to observe the things that I recount, even though physically, of course, they stay in their seats. But wait! I describe the tiger, her size, her big eyes, her teeth. I describe the two bloated cubs with their stomachs full of water, one drowned. But then, all of a sudden, the action shifts perspective. I transform myself into the tiger and I mime the gestures of the tiger. I raise my head . . . slowly . . . I begin to sniff around. This is the reverse angle.

Another shift: the movie camera moves again and the character of the tiger is in front of me, because I am the one telling the story, and it is through my eyes that the audience can see the snout, the jaws, the huge head of the tiger getting closer, the eyes getting bigger, the teeth, the approach of the tiger. . . . Another reversal: again I become the tiger who walks slinkingly toward the audience. . . . Another change to a reverse angle: there is the tiger, and I describe her, her eyes so big that they spill over the edges of the movie screen, like a big zoom lens that is swooping in for a close-up, the image is magnified beyond measure, approaching and overwhelming my own body. Then I take a breath and explode into a roar: "AHUGHAUA!" I stop roaring and leave. Is it clear? The scene consists of a sequence of quick cuts and splices, a classic montage of cinematic editing. And the spectators are obliged to follow me in this continuing change of camera angles.[22]

Although the words of each scene are simple and straightforward, Fo's cinematic conception of the action is highly sophisticated: "She's getting up. She's getting up. She's moving forward. The tiger is big, eyes wide open, teeth, huge mouth [mimes the tiger advancing, and turning her head away in disgust]. ROOOOAAARRR! [gestures suggest the tiger's retreat] Almost vomiting, she goes away . . . to the back of the cave."[23] The actor speaking these simple lines has to think like a movie camera and use his body like a split screen, creating narrative momentum from shifting camera angles punctuated by tiger roars. The pace builds slowly as the narrator describes the tiger's advance. The suspense rises to a climax as the detailed description creates the illusion of a camera lens zooming into the tiger's mouth. The roar is the scene's crescendo, and the slow fade-out comes as the disgusted tiger slinks away to the back of the cave.

Fo's vision of the story's structure is captured in a drawing he made to accompany it. An actor stands with his arms upraised; another man sits on his shoulders, pointing a movie camera toward a tiger. The tiger's mouth is open and her claws look ready to strike. The actor's fingers are curled like the tiger's claws, suggesting that the actor is either imitating the tiger or recoiling in fear from it. He seems to be narrating the story and

THIS PAGE AND OPPOSITE: Fo's sketches for *The Story of the Tiger*

143

participating in it at the same time, just as he seems to be looking at the tiger at the same time that he becomes it. The movie cameraman on his shoulders is a reminder of the audience that is watching from ever-shifting angles. Fo sees the play as a succession of images seen from changing viewpoints. It is the responsibility of the actor to carry the spectator on his shoulders into the action, with the help of the movie camera that Fo imagines them both to have wired into their brains.

Complicating the structure of Fo's pieces even farther, is his willingness to step completely outside the frame of the action and comment directly to the audience, as if the action had momentarily stopped and the narrator were taking the opportunity to provide the public with his most intimate thoughts before stepping back into the action. The soldier in *The Story of the Tiger* is surprised when the mother tiger does not eat him but tries to feed him instead, offering him her milk-swollen breast. Fo acts the tiger's roar of irritation when the soldier is too timid to accept her offer. Then he becomes the soldier gingerly holding the tiger's tit between his finger and his thumb and beginning to suck. After thanking the tiger for her hospitality he turns to the audience and comments, "It's good! Tiger's milk is good . . . a little bitter, but. . . ."[24] This is the moment Fo has chosen to have the narrator step self-consciously out of the screen. "Here the images are stopped," says Fo, "as if the movie camera has been momentarily turned off. TAC! It remains over there, and the audience is aware that the tiger is still in the same place, with her terrifying head over my shoulder to the right. I still have her nipple between my fingers . . . but I detach myself for a moment, almost as if I'm taking a time-out to say, 'Excuse me madam, but I've got to talk to my friends over here.' I turn to the audience and in an 'aside' I describe the quality of the milk: 'a little bitter, but very creamy when it goes down, so smooth . . . not bad at all !'"[25]

Asides like these have their own musical structures and can sometimes become elaborate plays within the play, using new characters and tonal qualities that don't exist in the main story line. For instance, when the soldier is licked by the tiger and starts to feel the healing qualities of her saliva in his skin, he recalls that itinerant medical charlatans would often come to his village when he was a child, hawking the restorative powers of tiger saliva that they sold in small bottles. Holding his wounded leg as he limps toward the audience, Fo steps out of the frame to re-enact this childhood flashback: "Step right up! Girls. Ladies. If your mammaries

are dried up and empty, just rub a little dab on your boobs and PLAF! Your jugs will be bursting with milk and spurting it out like fountains. Come on, ladies!"[26] The passage has the fast-talking tempo of medicine show patter, and Fo's gestures take on a corresponding pace as he delivers it. He inhabits the flashback sequence so completely that he stops limping, and it is only when he re-enters the frame of the central story, taking the tigers tit in his hand, that the effects of his wound become visible again, and the familiar cadences of the soldier's speech bring the audience back to the cave of the tiger.

Much of the rhythmic variation in Fo's texts comes from a playful use of language and dialects that calls attention to the musical nature of words. "In *The Story of the Tiger*", notes Fo,

> there are all the Italian dialects, from Sicilian to Provençal. There is a linguistic root for every situation, and every situation generates the right word in one dialect or another. The word "breast," for instance, in my show, changes at least ten times: mammary, boob, tit, etc. . . . . The word changes continually because everything depends on the situation in which it is employed. If it is violent it is a "tit." If it's sweet it's a "breast." "Mammary" is even more sweet in French. . . . There is also "jugs." All these terms come from different dialects. This has been a great innovation of theater throughout history. Euripides used this system, and that is what rendered his plays scandalous, not the fact that he mocked the religious functions of theater. His real crime was in his language and its rhythm. It was in this way that he betrayed catharsis, and showed how it was not very liberating at all.[27]

In Fo's vision of theater, the rhythms of language can be more subversive than its content. He argues that a free-form improvisational use of words is more liberating than the emotional catharsis of Greek tragedy, and claims Euripides as his role model for the jazz-like structure of plays like *The Story of the Tiger*.

When discussing the musical qualities of his texts, the collaborator Fo cites most often is the audience. "The audience is my co-conspirator," he says.[28] Fo takes great pleasure and pride in including the public in the creation of his works. Reading and watching his plays, one can see that they were written with an ongoing responsiveness to the vicissitudes of history, the physicality of the human body, and the quirkiness of language. All of these elements play a role in shaping the rhythms of the texts, but the audience has the most direct influence on the musicality of Fo's theater; he internalizes their responses and builds them into the structure of every phrase he writes. In a videotape of a workshop discussion of *The Story of the Tiger* Fo explains to the audience how he takes their reactions into account when he writes and performs. He isolates a passage from the play in which the tiger has developed a taste for cooked meat and tries to charm the soldier into preparing her a meal: "One, two, three, four . . . and one and two," counts Fo out loud, as he analyzes the rhythmic structure of the scene and imitates the feline caressing gestures the tiger makes when she wants to get her way. Then there is a pause before the soldier pronounces a mocking judgment of his hostess's suddenly tender behavior: "The trollop!"[29]

The audience laughs, only to hear Fo explain that their laughter is part of his musical score. "You didn't realize it, but here I am taking a breath," explains Fo, pausing before repeating his punch line: "The trollop!" He continues to explicate the audience's role in the segment, telling them that the pause is as much for their benefit as for his own: "I take the same breath you are taking. We breath together so that you have enough breath to make the sound of laughter. You laugh, and we continue on together. . . . We are telling the story together. I am compelling you to tell the story with me, to follow the rhythm and the timing of the story so that you can direct me, and give me the solution of how to move from one passage to another."[30]

As Fo tells the audience about the spaces in his story that he has left for their laughter, they laugh again. Delivering a technical analysis of the piece's comic structure, Fo uses the same comic structure he has built into the play, and the audience succumbs without thinking. It is as if Fo were conducting them and they were playing the musical notes of laughter that he has assigned to them. The same phenomenon occurs when Fo explains how a certain gesture—the soldier slapping himself in exasperation when the tiger throws him a piece of meat and growls, as if to say, "Cook it!"—is placed at a particular place in the text to draw their applause. "This is an invitation to applaud,"[31] he says. A few minutes later he repeats the same gesture in a different context, and the

audience watching his demonstration applauds again. The applause is not forced by the knowledge of Fo's technique; it is spontaneous, so spontaneous that everyone laughs in embarrassment when Fo calls it to their attention. By this time Fo is responding to all the nuances of their reactions, using them as inspirations for comic riffs to which they respond with still more laughter and applause. As he does in all his performances, Fo draws his audience into a participatory jam session where laughter, thought, and language tumble together with a musical momentum that takes on a life of its own.

The musical give and take between Fo and his audience is epitomized in a passage from *The Story of the Tiger* in which the soldier tells a group of villagers about his experience in the tiger's cave. Fo recapitulates the entire story in a rapid-fire condensation delivered so quickly that only a few key words and gestures are comprehensible.[32] But these key words trigger the audience's memory, so that they can replay the events of the story in their own minds. It is as if Fo had written a musical overture that captured all the highlights of the action, and had performed it in syncopated triple-time in the middle of the play. This high-velocity recapitulation is a comic device Fo borrowed from the tradition of commedia dell'arte. He uses it in several of his plays, and like many of his techniques, it serves as an invitation for the audience to participate by using their imaginations to fill in unseen actions and unspoken words. The laughter and applause that these segments generate is a sign that the spectators have accepted Fo's invitation to replay for themselves a new version of the story that they have been watching on the movie cameras in their minds. Fo is encouraging the audience to construct its own montage of actions and to re-edit it with new rhythms. The sequence is representative of Fo's fundamental beliefs about the relationship between the actor and his audience. Conducting the spectators at the same time that he is being conducted by them, Fo expresses his respect for the public by omitting the segments of the story he hopes they will intuit and orchestrate on their own.

PAGE 148: Poster for a German Production of *The Story of the Tiger*

EXCERPT FROM
THE STORY OF THE TIGER

By DARIO FO Translated by RON JENKINS

(The following scene is narrated by a Chinese soldier who was nursed to health by a tigress and her cub. After having lived with them in their cave for some time, the soldier watches the tigress and her son devour a goat she has brought home for her family's dinner.)

They ate the whole thing in an hour. Every bone sucked clean. The only thing left was a piece of the rear end with the tail, the thigh, the knee of the beast, and a hoof at the end. The tigress turned to me and said:

"Oaahaa," as if to say: "Are you hungry?"

She grabbed the leg and threw it over to me.

"Prooomm..." as if to say, "Have a little snack."

(He makes a gesture of impotence.)

"Fhuf... Me, eat that? That stuff's as tough as nails. I don't have teeth like yours.... Look how hard that is, like leather! And then there's the fat and the fur... all those bits of gristle... If there were a little fire to roast it over for a couple of hours! A fire, dammit! Sure, there's wood. The flood washed out all those roots and stumps."

I go out. I was already walking, with just a little limp. I went out in front of the cave where there were some tree trunks and stumps; I started to drag in some big pieces, and then some branches, then I made a pile like this. Then I took some dry grass, some leaves that were around, then I crossed the two horns, two bones, and over them I put the goat leg, like it was on a spit. Then I looked for some round stones, the white sulfur ones that make sparks when you rub them together. I found two nice ones, started scratching away, and... PSUT...PSUT...TAC. *(He mimes the rubbing of the rocks.)* Like shooting stars... tigers are afraid of fire. The tigress is back in the cave.

"OOOOAAHAAAAA."

(He makes menacing gestures as if to the tigress.)

"Hey, what's the matter? You ate your disgusting ugly meat! Raw and bloody! I like mine cooked, okay? If you don't like it, get lost." *(Mimes the tigress cowering in fear).*

You have to show a female who's boss from the start. Even if she's wild. I sat down with my rocks. FIT...PFITT... PFITTT... fire. Slowly catching, rising... the flames leaped: QUAACC... All the fat started to roast and the melted fat dripped down on the fire... It let off a thick black smoke... it drifted toward

the back of the cavern. The tigress, as soon as the cloud of smoke reached her, said:

"AAAHHIIAAAA" *(The roar sounds like a sneeze.)*

"Smoke bother you? Out! And you too, tiger baby."

(He threatens the cub with his fist and mimes the frightened response of the animal's cross-legged walk.)

"Out!"

And there I am roasting, roasting, roasting, basting, basting, and turning.

FLOM...PSOM...PSE... But it still gives off a disturbingly savage aroma. *(He goes out.)*

"If only I had some seasoning for this meat."

That's it! Outside I'd seen some wild garlic.

I go out, in the clearing in front of the cave, right there... I pull out a nice bunch of wild garlic. THUM... Then I see a green shoot. I pull:

"Wild onion."

I also find some hot peppers... I take a sharp piece of bone, make some cuts in the thigh and stuff in the garlic cloves with the onion and peppers. Then I look for some salt, because sometimes there's rock salt inside caves. I find some saltpeter.

"That'll do, even though saltpeter's a little bitter. There's also the problem that the fire might make it explode. But that's not important. I'll just be careful."

I stuff some pieces of saltpeter into the cuts of meat. And after a while, in fact, it flames up... PFUM... PFAAMM... PFIMMM... The tigress:

"OAAHHAAA...." *(He mimes the tigress getting scared.)*

"This is a man's work. Out. Get out of my kitchen."

Turn, turn, turn... now it's giving off a clear smoke, and what an aroma. After an hour, my friend, the aroma was heavenly.

"AHAH, so delicious."

SCIAAM: I peel off a piece of meat. *(Mimes tasting it.)* PCIUM, PCIUM. "Ah, so delicious."

It's been years and years since I ate anything like this. What sweet, heavenly flavor. I look around. It's the cub... he had come in and was standing there licking his whiskers.

"You want a taste too? But this stuff's disgusting to you. You really want some. Look. (*Indicates rapidly slicing some meat and throwing it to the cub who wolfs it down in a second.*) OHP."

He tasted it, swallowed and said:

"OAHA."

"Good? You like it?... Shameless brute. Take that. OPLA." (*Again mimes cutting and throwing the meat to the cub*)

"EHAAA...GLOP...CL...OEEE...GLOOO...OEH-AAAH-HAAA."

"Thank you, thank you... Yes, I made it myself. You want some more? Watch out your mother doesn't find out that you eat this stuff."

I cut off a nice piece of filet.

"I'll keep this for myself. The rest is too much for me so I'll leave it for you: take the whole leg." (*Mimes the action of throwing the goat leg to the cub.*)

BLUMMM... it hit him in the face and flattened him. He picked it up and staggered around with it like a drunk. Then mom shows up. What a scene!

"AAAHHAAAA what are you eating... this disgusting burnt meat? Come here. Give it to me. AAHHAAAAA."

"OOOHHOOOOCH!"

A piece of meat gets stuck in Mom's mouth. She swallows it. She likes it.

"UAAAHAAAA" says the mother.

"UUAHAAAA" answers the cub. (*He mimes the mother and son fighting over the meat.*)

An argument.

"PROEMMM... SCIOOOMMMM... UAAAMMMM..."

The bone. Licked clean. Then the tigress turns to me and says:

"OAAHAAAAA, isn't there any more?"

"Hey, this one's mine." (*Pointing to the piece he had cut a moment ago.*)

While I was eating, the tigress came over to me. I thought she wanted to eat my meat, but she just wanted to lick me. What a wonderful person. She licked me and then went over to her usual spot. She stretched out on the ground. The baby was already asleep, and pretty soon I fell asleep myself.

When I woke up in the morning, the tigers were already gone. It was getting to be a habit with them. I waited all day and they didn't come home. They didn't even show up that evening. I was a nervous wreck. The next day they still hadn't come back.

"Who's going to lick me? Who's going to take care of me? You can't go leaving people home alone like this."

They came back three days later. Now it was my turn to make a scene.

Instead I stood there dumbstruck, speechless: the tigress walked in with an entire beast in her mouth. Double the size of the last one. A wild bison, maybe. I don't know what. The cub was helping her carry it. They both stepped forward... BLUUMMM sideways... like they were drunk with fatigue...PROOOM... they came up to me. PHOOAAH-HAMMM.... (*He mimes the tigers unloading the dead animal.*) The tigress says:

"HAHAHA....HAHAHA..." (*He imitates the panting of the tigress.*)

And then: "AAAHHAAAAAAAA" As if to say "Cook it!"

(*Putting his hands to his face in desperation.*) Don't let tigers get away with bad manners.

"Excuse me, tiger, but you must be mistaken. You don't expect me to sweat and slave over a hot stove while you're out having fun. What do I look like? Your housewife, me?" (*Mimes the tiger preparing to attack him.*)

"OOAAHHAAOOAAHHAAAAOOO"

"Oh, stop it. OHO, OHO... OHO! So that's how you get your way. Can't we talk things over anymore? How about a little dialectics over here. Okay, okay... OHEOH... Don't get all hot and bothered about it. All right, I'll be the chef... I'll cook. But you two have to go out and get the wood."

"OOOAHHHAAAH?"

(*Indicating the tigress pretending not to understand.*)

"Don't play games. You know what wood is. Look here, come outside. That's wood. Those are stumps. Bring in all these pieces right away."

She understood all right: she gathered up the wood right away, all the stumps, back and forth, so that in an hour the cave was half-full.

"And you, tiger baby, nice life, eh? Standing around with your hands in your pockets?"

(*Turns to the audience*) He did have his hands in his pockets. He had his claws tucked in and was resting his paws on two black stripes just as if his hands were in pockets.

"Come on. Get to work. I'll tell you what you have to do: onions, wild garlic, wild peppers, everything wild."

"AHAAA."

"You don't understand? Okay, I'll show you. Look over there. That's an onion, that's a pepper."

The poor thing kept going back and forth with his mouth full of garlic, peppers and onions... ha... and after two or three days his breath was so bad you couldn't get near him: What a stink. And I was there all day, by the fire, roasting, falling apart. My knees were scorched, my testicles dried to a crisp. My face was burnt. My eyes were watering, and my hair was singed too. I was red in the front and white in the back. You couldn't expect me to cook with my ass. It was a dog's life. But they just ate, pissed, and came home to sleep. I ask you: "What kind of life is that?"

DOCUMENTARY SURREALISM: ACCIDENTAL DEATH OF AN ANARCHIST AND OTHER PLAYS

Toto [the Italian clown, variety artist, and film star, 1898–1967] *had a way of decomposing his body, of isolating its extremities —the head, the arms, the shoulders—of walking and moving by displacing his axis, of de-centering himself, which gave him a gait* [resembling that of] *a marionette, that is to say, something abstract, inhuman.*

At the heart of this inhumanity—or rather this non-humanity— there is violence. When speaking Toto touches his interlocutor but does not content himself with laying a hand on his arm or shoulder. He grabs him everywhere—in the face, by the hips, by the hand, by the elbow, by the foot. The violence of the comic tradition is replying to the violence of power. Toto is the timid person in revolt who, at the moment of giving in, in order to win the struggle or at least to re-establish equality in the face of power, begins to act—that is to say, to make gestures. He uses all his body—at first to resist and then to pass over to violence and madness. The play of madness and of the illogical is fundamental to Toto's theater. Toto works on the basis of paradox—at the limits of paranoia: he insults, he strikes, pretends to cry, shouts, and—this is fundamental—spits. He spits, bites, scratches, uses his elbows, sometimes gives great kicks in the stomach, sneezes. This famous prolonged sneeze is accepted as a cry, a pang, a sexual spasm, and presented as madness and frankness at one and the same time. Why so?

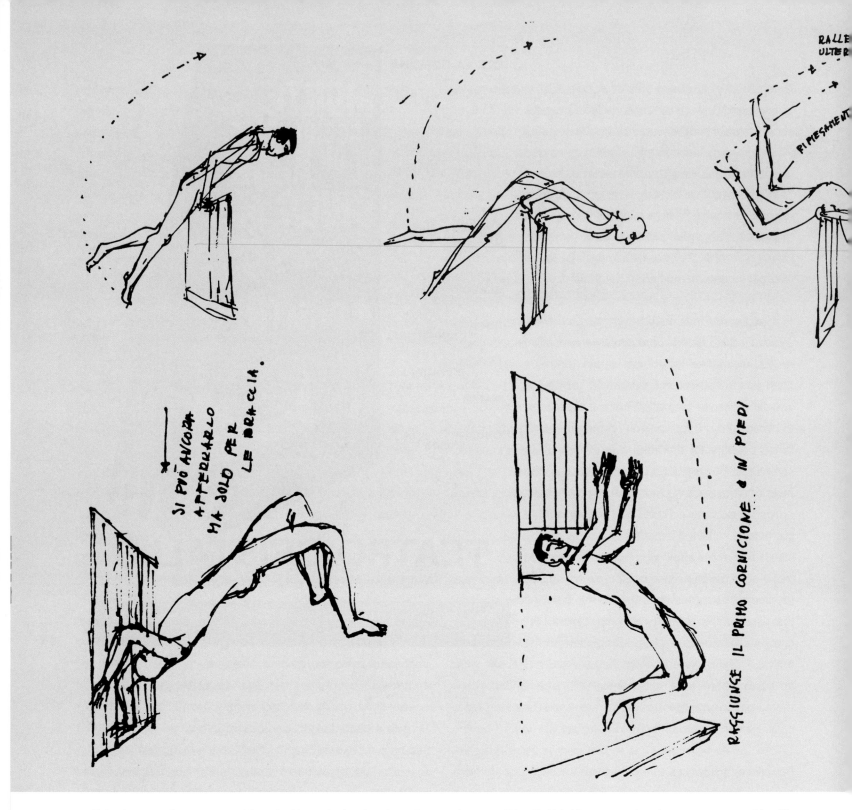

Fo's drawings function as a hieroglyphic code for the absurdity of the police testimony. In the second act of the play, a journalist enters the police station and draws sketches on a blackboard to indicate the parabola of flight the body would have taken if Pinelli had jumped on his own while he was still alive. This is the only time Fo's sketches make a literal appearance on the stage, but the play is full of physical actions and textual references that allude to the insights embedded in them. At one point the histrio-maniac threatens to jump out the window and assumes a position inspired by his sketch of the flying fish. Later, impersonating a government investigator from Rome who has discovered the police officers' crime, he advises them that the only way to save themselves is to throw themselves out the window, as

they say Pinelli did. He persuades them to assume Pinelli's position on the windowsill and nearly pushes them out himself, then claims he has only done this to help their case, by proving that it would actually be possible for someone to throw himself out of that window in a fit of depression brought on by an interrogation that was going badly. This was what the police said had driven Pinelli to jump. In fact they argued that his leaping out the window was proof that he was guilty of the bombing of Piazza Fontana. They called the suicide an act of self-accusation.

The police also argued that the anarchist must have committed an earlier train station bombing as well, because he was the only anarchist railroad worker in Milan. The histrio-maniac

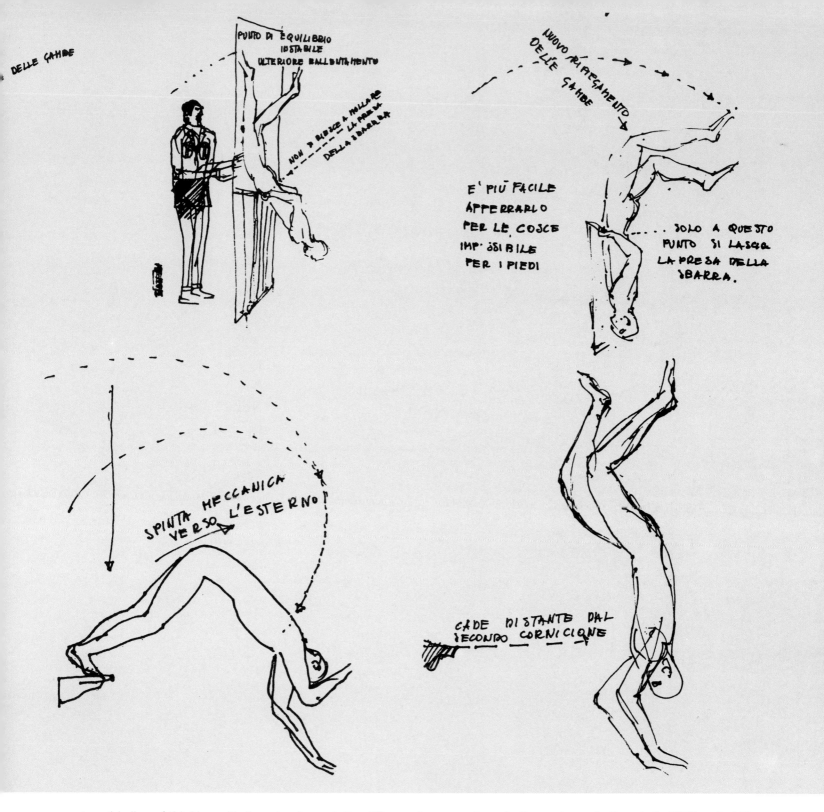

counters this line of thinking with its natural correlative: "So, if it's inevitable that the bomb in the train station was planted by a railway worker, then it is only logical to assume that the bomb at the courthouse in Rome was planted by a judge, and that the one at the monument for the unknown soldier was planted by the captain of the guards, and that the bomb at the Agricultural Bank was planted by either a banker or a farmer."[8]

Italian audiences greeted these farcical speeches with applause as well as laughter, an indication that they had been provoked into considering the implications of the histrio-maniac's jokes. Complementing the play's slapstick action, the verbal references in Fo's text kept the actual murder alive in the minds of the viewers, stimulating them to think and laugh at the same time. In the prologue to the play's 1987 revival Fo extended the frame of his farce even farther, explaining why he had transposed the original play to America: he said he had wanted to distance the play from its Italian reality just enough for people to see its absurdity. This is the kind of theatrical device advocated by Brecht in his writings on epic theater, to which Fo regularly refers. Although Fo's analysis of his technique was serious, he presented it with humor, telling the audience about the similar death of an anarchist named Salsedo in an American police station in 1921, which had generated documentation as absurd as that in the Italian investigation.

"The police said the anarchist fell quickly," noted Fo ironically. "As opposed to most people, who take their time and fall

slowly."[9] He then launched into a balletic comic fantasy in which he pantomimed the anarchist falling in slow motion, pausing to rest at a window on a lower story, cradling his head in his arms to get a view of the passing scenery, and waving to pretty women on the way down. Fo was preparing his audience for his treatment of the Pinelli case with a prologue that used the same style of documentary surrealism that had inspired his sequential drawings of the anarchist's flight out the window. Introducing the approach his audience was about to see in *Accidental Death*, he began with dry facts and chipped away at a few crucial details until he uncovered a carnival of absurdity lurking just beyond the illusion of truth. In both the prologue about the American anarchist and the farce about the Italian anarchist, Fo made the public laugh at death, but not without an aftertaste of horror.

As the master of ceremonies welcoming the public to his play, Fo was playing another incarnation of Harlequin, the figure he claims he has been impersonating his entire career. "My characters have always been in this key. Harlequin is a character who destroys all conventions. His personality and sense of morals are based on paradox. He comes out of nothing and can become anything."[10] This definition fits the histrio-maniac perfectly, and Fo explains the character's intentions through the metaphor of a scientific experiment: "My plays are provocations, like catalysts in a chemical solution. When you want to know what elements a particular liquid is composed of, you put in another liquid, and perhaps the mixture turns blue, or it boils, or it changes, forming precipitates. I do the same thing as a clown. I just put some drops of absurdity in this calm and tranquil liquid, which is society, and the reactions reveal things that were hidden before the absurdity brought them out into the open."[11]

In *Accidental Death*, the histrio-maniac provides the dose of absurdity that reveals the truth. "I was preoccupied with the issue of justice," recalls Fo.

I realized that a criminal act had been conducted by the state, but people were calmly accepting the results of the official investigation. When I injected absurdity into the situation, the lies became apparent. The maniac plays the role of the judge, taking the logic of the authorities to their absurd extremes, and he discovers that there are incongruities. For instance, if the police testimony were true, the victim would have had to have three feet. [One policeman corroborated his claim to have tried to prevent Pinelli's fall by producing a shoe he said had slipped off Pinelli's foot when he tried to save him. The

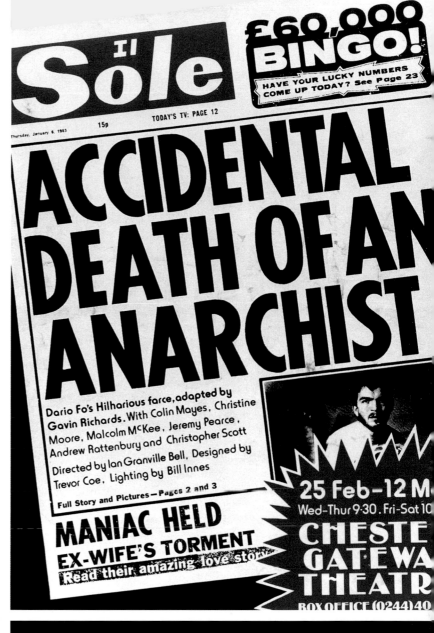

PAGES 154–156: Fo's sketches from *Accidental Death of an Anarchist* in which he demonstrates that it would have been physically impossible for Giovanni Pinelli to have committed suicide by intentionally jumping out of the window as the police claimed.

corpse, however, was found on the sidewalk wearing two shoes.] The clown maniac uses this incongruity to establish the truth of the situation. Absurdity becomes a form of logical reasoning based on paradox.[12]

The paradoxical logic of the absurd animates all of Fo's plays. Twenty-eight years after writing the first version of *Accidental Death*, he continued to explore the tragic absurdities of the Pinelli case and its aftermath in a work called *Marino Is Free! Marino Is Innocent!* This combination performance and illustrated lecture is based on the trials of Adriano Sofri and two other men who were accused of murdering Calabresi, the police commissioner suspected of orchestrating Pinelli's death. Calabresi was murdered in 1972, but it was not until 1988 that Leonardo Marino, a former colleague of Sofri's at the newspaper *Lotta Continua*, came forward and claimed that he had collaborated with Sofri and the others in the murder. In exchange for immunity, Marino gave testimony that was riddled with inaccuracies and contradictions. On the basis of that testimony alone, Sofri and the others were convicted of the murder. Fo examined the testimony and determined that Marino had told at least 121 lies. He drew an extensive series of colored designs that map out the evidence and reveal the absurd factual inaccuracies in Marino's account of the crime.

The assumption of Fo and thousands of other Italians is that Calabresi was killed by government officials who did not want him to reveal state secrets in the police corruption trials centering around the Pinelli case. Marino's testimony emerged only after he had been accused of armed robbery and spent eighteen days in police custody. When a judge asked prosecutors why they had withheld this information about the unusual circumstances surrounding the confession, one of them replied, "We didn't want to tell you because we were afraid that somebody would suspect that during those days we wanted to train Marino in his confession."[13] This is a sample of the absurd dialogue Fo re-enacted in his performance, during which he held a dummy on his knee dressed up as Marino. The visual metaphor reflected Fo's view that Marino was a puppet of the authorities, parroting a version of the crime that he had been trained to repeat but that was full of inconsistencies.

"I will wear the uniform of the public minister or the police chief," says Fo, introducing the theatrical device to the audience. "On my knee you will see the puppet of Marino, which I will animate, interrogate, scold, insult, and also slap." He demonstrates with a short ventriloquist's routine in which he

plays the role of the judge trying to determine how Marino and Pietrostefani could have planned the crime at an outdoor rally infiltrated by plainclothes police:

JUDGE: Don't tell any whoppers. Be careful.

MARINO: It's true. I swear that we were there in Pisa, me Sofri and Pietrostefani.

JUDGE: No. Pietrostefani was not there.

MARINO: Yes he was.

JUDGE: No he couldn't have been there, because there was a warrant out for his arrest.

MARINO: Oh, yeah. Well, okay, maybe he was over there, hiding behind a plant.

JUDGE: Stop talking nonsense. (He slaps him. Marino cries. Judge comforts him with kisses.) Come on. Come on. I won't hurt you. Let's take it from the top. Don't forget that there were a lot of policemen in the piazza.

MARINO: Dressed up as plants?[14]

Like the histrio-maniac in *Accidental Death*, Fo impersonates an authority figure and unleashes a torrent of slapstick violence to uncover lies that masquerade as truth. He turns the facts of the case into a grotesque Punch and Judy entertainment, abusing and cajoling the puppet the way he imagines the police abused and cajoled Marino. The logic behind this carnivalesque technique is mapped out in the ninety-one annotated drawings he made of the Marino case. There is a cartoon of Marino sitting on a policeman's lap that is the mirror image of the gestural relationship between Fo and his dummy.[15] Just as one can watch Fo's imagination take flight in the physical comedy of his stage performance, one can see his artistic sensibilities awakening to the case's increasing levels of absurdity in the pages of illustrations he drew to give physical dimension to the evidence at the trial. The sketches are animated cartoons of a judicial system gone haywire. One page is a portrait of a blonde woman whom witnesses had seen driving the killer's car. The next page shows the black-haired Marino with a bushy moustache and breasts; it is captioned, "After sixteen years Marino appears: 'It's me ... I'm the woman.'"[16] The drawings' other details of Marino's improbable testimony include the blue getaway car that Marino said was beige, and the deluge of rain that occurred on a day that Marino said was sunny. Many of the drawings are in bright pastels and have hand-painted captions. The words shift colors from phrase to phrase, as if the shapes and shadings of the letters were as elusive as justice itself.

PERFORMING UNDER THE THREAT OF DEATH WAS APPROPRIATE FOR A PLAY BASED ON ACTUAL MURDERS. FO WANTED TO BE SURE THAT HIS AUDIENCE NEVER LOST SIGHT OF THE FACT THAT HIS FARCE WAS ROOTED IN REALITY. "PINELLI, OR RATHER HIS CORPSE, AND WITH IT THE SIXTEEN CORPSES OF THE MASSACRE, WERE A CONSTANT PRESENCE ON THE STAGE," FO REMEMBERED.

Depicting the appeal of the case to a higher court, Fo's drawings explode into anarchy. Years after the initial conviction, a second trial ended with a majority of six judges declaring Sofri and his associates innocent. The job of putting the verdict in writing, however, was given to the dissenting judge who had voted them guilty. Fo claims that this judge sabotaged the verdict by writing what is known in Italy as a "suicide sentence," a document so full of flawed reasoning that it will inevitably be overturned in a higher court of appeals. This is what happened, sending Sofri and his associates back to jail. Fo depicts the legal shenanigans in a montage that shows the judge at the top of the page throwing the pages of his legal books into the air. The green sheets of paper cascade down the drawing, filtering through the words "suicide sentence" and landing on the heads of the judges in the court of appeals who are overturning the verdict. At the bottom of the page a chorus of green-robed figures leap into the air, their arms upraised in joy. Their reaction is labeled in ominous orange-shadowed letters: "The dance of the judges."[17] Fo's collage is a comic strip howl of indignation in the face of a judicial system running amok. In January 2000, when yet another team of judges announced that they had read the documents and decided that there was no need for a retrial, Fo's impulsive response summoned up the images embedded in the drawings he had sketched two years earlier: "The condemnation of Sofri is a dance of injustice, full of lies and deceits."[18]

Fo's drawings are a primal expression of his thought process. Even when unconnected to a particular play, they provide clues to the way he sees the world. A pattern that regularly emerges in both Fo's paintings and his plays is the juxtaposition of frames of fantasy over a foundation of reality. He accomplishes this blending of fact and imagination with an architectural precision that leaves the viewer with the impression that Fo's surrealistic vision was inherent in the original landscape. Just as the lunacy that erupts throughout *Accidental Death* is based on the documented facts of the trial transcripts, the fantastical elaborations in Fo's visual artwork are rooted in the concrete reality of whatever setting he chooses to portray.

THIS PAGE: From a performance of *The Pope and The Witch*; PAGES 160–161: From a performance of *About Face*; PAGE 163s: Dario Fo and Piero Scioto in a performance of *We Won't Pay! We Won't Pay!*; PAGES 164–165: Fo, Rame, and Ignazio Colnaghi in a 1953 performance of *A Finger in the Eye*; PAGES 166–167: Fo's preliminary sketch for *Isabella, Three Sailing Ships, and a Con Man*; PAGES 168–169: Fo's rendering of Saint Marks Place in Venice, from the exhibition *The Life and Art of Dario Fo and Franca Rame*, 2000

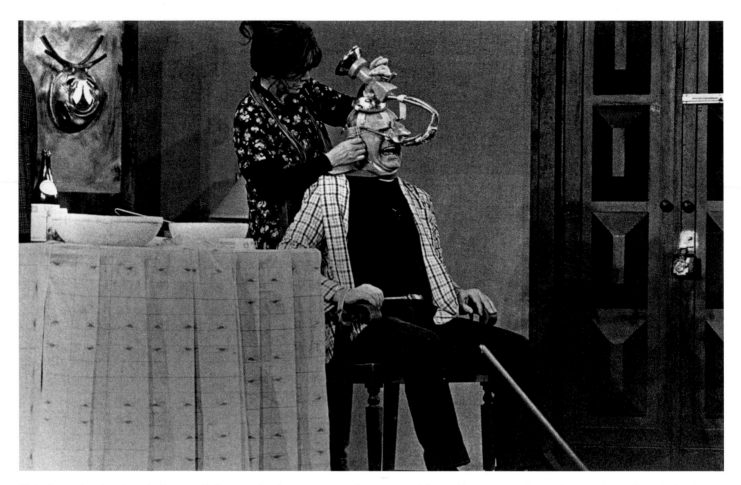

This is an instinctive choice on Fo's part. In the summer of 1998 he noticed a blank space on the wall of a gallery in Italy where his artwork was being exhibited. He offered to fill it by painting a picture of the medieval castle in which the gallery was housed. Using a realistic engraving of the castle as his model, Fo spent several hours inside the castle painting a likeness of its exterior. As the work progressed, he could not resist the impulse to paint exotic animals balanced on the castle turrets, and people flying through the air above the castle flags. He also used flecks of bright color to enliven the gray exterior of the edifice with banners and kites. By the time the work was hung in the gallery, the castle had been transformed into the setting for a medieval legend. People viewing the painting realized that they were seeing the building in which they were standing, but Fo's rendering had both undermined and preserved the reality of the structure. His colorful collection of animated figures suggested an invisible history to the castle, a secret past buried in the old stones.

Uncovering the invisible history of what is familiar or forgotten is a central principle of Fo's work. In his 1963 play about Christopher Columbus, *Isabella, Three Sailing Ships, and a Con Man*, Fo took a man with an established image in history and used information he had gleaned from historical documents to portray the explorer in a new light. The Columbus of Fo's play is a dreamer, a fraud, a spinner of tall tales, a *giullare* who uses his storytelling gifts to convince Queen Isabella of Spain to finance his voyages to the West. In an ink drawing he calls "an allegory for everything that is in the play,"[19] Fo has sketched Columbus as a manufacturer of pipe dreams. He is enveloped in a configuration of overlapping globes recalling Hieronymus Bosch's *Garden of Earthly Delights*, and each globe is crammed with epic action. In one sphere Columbus holds a globe of the earth in front of Queen Isabella in an effort to win her support. The other spheres teem with idyllic island scenes of naked native women, battle scenes, windmills, a mermaid, and a man hanging from the gallows. In some places the surfaces of the globes become the seas over which Columbus's ships sail toward discovery. The surreal montage is both violent and dreamy, bursting with the kinds of violent paradoxes that Fo uses in the play to satirize the colonialist spirit of profiteering that motivated Columbus and his sponsors. "I was inspired by Bosch," says Fo,

to draw circles inside which people were making love, embracing each other—even black and white lovers, an unthinkable union. And then I took this idea of the spheres and I put inside of them, instead of lovers, all the evil of Europe. If you look there you can see a man and a woman embracing. Inside is Christopher Columbus himself blowing soap bubbles into the sky, and then the globes suggest the shape of the earth. All the themes of the play are inside this allegory. There is the portrait of Columbus who tells stories, understanding that only by making things up about the New World will he be able to convince the great scientists, scholars, and bishops who surrounded Isabella to encourage the queen to support his future voyages. So he understood the reality, but he knew that reality would be rejected. No one would believe it. So he had to turn reality upside down.[20]

The drawing's imagery of grotesque inversion is reflected in Fo's play. The action takes place within multiple frames of reality. It is set during carnival, when an actor masquerading as a cleric is condemned to death, but is allowed to perform a play about Columbus on the gallows before he dies. Fo's ingenious set design and painted tapestries transform the gallows into both the palace chambers of Queen Isabella and the deck of a ship at sea. When the play within the play is over, the actor is executed. His headless body takes a bow with his head in his hand.

Fo's irreverent treatment of the Columbus myth caused great controversy when the play first toured Italy in 1963. Columbus was an icon of Italian history, and conservatives resented any revision of his image that varied from the hagiography of schoolroom textbooks. "We were attacked by fascists at the door of the Valle theater in Rome," recalls Rame. "Another evening the audience was evacuated during the show because a bomb threat had been received. Avalanches of threatening and insulting letters were arriving, and Dario was even challenged to a duel by a cavalry officer."[21]

While *Isabella* provided a topsy-turvy vision of history and its heroes, Fo was also interested in shaking up the world view of ordinary characters in contemporary settings. The action of a 1974 play called *We Won't Pay! We Won't Pay!* centers around two working class couples whose lives spiral into absurdity when the wives pretend to be pregnant to hide stolen food from their husbands and the police. The theft is part of a mass protest against the injustice of the economic conditions that have left them and their neighbors unable to afford the rising prices of food. A painting Fo made of one of the women captures the internal contradictions that animate the farce: he pictures Antonia running away from an unseen antagonist, her body twisted against itself. She looks backward while running forward, her hands clutching what seems to be a pregnant belly but is actually a hidden stash of rice, vegetables, and pasta swiped from the local supermarket. Although she is in flight, there is something triumphant in the openness of her body as her hair flies unbound behind her, as if she might be shouting one of her

lines from the play: "You have no idea how good it feels to shop without spending any money."[22]

Antonia and all the characters in the play are confronted with the dilemma of being forced into taking immoral actions for moral reasons, and into lying to stand up for the truth. Starting with the simple details of a neighborhood protest that actually happened in Italy, Fo catapults his characters into a chain reaction of farcical actions rooted in the paradoxical conditions of their lives. Like the Antonia of the painting, who seems to be full-bellied but is actually so hungry that she has to steal groceries, everyone in the play is famished. Fo uses their starvation to fuel the farce. Before the play ends they have turned dog food into a gourmet meal, given birth to cabbages, and convinced themselves that babies gestate in an amniotic fluid made from pickle juice. When liquids from the stolen groceries of Antonia's neighbor start dripping out from under her dress, Antonia tells a policeman that the woman has broken her water and is about to give birth. Later the same policeman's belly is pumped up with hydrogen and he believes he has become pregnant. Bodies in *We Won't Pay! We Won't Pay!* change size and shape with alarming rapidity. Identities are exchanged, authority is flaunted, and the laws of nature are turned upside-down. Beginning with the banal details of a shoplifting case, Fo turns the humdrum life of two ordinary families into a carnival assault against economic injustice.

Escalating the mundane rhythms of daily life into the frenetic pace of farce, Fo follows in the footsteps of artists like Molière, Charlie Chaplin, and the Marx Brothers. Many contemporary writers attempt to transform the details of everyday existence into heightened comedy, but what makes Fo unusual is the combination of precision and exuberance with which he executes his comic technique. The research behind his plays grounds them in solid reality, so that they are as full of persuasive details as an architectural blueprint. But this factual foundation does not prevent Fo's imagination from soaring into wild fantasy to make his satiric points. His painstakingly researched sketches of the fall of the anarchist Pinelli unleashed his impulse to envision ever more outrageous relationships between the police and the subjects of their interrogation. By the end of *Accidental Death's* first act the histrio-maniac and the police have cried in each other's arms, played choo-choo train together, and joined voices in singing the anarchists' anthem. The same blend of documentary detail and surrealistic elaboration occurs in all of Fo's plays. In *Marino Is Free! Marino Is Innocent!*, the exact transcripts of Marino's trial testimony are used as the text for a grotesquely violent puppet play. In an early

scene from *We Won't Pay!*, the welding equipment of Antonia's husband is described with great specificity, so that its particular functions can be used later in the play to make a male police officer believe he is both pregnant and blind. He makes his final exit shouting his thanks to the heavens for blessing him with the miracle of pregnancy. "God Bless Santa Eulalia," he bellows, patting his belly. "I'm a mother . . . I'm a mother!"[23]

Fo bases the factual foundation of many of his plays on the complex machinations of Italian politics. He has often referred indirectly to the infamous kidnapping of the late Prime Minister Aldo Moro. The government refused to negotiate with the kidnappers, who eventually murdered Moro, leading to speculation that he had been abandoned by his fellow politicians who disapproved of his efforts to bring left-wing parties into the government coalition. The Moro case, a landmark in Italian political history, has left the country with vivid and traumatic memories of their government's vulnerability. Fo toys with these memories in plays like *Elizabeth* (1984), in which an elaborate kidnapping plot is part of a conspiracy to remove the queen from her throne, and *About Face* (1981), in which Gianni Agnelli, the chairman of Fiat, is kidnapped. Agnelli is a well-known figure in Italy, and many details in the play are borrowed from the Moro

case, but these real-life elements are only Fo's point of departure: he uses the premise to launch a farcical plot in which Agnelli undergoes plastic surgery that makes him look like one of the workers on his Fiat assembly line. This leads to a continuing crisis of mistaken identities that culminates with a scene in which the worker's wife tries to feed him food that is funneled through a sausage grinder harnessed to his face. Agnelli, who looks like her husband, has told her that after his surgery the only way he can eat is to insert pureed foods through a tube directly into his trachea. When she tries this unusual feeding method on her husband he thinks she is trying to punish him for his extramarital affairs, and when

the police enter the scene, they make plans to adopt the meat-grinder device as an official interrogation method. There is real hunger and the shadow of a genuine national tragedy at the core of this absurd scenario, but Fo uses these elements of reality as a stepping stone for uninhibited lunacy.

Fo's method of mining laughter from actual events provokes his audience into seeing their world from fresh perspectives. In Brechtian terms, he makes the familiar strange, presenting situations that everyone thinks they understand in a context that forces a re-examination of what they have taken for granted. "Comedy is a form of madness," says Fo, but it confirms the superiority of reason. If you think of the techniques of comedy . . . they are always directed toward confirming the victory of reason in every discourse, in every story. The authority figure tries to cancel out reason and dialectic argument. He wants to substitute a rigid sense of order: "That's the rule and you have to accept it as written . . . you can't ask for the reason behind it . . . you can't challenge it." But in the comic's use of paradox there is always a slaughtering of the definitive rules of stability that allows you to watch the prince rolling around with his backside in the air. This changes your perspective on things so that you can see the contradictions and are given the possibility to shout: "Hey, the figures don't add up; the rules of the game are different; let's think the whole thing out again from the top."[24]

Rejecting the commonplace idea that comedy is a realm of irrationality, Fo argues that the disorder of comedy has a deeper purpose. "The irrationality of the comic is only in respect to the irrationality of the rules," says Fo.

In truth the comic is "rational." Walter Benjamin said, "If the Germans had had a better sense of humor, they would have realized how ridiculous they were and would never have accepted Nazism." In the moment in which one forgets how to use laughter, reason dies of suffocation. Irony is an irreplaceable dimension of reason. I don't know if you remember another famous paraphrasing of Benjamin, who toyed with a phrase of Goya's. Instead of "The sleep of reason gives birth to monsters" he said "The sleep of irony gives birth to monsters . . . who teach in German schools."[25]

In Fo's vision of the world, clowns are the opposite of dogmatic German schoolteachers. A clown uses the paradox of comic situations to re-imagine the world as it might be instead of accepting it blindly as it is. When the characters in Fo's plays unleash the spirit of carnival into the mundane landscapes they inhabit, there is a sense that justice is being restored. Inspired by the *giullari* of the Middle Ages, Fo's conception of comedy is similar to the Rabelaisian principles articulated by Mikhail Bakhtin, in which laughter possesses an "indissoluble and essential relation to freedom."[26] These paradoxical dynamics are visible in Fo's paintings. Mundane settings are liberated and transformed by fantastic visual contradictions. Bicycles fly in the air. Giraffes wander through the Italian seaside. A soldier goes to war riding naked on a pig.

Fo's comic cosmology is encapsulated in his painted rendering of Saint Mark's Square in Venice. Beginning with a realistic store-bought print of the piazza, Fo has enhanced its somber rust-hued tones with brightly animated figures that he has painted over the original. Dwarfing the serious figures walking across the square in everyday clothing, Fo superimposes a throng of larger-than-life revelers engaging in fantastical antics. A pinkish elephant strolls across a rooftop and trumpeting angels fly through the air. An aristocrat flails helplessly as he falls from a bell tower. Giant puppets manipulated by rods dance over the heads of the crowd, and an acrobat strikes a pose on a yellow-and-green-winged horse. As he does in his plays, Fo has altered the landscape to suggest that a realm of carnival lunacy lies just beneath the surface of the humdrum world. "It's a paradox," remarks Fo.

It's a paradoxical picture that uses the setting of Saint Mark's Square, with its usual everyday rituals, and superimposes a carnival that shakes everything up, where everything takes place outside the lines and there are no more rules. In short, it is freedom, the shattering of regulations. The original picture was banal. It was obvious, a conventional vision of Saint Mark's Square, and I chose it intentionally so that I could shatter it. I didn't choose Titian or Tintoretto. . . . I chose someone without a name, without imagination. I did it for pleasure, so that I could imagine the unseen possibilities of Venice more freely.[27]

The carnival that erupts in Fo's rendering of Saint Mark's Square is emblematic of his approach to comedy. Beginning with a meticulous depiction of realistic details, he achieves an effect of unfettered abandon. Whether he starts with tedious transcripts of an anarchist's trial, the annotated manuscript of Columbus's diary, or yellowed newspaper accounts of arcane political machinations, Fo's mastery of comic paradox enables him to sculpt creations of wild joy from sources of stifling banality.

EXCERPT FROM
ACCIDENTAL DEATH OF AN ANARCHIST

By DARIO FO Translated by RON JENKINS

(In this scene Fo plays the role of a 'histrio-maniac,' a con man obsessed with role-playing, who continues to change identities throughout the play. Here he pretends to be a federal judge sent from Rome to investigate the misconduct of a police sergeant and commissioner who, while interrogating a suspect, pushed him out of a window to his death. The suspect was a member of the anarchist party, and the police told the media that in spite of their efforts to save him, the anarchist threw himself out the window when he was seized by what they called a "raptus" of uncontrollable emotion. Although the play is a farce, it is based on a sequence of true and tragic events, and the term 'raptus' was taken from the actual transcripts of the trial.)

SERGEANT: Yes, I confess... we made a mistake.

MANIAC: Poor thing... any one can make a mistake. But you, I'm sorry to say, have gone too far. Let me explain: First of all you arbitrarily detained a free citizen. Then you misused your authority by holding him in custody beyond the legal limit. Furthermore you traumatized him with the pitiful ploy of saying you had proof that he was responsible for bombing the train station. Then you more or less intentionally threw him into a psychotic state by making him believe that he had lost his job, that his alibi had fallen through, and for the final stroke, that his friend and companion from Rome had pleaded guilty to the massacres in Milan. His friend was a heinous murderer?! He was so overwhelmed that he said despairingly: "It's the end of anarchism," and threw himself out the window! *(Pause)* Are we losing our minds? At this point why should we be surprised that a person taken advantage of in this manner would lose control of himself in a fit of "raptus"? No, no, I'm sorry, but in my opinion you are guilty. Do you understand me? You are entirely responsible for the death of the anarchist! You will be charged with instigation of suicide!

SERGEANT: But, your honor, how is that possible?! You admit yourself that our profession requires us to interrogate suspects, and to resort to any means necessary for trapping them into a confession. Surely a little psychological violence...

MANIAC: No, this is not a question of "a little", but of relentless violence! To start with, did you or did you not have definite proof that this poor railroad worker had lied about his alibi? Answer me!

SERGEANT: No, we didn't have definite proof, but....

MANIAC: I'm not interested in "buts"! Are there or are there not two or three pensioners who have already corroborated his alibi?

COMMISSIONER: Yes there are.

MANIAC: Then you also lied to the television and newspaper reporters when you said there were serious indications that his alibi would not stand up in court. So when you use the traps, the snares, and the lies, it's not only to deceive the suspect, but it's also to trick and misuse the faith of credulous and gullible people all over the country! Where did you get the information that the anarchist dancer had confessed?

COMMISSIONER: We made it up.

MANIAC: Oh, what vivid imaginations! You two should have been writers. And you still might have the chance, you know. There's plenty of time to write in prison. *(Pause)* You're feeling a little glum, eh! Well, to be honest I should add that in Rome they have definitive proof of your guilt in this case. You're both done for. The Minister of Justice has decided to sacrifice you, to make examples of you, and treat you as severely as possible to restore credibility to the police force!

SERGEANT: No, that's unbelievable!

COMMISSIONER: But how can they...

MANIAC: Of course that means two careers are ruined! That's politics, my friends! For a while you served a purpose: you helped prevent the growth of the unions by creating a climate in which it was acceptable to 'kill the subversives.' But now things have changed. People are indignant about the death of the defenestrated anarchist... they need a couple of heads... and that's what the government is going to give them!

SERGEANT: Ours?

COMMISSIONER: Exactly!

MANIAC: There's an old English proverb that says: "The master unleashes his watchdogs against the peasants. If the peasants complain to the king, the master pardons himself by killing his watchdogs."

SERGEANT: And you think... really... you're sure?

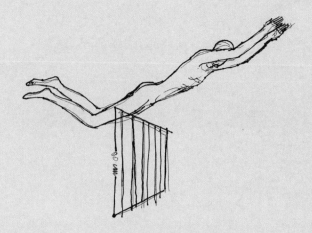

MANIAC: And who am I, if not your judge?

COMMISSIONER: Damned profession!!

SERGEANT: I built the gallows myself... and now I'm going to pay for it.

MANIAC: Of course there will be many who will take pleasure in your misfortune... who will sneer in satisfaction.

COMMISSIONER: Starting with our colleagues. That's what drives me wild.

SERGEANT: Not to mention the newspapers!

COMMISSIONER: Who knows what the headlines will be! Imagine what the tabloids will write!

SERGEANT: Who knows what they'll come up with, those worms, the same ones who used to kiss up to us to get a story... "COP GETS BOPPED!"

COMMISSIONER: "HE WAS A PSYCHOPATHIC SADIST!"

MANIAC: Not to mention the humiliation... the irony...

SERGEANT: And the mockery. Everyone will turn their backs on us... we won't even be able to find jobs as valet parking attendants.

COMMISSIONER: What a rotten world!

MANIAC: No, what a rotten government!

SERGEANT: At this point what do you think our options are? Give us some advice!

MANIAC: Me? What can I tell you?

COMMISSIONER: Please, tell us what to do!

MANIAC: If I were in your position...

SERGEANT: In our position?

MANIAC: I'd throw myself out the window!

COMMISSIONER AND SERGEANT: (*In unison*) What?!

MANIAC: You asked for my advice... and at this point, rather than endure that kind of humiliation... do yourselves a favor and jump! Come on, be brave!

SERGEANT: Sure, but what's bravery got to do with it?!

MANIAC: Nothing! That's the point. Just let yourself be seized by a 'raptus' and the jumping will take care of itself!

(*He pushes the two of them in the direction of the window.*)

COMMISSIONER AND SERGEANT: But no, wait! Wait!

MANIAC: What do you mean "wait?" What are you waiting for? What's left for you on this disgusting planet? What kind of life is this? Rotten world, rotten government.... Everything is rotten! Let's all jump! (*He drags them toward the window with increasing force.*)

SERGEANT: But no, your honor, what are you doing? I still have hope!

MANIAC: There's no more hope. You're finished... you understand, finished!!! Down you go!

COMMISSIONER AND SERGEANT: Help! Don't push... please!

MANIAC: It's not me that's pushing. It's the "raptus". Three cheers for the liberating "raptus"! (*He grabs them by their waists and forces them to stand up on the window sill. He continues trying to push them out from below.*)

COMMISSIONER AND SERGEANT: No, no, help! Help!

(*An officer enters*)

OFFICER: What's happening, your honor?

MANIAC: (*Releasing his grip*) Oh, nothing. Nothing's happening... isn't that right commissioner? Isn't that true, sergeant? Come on, calm down your officer.

SERGEANT: (*Descending shakily from the window sill*) Well, yes, don't worry... it was just...

MANIAC: A "raptus."

OFFICER: A "raptus?"

MANIAC: Yes, they wanted to throw themselves out the window.

OFFICER: Them too?

MANIAC: Yes, but don't say anything to the press, please!

OFFICER: No, of course not.

THE RHYTHMS OF RESURRECTION: JOHAN PADAN

Johan Padan is a kind of Ruzzante[1] . . . a Harlequin who finds himself engaged on a ship that is part of Columbus's fourth expedition. To tell the truth, I had not even thought of writing this play until the summer of 1991, when I was invited to Seville, in Spain, to make a presentation for a theater full of critics, actors, and cultural experts about Isabella, Three Sailing Ships, and a Con Man, *the play I was supposed to present in the spring of 1992 at the Exposition in honor of Columbus. It was a text I had staged with Franca about twenty-nine years earlier. At its debut and for the duration of its tour, the play aroused scandals, consensus, sensation, and polemics.*

In Seville, I talked about our debut in Genoa, Columbus's native city, where the press had published harsh criticisms of the play in defense of the explorer whom I had treated severely, presenting him as a cunning swindler, cynic, and even a thief. There was a great uproar. We had been warned that many spectators were coming to the theater armed with different vegetables: oversized cabbages, tomatoes, and zucchinis to throw at us. We began the play tensely, waiting for the insults, and . . . the vegetables. But instead we were thrown off balance: after a few minutes of perplexity, the audience began smiling and then letting themselves go in fits of laughter, with lots of belly-laughs and guffaws. Applauding, they shouted: "Yes, he's ONE OF US!"

But let's go back to the incident in Seville. I recounted the plot of the play to the Spanish critics and I reminded them that twenty years earlier, under the Franco regime, a company called Els Joglars had tried to stage the show in Barcelona, but had never made it to opening night. The entire company was arrested at the end of the dress rehearsal. The actors ended up in prison, together with the director, the stage technicians, and even the prompter . . . to teach him a lesson! The audience froze when they heard my punch line. Not a laugh. On the contrary, they looked at me as if I were some kind of impertinent provocateur. Unperturbed, I kept on talking about the diaspora of the Jews, who were thrown out of Spain when Columbus was getting ready to depart for the discovery of the Americas. I told how, at the end of the 1400s, Isabella had organized a veritable plundering of the possessions of the Jews. Before being thrown out, they were stripped of their belongings, furniture, and real estate, and then sent away, literally naked, to different countries throughout Europe. . . . Queen Isabella was history's first Nazi.

At this point I realized I was facing a genuine wall of hostility. Then I discovered why. I didn't know that precisely at that time, a campaign had begun in Spain to convince the Vatican to make Queen Isabella a saint. I had made a gaffe of epic proportions. Someone passed by my shoulder and whispered,

"Be careful, they still have the fires stoked up under the stakes." Making an impromptu attempt to recapture control of the situation, I said, "This is only one of the ideas I had in mind. The truth is that I would actually enjoy much more . . . staging for you . . . something else. It's a story about the adventurous voyages of a poor devil, a sailor in rags, a kind of Ruzzante who ends up in the Indies despite himself. He travels with Columbus and extraordinary things happen to him. It is the story of the discovery of the Americas seen from the viewpoint of a low-life who is one step away from the gallows. I spoke of this character with great enthusiasm . . . improvising. All of a sudden the climate in the room was turned around. There was an unexpected burst of applause, accompanied by a collective sigh of relief: "Beautiful! We like that! It's truly a thrilling story!" —Dario Fo, prologue to Johan Padan[2]

When Dario Fo performs the prologue to *Johan Padan* he is preparing the audience for an encounter with comedy as a survival strategy. Framing his narratives inside one another like a series of Chinese boxes, he introduces his tale about a comic storyteller who uses his wits to save his life by presenting himself as a comic storyteller who does the same thing. Fo ironically recounts how he braved the threat of flying vegetables for mocking Columbus in 1963, and then nearly got burned at the stake in Spain for satirizing Queen Isabella in 1991. His risky exploits as a traveling *giullare* mirror the adventures of his sixteenth-century protagonist, Johan Padan, a stowaway on Columbus's voyage who, like Fo, has the quick tongue of a *giullare*.

Opening a dialogue with history by evoking tyrannical regimes from the Spanish Inquisition to Franco and the Nazis, Fo establishes the dynamics of the story he is about to tell. It is a tale of oppression and resistance, featuring the comic antics of a powerless fool who uses his ingenuity to escape the tortures of the Inquisition in Europe and goes on to help the Indians outwit the Conquistadors in the New World. Fo gives this epic story a touch of intimacy by revealing its origins: at a moment when Fo was trying to rescue himself from a difficult situation in front of a hostile audience in Spain, he invented a story about a character who is a master at inventing stories to get himself out of difficult situations. *Johan Padan* is one of Fo's many stage doubles, a *giullare* who uses laughter to disarm his enemies, defend the downtrodden, and defy injustice.

The Johan Padan character is a composite of sixteenth-century explorers like Cabeza de Vaca and others, who published memoirs about their adventures in the Americas. The first thing

Fo did after reading about the exploration of the New World was to draw pictures of it. His visual imagination transformed the dry documents into dozens of vibrant sketches that capture the ferocious energy of two civilizations in conflict. Idyllic scenes of indigenous peoples fishing and swimming in tranquillity are countered by savage scenes of warfare. Forces of nature echo the clash of cultures in paintings of storm scenes with raging winds and crashing waves. The overall pattern that emerges in the drawings is the same as the overall pattern of Fo's story, which was based on improvised performances in which the drawings were Fo's only notes. The images are infused with a sense of freedom (expressed through human figures that dance, fly, feast, and make love) threatened by oppression (expressed through scenes of bondage, darkness, and violence) which is eventually overcome to restore a mood of harmony (expressed in montages of swaying hammocks, embracing couples, and serene waters).

What makes Fo's artwork and dramaturgy distinctive are the whimsical paradoxes and contradictions that flesh out his epic tale. In the final page of Fo's notebook, for instance, Johan Padan sways on a hammock in Florida dreaming of the Italian village where he was born. Above him, a man stands on a palm tree in a pose that would be impossible to sustain without snapping the tree trunk and plummeting to the ground.[3] The odd tension generated by this magical relationship between man and tree gives a strange vitality to what might otherwise be a banal depiction of a seaside idyll. Equally improbable details contribute to the tensions in Fo's text for the scene, which contrasts Padan's dreamy contentment with his poignant longing for home: "The fresh smell of the wind from my valley. I don't know how it gets here, but I smell it . . . it wafts through my nostrils and gives me goose bumps. . . . I smell the must of fermenting grapes from the tavern, I hear the wine bubbling in the barrels . . . the women singing . . . . My gullet tightens, my heartbeat quickens . . . and I run desperately to the hammock . . . I hug the netting . . . . Before long two young girls come by . . . they rock me slowly, slowly . . . they sing me the song from my village that I taught them . . . with the very same words, the same idiom of my dialect from home."

A few lines later Fo closes the piece with a song that underscores the tensions embedded in the drawings and the text. Based on a traditional folk song, its bittersweet melody is both mournful and joyous, like a spiritual hymn commemorating a costly victory. It is the song that Padan taught the Indians when giving them a crash course in the Gospels, hoping to make them Christians so that the

Spaniards could not justify slaughtering them by claiming they were pagans without souls. The walking oxymoron of Christian pagans infuriated the Spanish governor, but did indeed help to save Padan's adopted tribe, though only temporarily: Eventually the Spaniards resume using the tenets of Christianity to enslave and murder the Indians. Fo's song evokes this contradiction both in its words and through the context in which it is presented. Initially Padan sings the song to persuade the Indians that Christianity, at least as it is manifested in the rituals of his childhood village, can be life-affirming. "He brought us a religion fashioned from songs, happiness, dances, and joy," says an Indian leader to the Spanish governor, a representative of official Christian culture, who is threatening to execute Johan Padan. "You bring us a religion of sadness, melancholy, and death."

The song recalls the tension between official, institutional religion and the pagan-infused peasant traditions of Christianity that Fo first described in _Mistero Buffo_—festive, Dionysian traditions that Fo associates with "the must of fermenting grapes" and "the wine bubbling in the barrels." The song's text is handwritten in Fo's notebook, next to his drawing of Padan dreaming beneath the man balanced precariously on the palm tree. The lyrics begin with a celebration of Christ's Resurrection, but end with the audacious suggestion that the singer is thankful for being saved from the terrors wrought by Christians, who are viewed in the same category as pagan Turks and merciless storms:

> Oh what joy and oh what wonder,
> the son of heav'n is still alive.
> The son of Mary is still living!
> The Virgin Mary is full of cheer now
> and there's nothing for us to fear now
> not the Turks nor the stormy winds now
> not the winds nor the Christian soldiers
> not the Turks nor the Christian soldiers.

Like the narrative of Johan Padan and the paintings that inspired it, Fo's song is a collage of contradictions. Its placement in the story implicitly links the Resurrection of Jesus to the salvation of a _giullare_, a self-confessed Antichrist who preaches a comically and erotically charged version of the Gospels to frustrate the ambitions of a Spanish army that wants to Christianize a continent with a far more somber interpretation of the Bible's teachings. The lyrics contrast the restrictive forces that have been woven into the play (Christianity, violence, storms) with the freedom from fear that comes with their defeat.

After singing this musical reprise of the paradoxical dynamics that animate his play, Fo takes a bow, acknowledges the applause, and invites the audience onstage to look at the book of paintings he has been using as a prompter throughout the evening. In the early stages of creating the play, Fo improvised Padan's story, using the drawings as a mnemonic device to stimulate his verbal imagination. The text was born out of a few months of these impromptu encounters between Fo, his drawings, and his audience. The spectators who accept Fo's offer to come onstage find themselves leafing through the pages of an oversized sketchbook perched on an antique wooden lectern. The collage of paintings recapitulates the action of the play, depicting the multitude of characters, gestures, and settings that Fo embodies in his solo performance without props or costume changes.

At the beginning of the book are dark scenes with hooded judges of the Inquisition and bodies strapped to wheels of torture. These are set in Italy, from which Padan escapes only to find that the Inquisition in Spain is just as cruel. "Holy blood of God," exclaims Padan, seeing heretics burned alive in Seville, "I escape from Venice with a fire at my ass . . . and as soon as I get to Seville, there's another one in front of my balls." Fo's paintings of the scene capture the horror and absurdity as deftly as his text: he paints an unlikely montage of burning heretics, red-hot bodies floating into the sky, dancing girls, and a musician with a guitar. This visual juxtaposition of frivolity, death, and hypocrisy matches Padan's verbal impressions of the scenes he has witnessed. "These fanatics," observes Padan,

> were always setting people on fire: heretics who didn't want to repent, wizards who didn't want to renounce witchcraft, Moors who didn't want to convert . . . and Jews . . . for any reason at all. . . . They don't do it just for spite . . . they burn the body to free the soul. . . . the body turns to ashes and the happy soul goes off to heaven. What hearts they have! . . . The stench of burning flesh . . . but these people of Seville were not sad. No, on the contrary, as soon as they finished their acts of collective roasting . . . they ripped off the black vestments they were wearing, and all of them, men, women, and children, threw themselves into a joyous frenzy of singing and dancing. . . . I remember

they had castanets, that's what they called them . . . these wooden things that came from the Arabs . . . they beat them together to make music.

At this point Fo sings one of the songs Padan hears in Seville, using onomatopoeic sounds to create the illusion of the accompanying castanets. Surprisingly, Fo manages to create the same onomatopoeic effect in his painting: the text of the song is handwritten on the page of burning heretics below the feet of the dancing girls just to the right of a floating guitar. Popping through the lines at random are starbursts of red flames that seem to have jumped off the fires of the Inquisition; these punctuate the text with a crackling energy that serves as the visual equivalent of the "TATATATAT" sound that Fo uses with his voice to mimic the clacking of castanets. Equidistant from the burning heretics and the guitar, these starbursts could be musical notes or sparks of flame, an ambivalence appropriate to the irony in Fo's account of the event. The painting is as disorienting and contradictory as the scene of executions and dances it depicts. With a few splashes of color Fo mocks the paradoxical logic that fuels the Inquisition, and sets his satire to the fiery rhythm of Spanish castanets. The image of fire gains another layer of meaning from the song's lyrics, which refer to the passion of lovers, who bathe in a stream to cool off on a hot day.

The red sparks in Fo's montage also allude to the fireworks that Padan learns to make during his stay in Seville, a skill that later proves useful during his adventures in America. In performing this scene, Fo follows his imitation of castanets with an equally impressive imitation of fireworks. With sweeping arm circles, the well-placed fluttering of his fingers, and a mesmerizing array of vocal effects, Fo becomes a one-man pyrotechnic display, conveying all the details of a fireworks spectacle, including the time lag between the sound of the blasts and the lights that they generate. Over the course of a few minutes, Fo creates the stage illusions of heretics burning, castanets clattering, and fireworks exploding. Looking at the corresponding page from his notebook, it is clear that the blueprint for all of these theatrical effects was present in the visual collage he imagined before the scene was ever performed: a pyre of flames, a red-hot victim, dancing girls in swirling dresses, hooded figures, fiery starbursts, a guitar. In

a single montage of sensory images Fo was able to evoke "the stench of burning flesh", the "TATATATAT" of castanets, and "fireworks that burst into the lightened sky." The sounds, smells, and sights of sixteenth-century Seville, as well as the complexities of that historical context, are all captured with extraordinary economy in a page of painted images that inspired an equally succinct sequence of gestures, words, and vocalizations on the stage. In this passage Fo demonstrates the connection between his body, his text, and his drawings with an eloquent ease that belies the intricacy of his intertwining themes and techniques.

The Seville scene's pattern of paradoxical juxtapositions suggests a key to Fo's dramaturgy as an actor, writer, and designer. The theatrical structure of *Johan Padan* moves back and forth between violence and tranquillity, grimness and giddiness, near-death and salvation. This continual shift from darker moments to lighter ones creates a kind of theatrical chiaroscuro. The technique is apparent in the drawings Fo made for *Johan Padan*, which use an alternation of dark and light colors to contrast serious scenes with comic episodes, but the basic juxtaposition occurs in many variations. Fo's vocal technique, for instance, moves frequently from a deep bass to a comic falsetto. His gestures vary from a volcanic swirling of his limbs to tiny finger movements enacted while the rest of his body is still. These physical variations are an actor's response to the shifts from epic drama to light-hearted irony in the written text, which in turn takes its cues from the fluid changes in Fo's drawings.

The quality that most closely unites Fo's drawings, texts, and gestures is the kinetic physicality that animates them all. The constant changes in color, tone, and size generate a momentum that gives Fo's stories a narrative drive based more on paradox than on plot. The contradiction in each successive situation is established and resolved, so that the story moves dynamically from one paradox to another, pushed forward by shifting waves of contradictory action.

Fo's kinetic style is apparent from the opening passages of *Johan Padan*. Sailors are shouting as they prepare to set sail: "Faster! Faster! Let go the moorings! Haul up the yardarm! Hoist the mainsail! Weigh anchor! Heave away!" The mariners are hoisting, heaving, and hauling as their ship moves out to sea. Fo plays all the parts, voicing each of the sailor's cries with contrasting rhythms and tones. His gestures convey the multiple actions with motions that counterpoint each other by moving in opposite directions

as he changes voices. His sketch of the same scene pictures a bustling crew of sailors on a sixteenth-century brig. The urgency of the drawing comes to life in Fo's performance, a cinematic montage of sound and movement. Officers give orders. The crewmen throw their bodies into the work. Sails are unfurled. The ship crashes through the waves.

The momentum of the scene is provided by the sharp changes of pitch in Fo's voice and the athletic physicality of his body parts moving in opposition to one another. Suddenly Fo stops and turns to the audience, as if stepping out of the frame of a movie. "You don't understand this, do you?," he asks. In fact Fo has been performing in a dialect that is difficult to fully comprehend. He claims it is the language of sixteenth-century seamen. "You can't expect to make sense of it," says Fo, reassuringly. "I'm the one performing it and I don't understand either, so don't worry." Having set up a paradoxical dialogue with the audience about the incomprehensibility of the language he is using to tell them a story, Fo jumps back into the narrative. "Oh, how the wind rips and billows the sails," he shouts, creating the illusion of the ship moving out onto the open sea. "I'm saved!," he cries. Then he again steps out of the story to speak an aside, this time in the character of Johan Padan.

"Saved from what?" Fo asks, as if he can read the audience's mind, and wants to dispel their confusion. His tone shifts abruptly from epic bombast to intimate confession as he tells of his escape "from the Inquisition . . . from the gallows . . . from being burned alive." His lover, it seems, had been arrested for witchcraft, and Padan had been accused as her accomplice. Padan's description moves from the tortures of the Inquisition to the pleasures of making love with the witch. Fo's drawings for this sequence also shift from dark scenes of bodies tied to a torture wheel to carefree sketches of a naked couple caressing on the beach. Padan explains how their lovemaking was interrupted by a storm, that the witch predicted by reading the cloud formations around the moon. Storms appear throughout the story as violent counterpoints to episodes of calm. When Johan Padan arrives

in America he also finds blissful moments of lovemaking that are invariably followed by life-threatening encounters and howling tempests.

These recurring sequences of storms and serenity are displayed in the montage of drawings that depict Padan's trip across the Atlantic. He travels with the pigs, donkeys, horses, and cows in the ship's hold, which is shown in cross-section floating on a tranquil sea. Below this scene Fo paints a tempest, showing the same ship from a distance as it is tossed on its side by the swirling waves. At the bottom of the page Fo sketches another maritime scene, this time on the beach of Santo Domingo, where natives dive for pearls in clear-blue water. A few pages later there is a drawing of a shipwrecked Padan clinging to a pig that saves his life. "One should never go to sea without a pig," advises Padan, who relies on the pig's fat to keep him afloat. "A pig is so round and fat that he'll never sink! He goes under for a while, but then: GLUB, GLUB, GLUB, he always comes floating back up. It's a buoy made of fat! And he has that little curly tail, that's made just right for you to hold onto it, without slipping loose."

When he performs the pig-rescue episode, Fo uses his body and voice to create a mini-sequence of near drownings and comic resurrections. Padan and the pig keep sinking below the waves, but the pig's fat always buoys them back up again. Each time they come up to the surface, Padan, overjoyed to be alive, gives the pig "a big wet kiss." After a while the pig starts enjoying the attention and goes under even when there are no waves, just to get another kiss. Fo conveys the sequence of fear and relief with bobbing gestures that are accompanied by vocal effects whose tones rise up and down with Padan's chances for survival. The quick alternation of moods is a miniature mirroring of the shifting tones Fo captures in his drawings. Beneath the sketch of the pig bringing Padan to shore is a depiction of Padan and his pig freezing to death on the beach, followed by an attack from Indians with bows and arrows. By the time Fo gets to the bottom of the page, the assault has turned into a rescue in which both Padan and his pig are warmed by the Indians' blazing bonfire. The continuing shifts from danger to salvation are rendered on the page by streaks of sunshine yellow alternating with blood red and pale blue. The text also captures the difference between life and death in terms of color. "Ohhh! We were cold," laments Padan as he takes stock of the situation with his companions, who have also been saved from the shipwreck by pigs. "I looked at my skin . . . it was pastel blue. My companions were turning blue too. The pigs were shocking pink!"

As the narrative progresses, the paradoxes accumulate. Not only is Padan saved by a pig, and rescued again by the Indians he thinks want to kill him, but he ends up sounding an alarm that saves another tribe that had planned to eat him, a fact he discovers when they begin plucking out his hair in a manner resembling the way he has seen them plucking feathers from a turkey the day before. The plucking of the turkey and the plucking of Padan are represented in Fo's sketchbook by separate comic drawings. The sketch of Padan shows his body from four perspectives simultaneously, as if the viewer were seeing multiple camera angles at the same time, lined up on top of one another like a one-man time-lapsed totem pole. (Onstage Fo creates a similar illusion with rapidly shifting gestures.) The overlapping figures of Padan are all being painted with colored circles by women attendants, who caress and massage him before preparing him to be cooked. At first Padan interprets the painted circles as a ritual of affection. Only later does he realize the meaning of the markings: "They were reserving their favorite pieces of meat!"

In Fo's visual and verbal dramaturgy every action has a reaction. The lines in his drawings and the lines in his texts are structured in an architectural sequence of point and counterpoint that establishes the tension necessary to maintain a state of dynamic equilibrium. In the sketch of the cannibals' totem pole, the four animated depictions of Padan's body are designed to balance each other out. Padan's torso leans back to the left with outstretched arms as he asks in red letters superimposed over the images, "Do you take me for a turkey?" This action counteracts the movement of the body beneath him (also Padan's) that is leaning over in a back-bend toward the right, as if fainting in shock with the realization that he is about to be eaten. Underneath these two figures is another rendering of Padan, after the shock, in a flat-out position that serves as the base of the human pyramid. This horizontal foundation is counterbalanced at the top of the four-bodied structure by yet another version of Padan, here in a vertical position,

with outstretched legs in an inverted V-shape that seems to be an instinctive response to a woman who appears to be taking a sample bite out of his buttocks.

The composition of Fo's human tower functions soundly in both architectural and theatrical terms. On the page it has the effect of an intriguing comic edifice at the same time that it serves as a blueprint for Fo's physical interpretation of Padan's dilemma, which employs the same principles of point and counterpoint. As Fo moves his body parts in opposition to one another onstage, he creates the illusion achieved by his painting. His gestural montage collapses time, showing Padan's changing reactions to the situation in a quick succession of gestural jump-cuts. The narrative drive built into Fo's drawing is translated into a cinematic language of the body that gives a forward momentum to the words of Fo's text. Complementing the pyramid of the human totem pole in Fo's drawing is the inverted verbal pyramid formed by the quickening of Fo's phrases, which are also built on the opposition of action and reaction, question and response:

> They pulled out the hairs from my beard,
> from my armpits, and from down below too.
>
> Under the belly button!
>
> Oh how it hurts!
>
> "That's enough, you wretches!
> What do you take me for, a turkey?"
>
> "Yes!"
>
> "You want to eat me?"
>
> "Yes!"
>
> I fainted!

The synchrony between Fo's drawings and texts does not arise from any intellectual theories on his part. He is above all a practical professional, who structures the monologue this way because that's the way it works best in practice. His drawings follow the rules of perspective and composition he learned at the Brera academy. His plays follow the rules of dramaturgical structure that he learned onstage by studying the responses of the audience.

The dynamics of Fo's dramaturgy adhere to his principles of theatrical architecture. Conflicts between opposing forces are necessary to provide the tension that keeps a situation from collapsing. These basic concepts of theatrical equilibrium are implicit in Fo's description of Padan's first encounter with a hammock: each phrase of the passage is accompanied by gestures that alternate in opposition to one another, cumulatively creating the illusion of a man trying

QUEST L'E' OL FAMOSO MOSTRO

ME SPUSSA STO ZENTILEZZA

CANIBALI

STOR
AMERIGO
VESPUCU
ALFONSO CAMBERAN

ZELVAZI DOLZI ZENTIL

ME ME TOCANT COI DENCI CON LE
COI DIM DEI PIE ORECE

to master the physics of a swinging hammock. There is no hammock onstage, but its presence is suggested by the actions and reactions of Fo's body as he speaks:

> It's difficult to get up onto it. If you're not experienced, you may try sitting with your butt first and: [mimes a hammock turning upside down and a fall to the ground] PATAPUM! A whack in the ass! No! You have to do it with your knees! [Mimes mounting the hammock with a bent leg] . . . You stretch out this one [mimes opening the hammock], then you stretch out the other one [mimes extending his other leg] and then . . . PATAPUNFETE! [Mimes falling to the ground] Because it's not just a question of the knees. It's a question of balance . . . equilibrium . . . dynamics, because when you get on, you have to position your knee like this, but then give it a good strong kick! [Mimes making the hammock rock like a swing] Then you turn this one and that one, then you go JOM, you stretch out, you wait, one two, three . . . one pulls you, one goes down, the knee for support, twist here, turn there!!! [Mimes the success of a sustained and regular oscillation] It's all in the dynamics!

As Fo tells this story about the importance of equilibrium and balance he employs the dynamics he is describing. The rhythmic pattern of collapse and resurrection that has been employed regularly throughout the piece appears again. Twice Padan fails to mount the hammock. The reaction to his unbalanced actions is a rhythmically structured disequilibrium, and onomatopoeic sounds indicate his crash to the floor. On the third try the two falls are counter-balanced by a successful leap that leads to a sustained equilibrium, expressed in the gestural harmony of the "regular oscillations" he refers to in his stage directions.

This initial success is followed by a more complex variation of the same contradictory dynamics when Padan tries to make love in the hammock. The presence of two bodies in one hammock generates an even more complicated set of actions and reactions: "I fell with my head pointed down vertically toward the ground . . . but I didn't hit the ground! . . . My testicles were tangled up in the netting. 'AHHHHHH!!!!!'"

Padan's ignoble fate is pictured in Fo's sketchbook just below his rendering of Padan's successful rendezvous with his lover, achieved after relentless practicing of "equilibrium exercises" that eventually transform the awkward sailor into a hammock acrobat. "I tried it with one foot, with one hand," says Padan. "I tried it upside down, standing on my head. I became a hammock dancer like the world had never seen. I could make love hanging form my fingernails, from my feet, from my ears,

THIS PAGE: Drawings from Fo's notebook for *Johan Padan*

185

my teeth . . . my buttocks. . . . And when I was possessed by a twinge of folly . . . one, two, three [he mimes a full circle on the hammock] IHHEHHOHHAHH, a spinning wheel of love."

Later in the story it is a wild horse that ends up with his testicles squeezed by a rope when Padan tames him with a technique he claims to have learned in Bergamo. After recounting the falls he has suffered through the stallion's refusal to be mounted, Padan gives a detailed, almost geometrical description of his method. "Once the bridle has been attached," he warns,

> You can't approach him from the front because he'd bite you, so you pretend to talk to someone who's standing to your right . . . and you tie it over there . . . and he, the horse, . . . gets curious . . . so he comes over to listen and . . . then you go to the other side, but make sure you change the man that you're talking to. Otherwise the horse will get suspicious [he mimes the harnessing of the horse, the linking of the reins to the bridle]. You let the two ropes fall loosely in a line . . . [he mimes extending the ropes so that they reach the testicles of the stallion, and tying a knot around the testicles] . . . next it's the pectorals, you slide the ropes along the pectorals, then you slide them along the belly . . . when you get to the balls you make a little ring, you hook it around one testicle, without pulling . . . then another loop, also very gently, around the second testicle . . . then you wait for him to put his head down, you straddle onto his back as fast as you can: [mimes jumping onto the back of the horse, who reacts by lifting his head and neck so that he squeezes his

testicles by his own action and neighs desperately] TAN . . . right away he goes: TAK "AHHHHIIIII!" . . . he lifts his back: "AII-IIHHHIIIII!"... he raises his neck, TAK! "AHHHOIIIIII!" . . . by the third bucking . . . he's a new beast [mimes the obedient walk of a show horse on parade]. What elegance!

Fo depicts the training of this and other horses in a sequence of drawings that visualize some of the story's circular paradoxes. The central action of the narrative involves Padan's attempt to help the Indians free themselves from the repressive regime of the Spanish, but in doing so he ends up constraining the freedom of the horses, an element perhaps negated by the fact that the horses have escaped from the Spanish army in the first place, so that the more interesting paradox resides in the reversal that comes when the Indians defeat the Spanish with their own horses. This paradox is pictured in drawings that depict Spaniards on horseback massacring the Indians, who Padan says believed a horse and its rider to be a single creature of demonic origins. Eventually the positions are reversed, and it is the Spanish soldiers who are terrified. "INDIANS ON HORSEBACK LIKE CHRISTIANS?!" they exclaim, without realizing the irony of their words. "Nothing is sacred anymore."

Paradoxes like these are among the factors that make Fo's epic tale more intriguing than the typical story of "noble" Indians victimized by "greedy" conquistadors. In Fo's story the far-from-innocent Indians enslave and sometimes eat one another, a fact that Fo expects modern Americans to criticize as politically incorrect. "Americans want to continue enjoying their exploitation of the land they stole from the Indians," says Fo, pointing out a paradox in America's revision of its founding mythology, "but they insist on having the story told in terms that ennoble the people they massacred as if this nicety of storytelling will absolve them of responsibility for their actions. My story is based on documents that recount the cruelty of the American Indians to one another, and I should not be expected to censor that element of history to make it simpler for Americans to ease their consciences."[4]

Fo also acknowledges the politically sensitive contradiction that is raised by the story's focus on a European's efforts to help the Indians resist the invasion of Europeans. He confronts this paradox by raising another one: "In many senses," says Fo, "Johan Padan is an Indian. He comes from a class of Italians who were exploited just as horribly by their own countrymen as the Indians were by the Europeans. Padan is not part of the aristocratic class who will get rich from the

ME SCAGNAVA I CIAPP

PER UN TACHIN

ME CATAT

ALITARME ADOSO PER OL FIAT DE LA VITA

explorations of the Americas. He is one of the poor sailors who were used as slave labor on the ships. He has something in common with the Indians because they are both being abused by the conquistadors."[5]

The Indians in Fo's story are impressed by Padan for just these reasons. In a speech to the Spanish governor, the chief of Padan's adopted tribe compares Padan's humility to the arrogance of the conquistadors: "You arrived full of self-importance, in plumed helmets . . . he arrived as naked as we were. You arrived triumphantly riding on stallions . . . he arrived riding too . . . on the back of a pig." So when the Indians grow to revere Padan as a shaman, it is not because they are simple-minded savages who are awed by the conquistadors' shiny armor, but because they appreciate his honesty, humility, and generosity. Using the sewing skills he practiced when stitching up wounded pigs, donkeys, and cows during his journey across the Atlantic, Padan saves the lives of many Indians wounded in battle. These and other episodes of his adventures are borrowed from the journals of Cabeza da Vaca,[6] but Fo weaves his own threads of fantasy into the documentary sources of the narrative. As the story progresses, Fo's Padan becomes a pagan Christ figure, performing miracles that recall at some moments the New Testament (multiplication of fishes for a hungry tribe), and at other moments the mythical tales of peasant folklore (ending a drought by making the son of the rain god laugh and shed tears of joy). But Padan's miracles are not based on supernatural powers. They are connected to his skills as a storyteller and his luck as a fool. Padan's gift for comedy brings the rain, and his yarn-spinning chutzpah brings him credit for the sudden appearance of fish. The miracles he performs are the secular miracles of a *giullare* following in the footsteps of his medieval predecessors, who raised their voices against hunger and injustice.

Like the medieval *giullari*, Padan tells his own version of the Gospels, humanizing the story to bring it to life with particular relevance for his audience. The Gospels that Padan preaches to the Indians are loaded with multiple ironies, the first being that Padan was branded a blasphemer by the court of the Inquisition. Furthermore, the Gospels were the stories used by the Spaniards to justify their plundering of the Indians' land in the name of Christianity. Padan wants to use the same Christian stories to outwit the Spaniards at their own absurd game. If he can teach the Indians enough of the Gospels to convince the Spaniards that they are Christians, the Spaniards won't be able to justify their massacre of the Indians by claiming that they have no Christian souls. In Fo's narrative, the story and the storyteller have the power to save lives or end them. The *giullare's* miracles are fashioned from the humble and secular magic of words.

Adopting the classic technique of the *giullare*, Padan inserts local details to render his Gospel story more immediate to the audience at hand. When he tells the story of Adam and Eve in the Garden of Eden, he realizes that the Indians have no apples, so he substitutes a forbidden fruit that is more familiar to them: in his version of the story, the snake tempts Eve with a mango, but because it is much bigger than an apple, the reptile has a hard time fitting it into his mouth and can barely get his message of sin across. "Eeeaatthisssssssmaaaangggmaaaangmaaannngo," the snake urges, his mouth stuffed, in a slapstick gag that grew out of Fo's drawings of the scene, in which the mango is the size of a watermelon.

Apparently, Padan's strategy is successful. The Indians identify so strongly with the story that when Padan tells them about the angel with a sword coming to chase Adam and Eve out of Paradise, they all shout out, "That one must be a Spaniard." In fact, Padan tells his tale so skillfully that the Indians become deeply attached to the character of Jesus and refuse to accept his death. They mourn Him with wailing and self-flagellation, as if Christ had been one of their children. At first they think Padan is fabricating the Resurrection just to make them feel better, but when they finally accept Jesus' return, they erupt into wild and raucous rituals of celebration. Padan cautions them that love-making and cocaine intoxication are not acceptable Christian forms of thanksgiving.

"It's not allowed."

"No, it's not."

"You can't dance in front of God?"

"NO!"

"You can't make love in front of God?"

"NO!"

"You can't drink?"

"Only the priests drink. Everybody else watches."

"And we can't blow through the reeds?"

"NO!"

"Not even a little snort?"

"NOOO!!!!"

"Oh, what kind of dead religion is this?"

To prove to the Indians that Christianity is not dead, Padan reaches back to his religion's peasant roots and teaches them a song about the Resurrection that the people in his village sang during Easter. The Indians jazz up the song with their own rhythms, which help give them the courage to march in procession with crosses to the settlement of the Spanish governor—who condemns Padan to death as a blasphemer "because he started a religion full of songs, dances, . . . and laughter."

Then, at the moment of Padan's hanging, Fo orchestrates one of the play's most surprising resurrections, infusing the scene with a hallucinatory beauty that emerges from the cinematic scope of his language as it has evolved from the epic action of his paintings. "They put the noose around my neck," Padan narrates, "and two hangmen tightened it. I could feel myself hanging, hanging there in the sky, my throat was choking . . . I saw red fire . . . the sky was burning: 'Am I in hell?!' No! No! The sky was really burning! All the Indians, twenty-five thousand Indians, had come with torches and were standing on the bell towers, the plantations, and even the ships. Twenty-five thousand Indians! Fifty thousand torches! The sky was burning."

Padan's adopted tribe had come to save him by threatening to burn the governor's settlement if he did not release their friend. Fo moves from a close-up to a long shot in the text, just as he does in his paintings of the scene. Standing on the gallows, Padan's body is red, as are the torches of the Indians who line the rooftops of the Spanish settlement. The fiery hell of Padan's imagination becomes the fiery nightmare of the Christian governor. He orders his men to shoot at the Indians, but the cannon fuses are too wet to ignite: the Indians had urinated on them the night before. Then the Indians set off the fireworks that Padan had taught them to use. In Fo's tale of the *giullare* humiliation and spectacle are more powerful than guns. The Spaniards are shamed and terrified into submission, defeated by mockery.

According to Padan, subsequent attempts to conquer Florida were unsuccessful for forty years, forcing the Spanish king to declare it an "impregnable territory." The *giullare* Padan remains with the Indians, paradoxically living a more peaceful and fear-free life than he could have in the Inquisition-plagued Christian countries of Europe—an irony alluded to in the Easter song from his Italian village, which the Indians sing to him as he sways on his hammock in his old age. Fo's resonant voice captures the ambiguous tone of the paintings that close his sketchbook, a bittersweet rendering of an impossible landscape, a temporary paradise where the hammock is suspended in the air with no visible means of support. The European soldiers are bound to return some day, but for the moment at least, a miraculous equilibrium has been achieved. The fragile balance of irreconcilable forces is expressed in the final reprise of Fo's song.

Oh what joy and oh what wonder,

the son of heav'n is still alive.

The son of Mary is still living!

The Virgin Mary is full of cheer now

and there's nothing for us to fear now

not the Turks nor the stormy winds now

not the winds nor the Christian soldiers

not the Turks nor the Christian soldiers.

EXCERPT FROM
JOHAN PADAN
AND THE DISCOVERY OF THE AMERICAS

By DARIO FO Translated by **RON JENKINS** with assistance from **STEFANIA TAVIANO**
(reprinted with the permission of **GROVE/ATLANTIC**)

(This segment of the story begins when Johan Padan, a stowaway on one of Columbus's voyages to the New World, is preparing for what he thinks will be a voyage back to Europe.)

I was almost disappointed when the orders came: "We're going back home!"

But I was so happy to be heading back, that I loaded twice as much onto the ships as everyone else: I loaded water, I loaded vegetables... I even loaded five fat pigs that we had to take to Santo Domingo. Meanwhile the others loaded throngs of Indians onto the ship, enslaved prisoners... a hundred and twenty-five of them locked up in the hold, below deck, in place of the ballast... and to stop them from screaming they stuffed their mouths with chaff down to their throats.

We left. It was burning hot. Not much to eat... not much to drink. The poor Indians started dying. The sailors took the corpses and threw them into the sea.

After a few days, behind the stern in the ship's wake, we caught sight of a bunch of big fish following us: they were waiting for their meal of Indians.

They liked Indians.

So the sailors said: "Why don't we fish with these savages?" They took some dead Indians, fresh from that morning, stuck them on hooks, threw them into the sea and went fishing.

But it just so happens that there is a God in heaven, who every once in a while gets so mad that his halo starts spinning, and he sent a storm with a wind so strong that you could see it scoop the waves out of the rolling sea. Our sails were ripped to shreds, and we were all staggering around like drunkards.

We heard a tremendous crash. We had smashed into a rock! "We're sinking! We're going to sink!"

"Bring out the rowboats!"

There were only three. I asked the captain: "Where should I go?" There were three boats.

"No, there's no room for you five animal keepers... Go sink with the Indians and the pigs!"

I don't know what got into me, maybe it was out of anger... maybe it was pity: I threw open the door to the hold and all the Indians leapt out on top of me... I was trampled under their feet and they threw themselves into the sea!

Luckily my four fellow animal keepers were around to help me up.

"Get moving! Quick, the ship is going under!"

Down in the hold the pigs were still squealing desperately,

"Save the pigs!"

"Why?"

"One should never go into the sea without a pig!"

Because these animals have an unrivaled sense of direction. They can orient themselves in the sea even during a storm. You throw them in the water and: TAK! They immediately point their snouts in the direction of the closest shore.... When they go: "OINK, OINK, OINK, OINK!" four times, you're headed to land, and they're never wrong!

And that's why the Genoese people say: "On every ship you should always bring aboard an authentic pig... besides the captain... who's just an ordinary pig."

My companions and I went down and grabbed five pigs. One by one we strapped ourselves to the pigs with ropes tied around our waists... and then, all together, each one of us embracing his own pig: "Bon voyage!... OHOHOHHHHHH... BOOOM!"

It's not that I was possessed by a sudden Christian passion for pigs.

It was just that I knew about a story by Homer, the poet... where he talked about shipwrecked Greeks who were saved embracing pigs, because a pig is so round and fat that he'll never sink! He goes under for a while, but then: GLUB, GLUB, GLUB! (mimes a pig floating up to the surface) he always comes floating back up. It's a buoy made of fat! And he has that little curly tail, that's made just right for you to hold onto it without slipping loose. You grab onto that tail, and he's off... (mimes the swift swimming of a pig) SSCITTSS... TRITRI TRI... Its a buoy with hooves!

We were holding onto our pigs like this when the waves came: "No, we're not going under!" (Mimes kissing the pig as soon as he resurfaces) SMACK...a big wet kiss! Another wave and "OHOOOO...." SMACK! Another wet kiss... After a while the pigs started liking it... they went under even when there weren't any waves! So the five of us, each embracing his own life-saving animal, and smooching it too... traversed the thrashing waves that ripped off our shirts and trousers, and made it to land... naked! If the Tribunal of the Inquisition had discovered us, they would have burned us alive!

We made it to shore! The pigs had saved us... and now there we were, on the sand of the bay, naked, embracing our pigs... who were also naked.

Ohhhh! We were cold! I looked at my skin... it was pastel blue. My companions were turning blue too. The pigs were shocking pink!

The only one in good shape was the Catalan, who was so fat we called him Jelly Belly. With that gut he didn't need a pig... in fact he was the one who saved his pig! Then there was another one who had red hair and we called him Red. Then there was a Negro, a Muslim from Tripoli. We called him Negro. And there was the skinny one that we called Skinny... because we men of the sea have a great imagination when it comes to nicknames!

I said: "It doesn't matter that we were saved, because now we're going to freeze to death."

So much for miracles.

I look at the hills along the shore and there are people! Savages come running down. A hundred of them, two hundred, all armed with bows and arrows. "Uh-oh," I say. "If they've met Christians before, we're screwed. They'll cut us to pieces."

I gathered my courage... and started shouting words from their language that I had learned: *"Aghiudu, en li sala... chiome saridde aabasjia Jaspania..."* They understood everything! *"Mujacia cocecajo mobaputio* Christian*!"*

"Eh?"

The only word they didn't understand was "Christian." We were saved. (He begins a dialogue in grammelot-gibberish in which he translates for his companions the things he has just said.) "Give us something to cover ourselves with, because this cold is going to turn us to ice, stone-cold dead!"

"But what can we give you to cover yourselves with when we're just as naked as you are?"

But listen to how intelligent those savages were: they took some chaff and burned it. They made a bonfire and then circled around us to protect us from the wind... Then, since their village was far away, they made lots of bonfires... every hundred feet there was a bonfire... then they took us in their arms.... there were two hundred of them... and carried us to the next bonfire.... a little toasting and then we were off again.... a little toasting and off we go.... a little toasting.... and they did the same thing for the pigs... toasting, toasting... oink oink!

Because they had never seen pigs before and thought that they were another race of Christians... just a little fatter.

CHAPTER 9

A NOBEL JESTER: DRAWING CONTROVERSY

Dario Fo . . . emulates the jesters[1] of the Middle Ages in scourging authority and upholding the dignity of the downtrodden. . . . For many years Fo has been performed all over the world, perhaps more than any other contemporary dramatist, and his influence has been considerable. He, if anyone, merits the epithet of jester in the true meaning of that word. With a blend of laughter and gravity he opens our eyes to abuses and injustices in society and also the wider historical perspectives in which they can be placed.

—Citation of the Swedish Academy
awarding Fo the 1997 Nobel Prize In Literature[2]

By recognizing Mr. Fo, the Swedish Academy expands the boundaries of literature and underscores the immediacy of theater. It legitimizes the world of performance and recognizes the contribution of comedy, and in particular of political satire. All outspoken monologists, clowns, and cartoonists should be aware of the importance of the award. Jonathan Swift takes his position in the Pantheon with Shakespeare.

—Mel Gussow, NEW YORK TIMES[3]

A body of work that has reestablished a unified stage language based on the word, the gesture, and the idea. . . . A body of work that (and this is the most authentic impulse that motivated Stockholm) substituted for the worn-out words of the literary garden a Renaissance language that is vital, vibrant, joyous, and physical. . . . Fo's grammelot in Stockholm has perhaps announced the end of an era in literature, and the rise of new stage languages of multiple codes that bring the world in which we live back to the stage.

—Ugo Ronfani, HYSTRIO[4]

Dario Fo is a man at the crossroads of popular theater, the inheritor of a very ancient tradition at the same time that he is open to the contemporary world. His art is often considered to be that of a medieval jester transposed into the modern world. His art is both refined and close to the people, to the questions, the conflicts, and the hopes of the world.

—Former French Minister of Culture Jack Lang,
LE JOURNAL DU DIMANCHE[5]

I am very happy. This prize compensates Dario for all the humiliations he has suffered.

—Franca Rame, GENTE[6]

What does this mean? Everything changes, even literature changes.

—Italian scholar Carlo Bo, L'ESPRESSO[7]

I doubt that Fo is an author of the first rank. Even in the Nobel, as in other prizes, mistakes happen.

—Mario Vargas Llosa, LA REPUBLICA[8]

A clown who is worthy of a circus, but not of a prize of this significance.

—National Alliance Party Deputy Maurizio Gasparri, L'ESPRESSO[9]

Might it not be possible that the choice of the judges in Stockholm has been conditioned, in a more or less unconscious way, by a strange and not altogether flattering image of our country as a country of improvisers, of mountebanks, of charlatans, of people who pretend to be what they are not; a country inhabited not by saints, sailors and poets, but by Zanies, and Pulcinellas?

—Giovanni Raboni, CORRIERE DELLA SERA[10]

It's like pissing outside the toilet. What does Fo have to do with Literature?

— Actor and director Carmelo Bene, OGGI [11]

It's total madness, signifying that thirty-five years of Social Democratic Government has infantilized the brains of the Swedes.

—Philosopher & ForzaItalia Party Deputy Lucio Colletti, OGGI [12]

"When I think of the Nazis nothing comes into my mind," wrote Karl Kraus, overwhelmed by horror. In front of a phenomenon so vast and unfathomable, one is struck dumb by aphasia. It is a little like what happens when one considers the Nobel Prize in Literature being awarded to Dario Fo, even more so after the great uproar that has been raised over it. But it is an aphasia that is suffocated by indignation . . . indignation for the affront to literature . . . indignation for the affront to Italian culture.

— Editorial, CATHOLIC STUDIES [13]

Dario Fo. I don't know him, but I've heard his name before. Is he Italian?

—Rita Montalcini, Nobel Laureate in Medicine for 1986, L'ESPRESSO [14]

Just today one of Italy's most accomplished cultural experts said, "But who is Fo?" …this gives you an idea of the consideration with which actors are held in our culture.

—Dario Fo, CORRIERE DELLA SERA [15]

Fo is the sixth Nobel from Italy after Carducci, Deledda, Pirandello, Quasimodo, Montale. After these sages, a clown.

—Vatican newspaper L'OSSERVATORE ROMANO [16]

The newspaper of the Vatican accused the judges of giving the prize to a clown. It's true. But the church should also remember how many of them they burned [during the Inquisition]. God is also a clown. . . . God is a prankster, because with this prize, he's made a lot of people cry.

—Dario Fo, LA REPUBLICA [17]

This Nobel is not only for me, but for all the people of the theater. It is the first time that the prize has been given to an author who was also an actor. The first time that they have recognized the value not only of the written word but also of the spoken word. . . . and so this Nobel rings out like an extraordinary vendetta, the revenge of the actor who is always banished from

power, suddenly brought to the table of the king. The poor giullare is now with this prize rehabilitated, even more than that, called to the court and decorated with the most prestigious prize. And even more extraordinary is that this Nobel goes to a comic, one who makes people laugh and has the audacity to write. A scandalous combination.

—Dario Fo, CORRIERE DELLA SERA [18]

The *New York Times* called the announcement of Dario Fo's Nobel Prize in Literature "among the most unexpected and controversial in the ninety-seven-year history of the award." [19] A headline in an Italian theater journal called Fo's award the "dynamite Nobel," [20] referring to the explosion of controversy set off by the news (an appropriate response to a prize named after a pioneer in the invention of explosives). Some writers, politicians, clergymen, and self-proclaimed arbiters of culture were outraged by Fo's selection. Others sensed that the choice was courageous, not because of Fo's unorthodox politics but because of his unorthodox use of language. In honoring for the first time a writer who is also an actor, the Swedish Academy expanded the officially recognized boundaries of literature.

Fo's approach to language is visceral: his syntax is sculpted by the instincts of his muscles as he performs. His phrasing is orchestrated by the responses of his audiences. His texts are a collage of medieval sources, forgotten dialects, onomatopoeic inventions, current events culled from newspapers, and codified improvisations. Fo's eclectic style could be termed postmodern, but it also recalls the oral epics of Homer and the texts of Shakespeare and Molière, which were forged in performance as well. "I believe that this Nobel is actually a recognition of the value that the word has onstage," reflects Fo, "the word that is written after it has been used, after it has been chewed many times on the stage." [21]

Fo's most eloquent response to his critics can be found in his Nobel acceptance speech to the Swedish Academy, an extraordinary performance of self-dissection in which Fo explains his approach to writing while simultaneously demonstrating it in action. The kinetic power, visual density,

"IT IS THE FIRST TIME THAT THE PRIZE HAS BEEN GIVEN TO AN AUTHOR WHO WAS ALSO AN ACTOR. THE FIRST TIME THAT THEY HAVE RECOGNIZED THE VALUE NOT ONLY OF THE WRITTEN WORD BUT ALSO OF THE SPOKEN WORD. . . . AND SO THIS NOBEL RINGS OUT LIKE AN EXTRAORDINARY VENDETTA, THE REVENGE OF THE ACTOR WHO IS ALWAYS BANISHED FROM POWER, SUDDENLY BROUGHT TO THE TABLE OF THE KING."

and verbal textures of Fo's style are on display throughout the presentation. In short, Fo is using the opportunity to stage the inner workings of his creative process. He embodies the poetics of the *giullare*, giving his audience a glimpse into the landscape of his unorthodox literary imagination.

First, Fo makes it clear that he thinks in pictures. Before delivering his speech in Stockholm he handed out reproductions of the drawings he had made while writing it. "For a long time I've been accustomed to fashioning my speeches out of images," Fo tells his audience. "Instead of writing things down, I draw them. This allows me to make things up as I go along, to improvise, to use my imagination and to oblige you to use yours."[22] Later he gives a reporter a more practical reason for using pictures. "I illustrated the talk because the drawings help me," Fo says. "They are my prompters."[23]

In one sense Fo uses the drawings as mnemonic devices that free him to invent variations on his topics as he speaks. On a deeper level, though, he believes that this method liberates not only his own imagination but that of the audience. Fo's constant concern for the audience's involvement is evident throughout his talk. He uses the drawings to make the event as interactive as possible, so that his dialogue with the audience is enhanced by their interaction with the drawings as they try to discern the relationship between what Fo says and what he has drawn. When Fo performs with his epic tapestries behind him as a backdrop, this often happens subliminally, but in the intimate setting of the Nobel lecture, where Fo is able to give each audience member a copy of his drawings, he can call direct attention to the visual aspect of his dramaturgy. Pointing to enlargements of the drawings that are propped up on an easel beside him, he invites the audience's participation: "You have been given slightly smaller copies of these images," says Fo. "Every once in a while I will stop to show you where we are, so you won't lose the thread. This will be especially useful for those of you who don't know either Italian or Swedish. [Fo's talk is translated simultaneously into Swedish.] The English will have a special advantage because they will imagine things that I have never said or even thought about."[24]

Before beginning his address, Fo creates a bond with the audience that he will strengthen throughout his talk whenever he steps out of his text to ask the audience to focus on the drawings. He also establishes an elasticity of language, suggesting that the drawings serve as an alternate form of translation that may convey to some audience members a new meaning that is just as acceptable as the meaning conveyed by his Italian words or their Swedish translation.

PAGE 193: Fo receiving the Nobel Prize in Literature from the King of Sweden, Stockholm, 1997; THIS PAGE: Fo and Rame at the Nobel Prize ceremony, Stockholm, 1997; PAGES 196–197: Drawings from Fo's notes for his Nobel acceptance speech

The borders between verbal and visual languages are playfully blurred, as is the boundary between the actor and the spectators, who in this case are being urged to use their imaginations to create their own version of the performance. As he continues, Fo also blurs the boundaries between past and present, using his drawings to set up a playful dialogue with history that will unfold concurrently with the other ongoing dialogues in his performance.

The title page of Fo's speech is particularly revealing. Depicting a *giullare* being throttled in a choke hold by a scowling adversary, it can be seen as a visual metaphor for the attacks to which Fo has been subjected since the announcement of his award, but it is actually Fo's illustration of a medieval decree known as "*Contra Jogulatores Obloquentes*." Fo has wrapped these Latin words around his drawing, literally framing the struggle in medieval terms.

"This is the frontispiece [title page]," says Fo, "of a law that was instituted in 1221 in Sicily by the Emperor Frederico II of Swabia, a respected leader who in schools is presented to us as an extraordinarily liberal and enlightened emperor. Now you can decide for yourself from what follows just how liberal this heavenly anointed leader really was. 'Jogulatores obloquentes' means 'insultingly obstreperous jesters.' The law in question

CONTRA JOCULA TORES OBLOQUENTES DALL'INFAME PAROL DIFFAMANTI

CONTRA JOGULATORES OBLOQUENTES 3

AMICI LETTERATI ARTISTI FAMOSI

MEMBRI DELL'ACCADEMIA

INTERVISTA

GIULLARE

PROVOCAZIONE

PUTIFERIO

PARNASO DEGLI ELETTI 2

POETI E PENSATORI SUBLIMI CHE VOLANO ALTO

TRAVOLTI DA UNA TROMBA D'ARIA

IMPROPERI TREMENDI AI MEMBRI

ABBASSO IL RE DI NORVEGIA

SCIVOLA 6 LA SCHEGGIA

7

PERSONALMENTE 8

IO DEVO MOLTO AI MAESTRI SOFFIATORI

FOLLEMENTE ESPLOSIVO

CULTURA TELE VIDEO 13

PROGETTO: BREVETTARE ORGANISMI VIVENTI 14

FRATELLO PORCO DI FRANKESTEIN

MANIPOLAZIONE GENETICA

15

METTERE LE MANI NEL CORREDO GENETICO DI UN MAIALE

RIESCE A RENDERLO

FEGATO RENE

DA TRAPIANTO

MA CHE? PAZIAMMO?

LA CURIA È IMPAZZITA

TEATRANTI
HANNO
STRAGIOITO

GUITTI
GIULLARI
CLOWN
SALTIMBANCHI
FABULATORI DEL LAGO

FAVOLE ASSURDE CHE NOI RAGAZZI
COMMENTAVAMO CON SGHIGNAZZI

SILENZI   PER LA TRAGICA 5
ALLEGORIA

TANTI ANNI FA
RACCONTAVA IL
MAESTRO
SOFFIATORE

STAVA
ARROCCATO
UN PAESE
DI NOME
CALDÉ

CHE GIORNO   DOPO GIORNO

FRANAVA TUTTO
IN BLOCCO

SI LEVA SOLENNE E
FRAGOROSO IL SALUTO

RUZZANTE

SHAKESPEARE
MOLIÈRE

ENTRAMBI
DISPREZZATI

DAI SACCENTI

TURCHIA   11

STRAGE DI   SIVAS

37   IN ANATOLIA

SCRITORI   AUTORI
ATTORI   DANZATRICI
RITO   CURDO

ASCOLTAVANO INCREDULI   12

IGNORANZA
DEL NOSTRO

TEMPO
SA VINIO L'IGNORANZA DIFFUSA
DEI FATTI È IL MAGGIOR
SUPPORTO
ALL'INGIUSTIZIA

L'ASSENZA-   IL SILENZIO

GENI

PARTICELLE
AVREMO   L'UOMO
MAIALE

IMPORRE A OGNI PARTE
IL COPY-RIGHT

BREVETTARE

PAGARE I DIRITTI D'AUTORE
PER OGNI PEZZO
ALL'INDUSTRIA
PADRONA DEL BREVETTO

INFORMARE   18
CRITICAMENTE

I GIOVANI

NON SANNO DELLE STRAGI
DI STATO

INCHIESTE DEVIATE
PROCESSI FARSA
DI STATO

MI
STO   ALLENANDO

SENZA DI LEI

permits all the citizens to insult the jesters, to beat them, and if they get a little carried away even to kill them without risking any trial or retribution. I warn you right away that this law is no longer in effect, so I can continue without worrying."[25]

By giving his speech a medieval Latin title, Fo makes his dialogue with language and history an integral part of his performance from the start. His ironic punch line makes it clear that he considers himself a potential target of the open season on jesters, and in Italian he translates the word "*jogulatores*" as "*giullari*," the medieval term for clowns, satirists, or jesters, and a word that Fo uses regularly to define his own work. His assault on the schoolbook presentation of Frederico II as an enlightened king is a typical provocation on Fo's part, challenging the audience to re-evaluate a commonly accepted version of history.

The next sequence of drawings continues Fo's playful use of anachronism. He sketches a collage of figures that includes the members of the Swedish Academy, a chorus pointing their fingers at the Academy members, and a motley-clad medieval *giullare* dancing beneath them all. As always, the figures in Fo's drawings are swept up in a whirlwind of action. The Academy members seem to be recoiling from all the attention—the proceedings are being filmed by a television journalist—as the *giullare* leaps on top of the letters of the words Fo has inserted into the collage: "Provocation." "*Giullare.*" "Pandemonium." These and other words are as much a part of the action as the figures in the sketch. The "MEMBERS of the Academy" are endowed with power by the boldface script in which Fo has labeled them, as well as by the dais on which they stand at the top of the page, just below the Latin title phrase "*Contra Jogulatores Obloquentes*," which again appears to frame the conflict. Thanking the Academy members (who are in the room among his audience) for their controversial choice to honor a *giullare*, Fo speaks directly to them with words that echo the mood of his drawings. "Yours is an act of courage verging on provocation."[26]

The subsequent drawings are infused with still more action. They depict the traditional literary figures and church officials who were scandalized by the Academy's choice. "At this point," announces Fo, "you can turn the page and you will see a naked poet knocked off his feet by a blast of air." The trumpets of air bringing the news of Fo's award are pictured as swirling colored funnels that send the poet head-over-heels and dislodge the "elected elite of Parnassus" from their comfortable place at the top of the literary world. Writhing in frustration is

one of the clergymen who, Fo claims, have called for "the reinstatement of the laws that allow the *giullari* to be burned at the stake . . . delicately, over a slow fire." In yet another display of the world being turned topsy-turvy, indignant citizens protest the academy's choice of Fo by shouting "Down with the king of Norway." The word "Norway', is encased in a crown that has tumbled to the bottom of the page. "With all the commotion," jokes Fo, "they insulted the wrong dynasty."[27]

But the pages of Fo's drawings are also teeming with figures who celebrate the award. Clowns, actors, acrobats, troubadours, and jesters kick up their heels and turn back flips for joy at the news that one of their own has been given a prize for literature. Having introduced these humble purveyors of popular entertainment, Fo brings the discussion to the origins of his training and the glassblowers of Lake Maggiore, who taught him the art of storytelling when he was growing up. On the same page as the leaping performers, Fo draws the glassblowing artisans of the village in which he was born, where he says the pride over his selection for the Nobel Prize was manifested with such wild joy that "in a glass factory that had been closed for fifty years one of the big kilns exploded with fiery lava that sent myriads of colored glass shards soaring into the sky like the finale of a fireworks display." The visualization of this colorful explosion fills a page of Fo's notes, coming at the point in the speech where he thanks the glassblowers for everything they have taught him about telling "absurd fables to which we listened and responded with snickers that were quickly choked into silence by tragic allegories that transcended all sarcasm."[28]

The centerpiece of Fo's performance is his recounting of one of the fables he learned from the Lake Maggiore glassblowers. It is the story of a town called Caldé, which stands on a promontory above the water. The foundations of the town rest on a slab of stone that is slowly slipping down toward the lake, but the inhabitants refuse to acknowledge that they are sliding toward disaster. They ignore all warnings. When it is pointed out to them that the rocks under their houses are moving, they reassure themselves that it is just the normal settling of the buildings. When the flood level reaches their streets, they just wade through the waves and tell each other the fountains are overflowing. And even after the town is entirely submerged, they go about their business, noticing only that the weather is more humid than usual.

"The fish pass back and forth in front of their eyes," says Fo, mimicking the town's inhabitants in words and gestures,

"'Nothing to fear,' they insisted. 'It's just one of those kinds of fish that learn how to swim in the air.' . . . 'Achoo!' . . . 'Bless you.' . . . 'Thanks.' . . . 'It's a little humid today . . . more humid than yesterday . . . but everything's fine.' They had sunk to the bottom . . . but as far as they were concerned, nothing had happened."[29] Fo's retelling of the story bubbles with the onomatopoeic sounds of gurgling waters and flooded conversations that comically convey the allegory of a population drowning in its own ignorance. A nun is submerged in mid-confession, while the words of the priest are washed away as he speaks: "You are absolved. . . Holy . . . glub . . . Spirit . . . glub . . . aahmen . . . glub. . . ."[30]

Fo's drawings convey the same sense of slipping into incomprehensibility that he portrays in the sputtering dialogue of his characters. A series of illustrations depicts the once orderly town disintegrating into watery chaos as it slides into the lake, a visual analogue to the dissolution of the dialogue spoken by Fo's waterlogged characters. The handwritten words on Fo's drawings also diminish in number as the sequence progresses, until the last blurry image of the sunken town illuminated by lightning has no words at all. "It is a town that once existed," narrates Fo, "but is no longer there: in 1400 it disappeared." The colors Fo uses to tell his story in pictures become progressively darker. Vocally, Fo achieves the same effect with a tone of lamentation that conveys the solemn underside of the comic allegory. "It is undeniable that a fable of this nature would still be unsettling today,"[31] he concludes.

The double nature of the fable is also conveyed in Fo's two drawings of the children of Lake Maggiore listening to the glassblower telling the story. In the first picture they are applauding and laughing. In the second they are subdued into silence. It is representative of Fo's respect for the audience that he includes them in his drawings along with the images of the stories he tells. In these particular images Fo himself is one of the spectators, portrayed as a child listening to the tale, as he imagines his audience will be listening to him.

Fo also includes the audience in other pages of his Nobel drawings that depict a group of young people to whom he had spoken recently about current events. He was astonished to discover that they knew nothing about genetic engineering experiments and the copyrighting of biological materials. Fo pictures their upturned faces encircled by the handwritten words, "They listened incredulously . . . the ignorance of our times." Below this collage is a quote from the Italian writer Savinio: "The primary pillar of injustice is a general ignorance of the facts."[32]

The links between Fo's present-day audience, the storytellers of his childhood, and the fifteenth-century allegory of ignorance are never mentioned directly in Fo's Nobel speech, but his drawings make the connection in visual terms. The page following Savinio's quote is labeled "tele-video culture." It is a collage of figures engaged in sexual violence, gun shootings, and car crashes. The images fall down the page into an ocean that is sketched onto the outline of the globe, as if the inhabitants of the modern world were cascading into ignorance with the same downward momentum depicted in Fo's drawings of the town that slid into the sea. In Fo's kinetic imagination it is this downward momentum that links the various episodes of his performance/lecture. The actions of plunging and plummeting convey the plague of ignorance that is his central theme. The same visual motif is seen in Fo's illustrations of his critics, like the poets of the Parnassian heights and the bitter clergyman, who are also depicted tumbling downward as they drag the crown of Norway's king down with them.

Fo's comic dramaturgy turns the world upside-down by depicting paradox in motion. While kings and poets are brought low, clowns and jesters rise up and dance. The acrobats and *giullari* in Fo's Nobel drawings manage to defy gravity, leaping into the air alongside Shakespeare and Molière, two actor/writers who also appear in Fo's drawings as fellow artists fighting against ignorance by mocking hypocrisy and injustice.

While Fo praises Shakespeare and Molière as his teachers and role models, he saves the final passages of his speech for his contemporary teacher and partner Franca Rame, without whom, he tells the Stockholm audience, he would never have won the Nobel Prize. Fo underscores his debt to Rame with a drawing that depicts his wife on her hands and knees while Fo stands on her back. It is an ironic reference to Rame's self-deprecating remarks to reporters who had asked her what it would be like to live with a monument. "I'm not worried," she replied. "I'll be able to handle it with ease, because I've been training for the role. Every morning I do stretching exercises: I get down on my hands and knees so that I can get used to serving as the pedestal for a monument. I'm very good at it."[33]

Fo closes his speech with a story that brings him together with Franca and their public in another moment full of paradox. In Milan, shortly after his award was announced, Fo was waiting outside the theater where Franca was performing in their play *The Devil with Boobs*. Seeing him on the street, a bus driver stopped his bus so that the passengers could get out and congratulate Fo. A crowd gathered, and soon started shouting for Franca, chanting "Where is Franca?" Next an amateur brass band from the neighborhood came around the corner by chance and started playing. "I've never heard a band play so out of tune," recalls Fo, "but it was the most beautiful music that Franca and I had ever heard."[34] Fo captures the moment in a pair of drawings that spiral up the pages of his notebook in festive patterns of celebration. He draws himself and Franca into the tableau enjoying the impromptu carnival in their honor. It is an apt conclusion to a speech that began with the negative critiques Fo received from elite literary figures horrified by his award. Fo is content to have the support of the ordinary people who ride the bus to work every day, and he enjoys the role reversal of having them perform for him, carrying the tradition of the medieval *giullare* into the streets of modern Milan.

As Fo delivers his speech to the Swedish Academy, he is conscious of the contrast between the ragtag reception he is describing in Milan and the formal event in which he is participating in Stockholm. Playing the role of the fool in the king's court, he uses every opportunity to subtly undermine the prestigious ritual and bring it down to earth. The cartoonish drawings he has distributed to the audience are only the beginning: once he finished the talk, he could not resist performing a comic improvisation based on a play by the Italian Renaissance writer Beolco Ruzzante, one of the *giullari* he cited as a role model in his talk. It is a war story that Fo presents in the invented language of "grammelot," using onomatopoeic sounds and fluid gestures to convey the rhythms of battle: the blaring of bugles, the waving of flags, the thud of steel piercing flesh, and the shrieks of pain. This is Fo's response to the critics who question his work's value as literature—he goes back to a Renaissance writer who invented his own language, and demonstrates the performance techniques through which that language can be reinvented for the present. The comic hero of the story is so terrified of the carnage around him that he straps himself to the underbelly of a horse that is running away from the battle. After a while he realizes that he is running faster than the horse—his fear has given him the strength to carry the horse on his back in an absurd dash for survival. Fo's physically imaginative performance demonstrates the intimate relationship between literature and the body. His excerpt from Ruzzante condenses the main points of his lecture into a two-minute master class on the muscularity of theatrical language.

Fo gave free rein to his comic imagination throughout his stay in Stockholm. During the official ceremony, when the king gave him

his prize, the royal orchestra played Stravinsky's "Circus Polka for a Young Elephant." Fo responded by speaking to the king in the invented language of grammelot: "He answered me back in the same language," joked Fo a few months later in Italy, imitating the king's Swedish. "He didn't speak Italian and I didn't speak Swedish, but we had a very nice conversation. The king is very good at grammelot."[35] Fo sometimes performs a comic re-creation of his meeting with the king as a prologue to his plays. The encounter has become another chapter in his ongoing efforts to update the figure of the medieval *giullare*, whose comic antics brought the king and the clown onto common ground. When he tells the story to audiences and friends, Fo mocks the stiff-necked walk of the palace guards, and the queen's boast that her dinner table was in the *Guinness Book of Records* as the longest single piece of wood ever used as a piece of furniture. (It sits 300 guests.) One of Fo's recent drawings depicting the event is called *The Clown and the King*. For Fo it was all a comic fairy tale, a paradoxical fable of a jester and a monarch that was worthy of the storytellers on Lake Maggiore. "The luncheon was like 'Cinderella,'" quips Fo. "It had everything but the pumpkin carriage."[36] Rame has a similarly light-hearted attitude to the proceedings, making fun of the Italian ambassador who was so impressed by the fact that she had flown to Stockholm in a private plane that she couldn't resist asking how much it cost to rent it. Still, Rame did her part to play along with the ritual: "I wore shoes with heels so high," she laughs, "that they pushed my ovaries all the way up into my mouth."[37]

Many left-wing radicals in Italy criticized Fo for accepting the Nobel Prize, arguing that he should not have taken an award from the cultural and political establishment he usually satirizes so harshly. Some reminded him of remarks he had made in 1975, when he was nominated for the award but did not receive it. The literary establishment then had been scandalized that Fo's name was even mentioned in association with the prize, and Fo in turn had said he could not imagine himself getting dressed up in an evening suit and tails to receive an award from a king. Twenty-two years later the press dug up Fo's old remarks and chastised him for contradicting himself. Fo, whose comic artistry is based on contradiction, responded to these critics by changing the frame of the debate: turning to a paradoxical comic fable by Bertolt Brecht, he imagined his encounter with the Academy as an event in which theater and reality converged in an ironic reversal of social and historic forces. "No, I am not embarrassed," Fo told a reporter.

For me the evening dress and tails were my stage costume for the play of the Nobel Prize. It is a stage costume. . . . Recently some one else asked me, "What does Fo have to say about the evening suit and tails, when he said twenty years ago that he would never wear them since he would never be awarded the Nobel prize." Yes, I said that. How did I respond? I responded by citing the allegory of Brecht in his play *The Exception and the Rule*. [In that play] the servant who had killed his master was absolved because the master had raised his hand against him and the servant only discovered later in the testimony that the master was trying to offer him a gesture of affection. But the servant didn't know that and since it had been the rule that every time the master raised his hand it was to beat him, the servant had rebelled and killed him. He couldn't imagine that this would be an exception, so he conducted himself according to the rule and he was absolved. So twenty years ago I was comporting myself according to the rule. The rule was that the Swedish Academy would absolutely never give me the prize. But then gradually they began to make exceptions. They gave the prize to a black. That had never happened before. And then they gave the prize to a Jew, another first. And now they have given the prize to a *giullare* and it has entered the list of exceptions. But back then I was speaking according to the rule and not the exceptions.[38]

The elaborate irony of Fo's response is typical. Provocatively blurring the boundaries between theater and reality, Fo sees his tailcoat as a costume in a performance that he hopes will spark a re-evaluation of the entire history of the Swedish Academy, as well as of the prejudices and political machinations behind its decisions. Seeing his relationship to the Academy in the terms of Brecht's fable, a paradoxical satire on the relationship between the powerful and the powerless, Fo imagines himself as the servant, the Harlequin figure, while the Nobel jury are the authority figures who break their own rules and suffer the consequences.

Fo has made a career of breaking rules, and enjoys portraying the Swedish Academy as a group that is also making exceptions. His Brechtian interpretation of the event turns the Nobel ceremony into a comedy in which everyone is improvising, including the jurors. Fo sees the 1975 Nobel nomination and his response to it as the first act of a play that climaxed with his 1997 award and the controversy it evoked. Not only did he turn the Stockholm ceremonies into a spectacle, he used the opportunity to do what he does in all his performances: open up a dialogue that expands the boundaries of the discussion at hand. Aristophanes, Molière, Shakespeare, and Ruzzante became part of a discourse on literature that included illiterate fishermen, glassblowers, and genetic engineers.

THIS PAGE: A Poster honoring Fo for his Nobel Prize; PAGES 204-205: Portrait of Fo and Rame by Sylvia Plachy

Fo's presence in Stockholm compelled the academy, the press, and the literary establishment to reconsider the definition of literature and re-examine the history of the Nobel Prize. Fo made it clear that he was accepting the award on behalf of all of history's famous and anonymous writer/performers who were considered inferior in some way because they did not follow the rules, and he welcomed the members of the academy into the ranks of the rule-breakers. Now that the jurors had broken with precedent, he included them in his drawings as part of a carnival collage on the side of clowns, jesters, and *giullari*, and in exchange he agreed to wear their formal evening wear as a costume to the ceremony, which his presence had transformed into a comic performance. In the end Fo changed the Academy more than he had been changed by them, challenging the structure of the Nobel ritual—and also the definition of literature —with a lecture that used cartoon drawings and gestures as well as words to make its points. His work has remained unorthodox, unpredictable, and provocative in the years since he was honored with the world's most prestigious literary award. Still reveling in paradox, Fo continues his kinetic dialogues with history, visual art, language, the human body, and his audience. The Nobel Prize has simply become part of the conversation.

EXCERPT FROM
CONTRA JOGULATORES OBLOQUENTES

("In opposition to insultingly obstreperous jesters")
Excerpt from 1997 acceptance speech for THE NOBEL PRIZE IN LITERATURE
delivered in Stolckhom by DARIO FO translated by RON JENKINS

(In acknowledging the many artists who inspired his work from Aristophanes, Molière, and Ruzzante to his wife and collaborator Franca Rame, Fo included an appreciation of the storytellers from his childhood village on Lake Maggiore)

Now we are here. *{Fo points to figure number five in the drawings he has sketched as an outline for his lecture. He has distributed reproductions of these drawings to the members of the Swedish Academy so they can follow the illustrations as he speaks.}*

And while we are speaking of "cantastorie" [the Italian traditional folk art of sung narrative] we should not leave out the storytellers of my village on Lake Maggiore, where I was born and raised and where there is a great tradition of storytellers; the old storytellers, master glassblowers [many village residents earned their living in the local glass factory], taught me and the other children their profession, the art of telling absurd fables to which we listened and responded with snickers that were quickly choked into silence by tragic allegories that transcended all sarcasm. I still remember the fable about "The Rock of Caldé."

"Many years ago..." recounted the master glassblower, "on the steep slope of that rocky summit that rises up out of the lake... just over there, was a town by the name of Caldé, that was ensconced on a stone ledge that day after day was sliding gradually down toward the base of the precipice. It was a magnificent town with a bell tower, a fortress on its highest peak, and houses that were built into the rock one behind the other. It is a town that once existed, but is no longer there: in 1400 it disappeared.

'Hey...' shouted the farmers and fishcrman from the valley below, 'you're sliding... you're slipping down to the water'

But the inhabitants of the rock didn't listen. They just laughed, joked, and mocked them: 'You think you're pretty clever, trying to frighten us into running away and leaving our houses and land so you can grab them for yourselves. We're not falling for it.'

And so they continued to cultivate their vines, farm their fields, get married, and make love. They went to mass. They felt the rock shifting under the foundations of their houses... but they

didn't worry much about it: 'It's just the normal settling of the ground,' they reassured themselves.

The huge shard of rock was sinking into the lake. 'Be careful, your feet are in the water,' shouted people from the coast.

'What do you mean, that's the overflow from our fountains. It's just a little humid, that's all.'

And so, little by little, but inexorably, the entire town sunk into the lake.

Glug...glug...pluf....they sunk...houses, men, women, two horses, three donkeys... iaaa... glug... Unperturbed the priest continued to take confession from a nun: 'You are absolved.... Holy...Spirit... glug.... Amen...glug...' The fortress disappeared. The bell tower went under, with the bells: dong...ding... dop...plop..."

"Still today," the old glassblower told us, "if you happen to be leaning over the edge of the rocks that are still there hanging above that part of the lake... during a storm, just at the moment when a bolt of lightning illuminates the bottom of the water,

you will see something incredible: there down below is the sunken town with its houses and streets still intact. And you can look at the inhabitants, as if they were in an animated manger scene, still walking around unperturbed, telling each other, 'Nothing's happened.' The fish pass back and forth in front of their eyes... sometimes in their ears... 'Nothing to fear!... It's just one of those kinds of fish that learn how to swim in the air.' And they continue on their way, 'Achoo!' 'Bless you.' 'Thanks... it's a little humid today... more humid than yesterday... but everything's fine!'

They had sunk to the bottom... but as far as they were concerned, absolutely nothing had happened."

It is undeniable that a fable of this nature would still be unsettling today.

I repeat that I owe a lot to my teachers, the glassblowers, and I'm sure that today they too are immensely grateful to you, Honorable Members of the Academy, for having awarded a prize to their student.

ENDNOTES

Unless otherwise noted, all quotations in the book are translated from the Italian by the author.

Preface

1. Dario Fo, interview with the author, Delphi, Greece, July 2, 2000. The epigraph to this chapter comes from the same interview.

2. Fo, performing the prologue of *Mistero Buffo*, Joyce Theater, New York, June 4, 1986.

3. Franca Rame, performing the prologue to *Sex? Don't Mind if I Do!* in Toronto, June 6, 1995.

4. Rame, in conversation with the author, Washington, D.C., June 12, 1986.

5. Fo, *Fabulazzo*, ed. Lorenzo Ruggiero and Walter Valeri (Milan: Kaos, 1992), p. 95.

6. Fo, interview with the author, Delphi, Greece, July 2, 2000.

7. Fo, lecture/demonstration at a meeting of the International School of Theater Anthropology, Copenhagen, May 10, 1996.

8. Fo, lecture/demonstration at an international management symposium hosted by Milan's graduate school of business. Milan, November 8, 1989.

9. Fo, lecture/demonstration at the international theater symposium "From Aristophanes to Dario Fo," Delphi, July 2, 2000.

10. Fo, prologue to *Mistero Buffo*, Kennedy Center, Washington, D.C., June 12, 1986. This and the following quotations about Ronald Reagan are taken from tapes of this performance.

11. Fo, prologue to *Mistero Buffo*, Joyce Theater, New York, June 4, 1986. This and the following quotations about Pope John Paul II are taken from tapes of this performance.

Prologue

1. Except where otherwise noted, all of Fo's quotes in this chapter are from the informal tours he conducted during the opening days of his exhibition *La vita e l'arte di Dario Fo e Franca Rame* (The Life and Art of Dario Fo and Franca Rame) at the Citadella dei Muesi in Cagliari, Sardinia, January 20–24, 2000. In a slightly different version, and under the title *Pupazzi con rabbia e sentimento* (Puppets with Anger and Emotion), the exhibition had first opened in Cesenatico, Italy, in the summer of 1998. It has also been shown in Milan, Rome, Paris, and other European cities.

2. Fo, interview with the author, Milan, June 28, 1999.

3. Francesco Madedou, interview with the author, Cagliari, January 21, 2000.

4. Fo, *La vera storia di ravenna* (Modena: Franco Cosimo Panini, 1999). Here Fo uses paintings, drawings, and texts to create an alternative history for the town of Ravenna.

5. Sergio Pernaciano, interview with the author, Cagliari, January 22, 2000.

6. Ibid.

7. Fulvio Fo, interview with the author, Cagliari, January 22, 2000.

Chapter One

1. Fo, quoted by Lanfranco Binni in *Attento Te...!* (Verona: Bertani, 1975), p. 193.

2. Fo, interview with the author, Milan, August 10, 1985.

3. Fo, *Poer nano* (Milan: Ottaviano, 1976), pp. 5–6.

4. Fo, in conversation with Luigi Allegri, in *Dialogo provocatorio sul comico, il tragico, la follia e la ragione* (Rome: Laterza, 1990), p. 21.

5. Ibid., p. 24.

6. Ibid., p. 23.

7. Ibid., pp. 22–23.

8. Ibid., p. 24–25.

9. Ibid., p. 22.

10. Fo, quoted in *La Repubblica*, Milan, November 1999. Newspaper clipping from Fo's archive in Milan.

11. Fo, in a press conference in Cagliari, January 19, 2000.

12. Fo, in *Dialogo provocatorio*, p. 28.

13. Fo, *Il teatro dell'occhio*, ed. Sergio Martin (Florence: Usher, 1984) p.17.

14. Fo, *Fabulazzo*, ed. Lorenzo Ruggiero and Walter Valeri (Milan: Kaos, 1992), p. 21.

15. Fo, interview with the author, Milan, August 10, 1985.

16. Fo, in *Dialogo provocatorio*, p. 125.

17. Ibid., pp. 135–36.

18. Ibid., pp. 136–37.

19. Fo, *Fabulazzo*, p. 18.

20. Fo, *Manuale minimo dell'attore* (Turin: Einaudi, 1987), p. 70.

21. Fo, interview with the author, Milan, June 22, 1999.

22. Fo, in a press conference in Cagliari, January 19, 2000.

23. Fo, *Manuale minimo dell'attore*, p. 190.

24. Ibid., p. 64.

25. Ibid.

26. Ibid.

27. Ibid.

28. Fo, *Dialogo provocatorio*, p.113.

29. Fo, interview with the author, Milan, August 10, 1985.

30. Fo, quoted in *La Provincia di Cremona*, September 9, 1999. Newspaper clipping from Fo's archive in Milan.

Chapter Two

1. Except where otherwise noted, this and all other quotations from Rame and Fo in this chapter come from the author's interviews and observations during the month preceding the premiere of *Lu Santo Jullare Francesco*, in Spoleto, on July 8, 1999. These interviews and observations took place in Milan, where Fo and Rame allowed the author to document their working process at home in their apartment; in Umbria, where Fo and Rame continued their work at the estate of their son Jacopo; and in Spoleto, where the development process went on during the play's preview performances.

2. This and all other quotations from the prologue and text of *Lu Santo Jullare Francesco* are taken from recordings of the play's premiere presentations at the 1999 Spoleto Festival on July 8 and 10, 1999. These excerpts differ slightly from the printed version of the play, which underwent further revisions during Fo's subsequent performances on tour. For the final version of the play see Fo, *Lu Santo Jullare Francesco*, ed. Franca Rame (Turin: Einaudi, 1999).

3. *Vita di un uomo: Francesco d'Assisi* by Chiara Frugoni (Milan: Einaudi, 1995) p. 8.

4. Ibid. p. 6.

5. Fo, Interview with the author, Milan, June 28, 1999.

6. In June 1999, Fo's son Jacopo hosted a week-long conference on clowning and therapy at his estate in Umbria. Fo attended some of the

conference sessions while he continued working on his text of *Lu Santo Jullare Francesco*.

Chapter Three

1. Fo and Rame, lecture/demonstration at Casa Italiana, Columbia University, New York, September 23, 2000.

2. Ibid.

3. Rame, interview with the author, Milan, June 4, 1999.

4. Ibid.

5. Fo, *Il teatro politico di Dario Fo*, (Milan: Mazzotta, 1977), p. 148.

6. Fo and Rame, Preface, *Venticinque monologhi per una donna* (Turin: Einaudi, 1989), n.p.

7. Rame, interview with the author, Milan, June 4, 1999.

8. Ibid.

9. Fo, *Il teatro politico di Dario Fo*, p. 150.

10. Rame, in a performance of *Sex? Don't Mind if I Do!* on June 18, 1999, that was part of a conference on humor and therapy organized by her son Jacopo at his estate in Santa Cristina, Umbria.

11. Ibid.

12. Rame, interview with the author, Milan, June 4, 1999.

13. Ibid. This is a variant of a line that Rame often uses in the prologues of her shows.

14. Rame and Jacopo and Dario Fo, *Sex? Don't Mind if I Do!*, translated by Ron Jenkins, in *Franca Rame: A Woman on Stage*, ed. Walter Valeri (West Lafayette: Bordihgera, 2000), p. 65.

15. Ibid., p. 75.

16. Ibid., p. 77.

17. Ibid., p. 73.

18. Rame, improvisation from performance of *Sex? Don't Mind if I Do!*, Santa Cristina, Umbria, June 18, 1999.

19. Rame, "The Rape", translated by Jenkins, in *Franca Rame: A Woman on Stage*, pp. 107–10.

20. Rame, interview with the author, Milan, June 4, 1999.

21. *Dario Fo and Franca Rame: Theatre Workshops at Riverside Studios London* (London: Red Notes, 1983), p. 50.

22. Rame, from a tape of the prologue to a performance of excerpts from *Tutta casa letto e chiesa*, San Francisco, June, 1987.

23. Rame and Fo, "Una Donna Sola," in *Tutta casa letto e chiesa* (Milan: La Comune, 1981), pp. 17–36.

24. Rame and Fo, *Tutta casa letto e chiesa*, p. 81.

25. Rame, interview with the author, Cesenatico, July 10, 1994.

26. Fo, *Elizabeth: Almost by Chance a Woman*, translated by Jenkins (New York: Samuel French, 1989), p. 46. This exchange between Fo and Rame began as an improvisation and was eventually written into the script.

27. Ibid.

28. Fo, in Jenkins, *Subversive Laughter* (New York: Free Press, 1994), pp. 111–12.

29. Rame, in L'Unita, December 11, 1999. Unpaginated newspaper clipping from the Fo/Rame archive in Milan.

30. Fo and Rame, "Io, Ulrike, grido . . . ," *Venticinque monologhi per una donna*, pp. 247–48.

31. Author's interview with the sister of Sylvia Baraldini, who asked that her name not be used.

Chapter Four

1. Dario Fo and Franco Zeffirelli, debate in *La Repubblica* (Milan), April 27,1977. From the Fo/Rame archive in Milan.

2. *L'Osservatore* (Rome), April 24, 1977. Quoted by Tom Behan in *Dario Fo: Revolutionary Theatre* (London: Pluto, 2000), p. 102.

3. Fo, in *La Repubblica* (Milan), April 25, 1977, quoted in Behan, *Dario Fo: Revolutionary Theater*.

4. Quoted in Behan, *Dario Fo: Revolutionary Theatre*, p. 102.

5. Fo, in *Panorama*, April 26, 1977. Quoted in Chiara Valentini, *La storia di Dario Fo* (Milan: Feltrinelli, 1977), p.176. Parts of the quotation also appear in Behan, *Dario Fo: Revolutionary Theatre*, p. 102, and Tony Mitchell, *File on Fo* (London: Methuen, 1989), p. 100.

6. Fo, *Mistero Buffo* (Turin: Einaudi, 1977), p. 66.

7. Ibid., pp. 53–54.

8. Fo, *Mistero Buffo*, in the televised version broadcast on RAI Italian National Television in 1977.

9. Fo, *Mistero Buffo*, p. 58.

10. Ibid., p. 62.

11. Ibid.

12. Ibid., p. 64.

13. This quotation and all others from the prologue to "The Wedding at Cana" are taken from the televised version of *Mistero Buffo* broadcast by RAI. Later versions of the prologue do not always include these detailed discussions of artworks, but the early prologues are valuable in illuminating the visual sources at the root of Fo's creative process.

14. Fo, *Mistero Buffo*, in the televised version broadcast by RAI.

15. Ibid.

16. Fo, *Mistero Buffo*, p. 160.

17. Ibid., p. 168.

18. Fo quoted in Ron Jenkins, "Clowns, Politics, and Miracles," *American Theater*, June 1986, p. 16.

19. Fo, *Mistero Buffo*, p. 97.

20. Ibid., p. 100.

21. Ibid.

22. Fo, in a televised version of "The Resurrection of Lazarus" broadcast by RAI as part of Fo's lecture/demonstration "The Tricks of the Trade," 1985.

23. Fo, *Manuale minimo dell'attore* (Turin: Einaudi, 1987), p. 155.

24. Ibid., p. 146.

25. Ibid.

26. Ibid., p. 147.

27. Ibid., p. 146.

28. Fo, *Mistero Buffo*, p. 104.

29. Fo, quoted in Jenkins, "Clowns, Politics, and Miracles," p. 14.

30. Fo, *Mistero Buffo*, p. 72.

31. Ibid., p. 105.

32. Fo, interview with the author, Milan, July 2, 1999.

33. Fo, quoted in Marisa Pizza, *Il Gesto, la parola, l'azione: Poetica, drammaturgia e storia dei monologhi di Dario Fo* (Rome: Bulzoni, 1996), p. 221.

34. Fo, *Mistero Buffo*, p. 116.

35. Fo, from a tape of "Boniface VIII" in performance at the Joyce

Theater, New York, June 4, 1986.

36. Ibid.

37. Ibid.

38. Ibid.

39. Behan, *Dario Fo: Revolutionary Theatre*, p. 102.

40. Fo, in *Panorama*, April 26, 1977, quoted in Valentini, *La Storia di Dario Fo*, pp.176–77.

Chapter Five

1. Fo, Interview with the author, Milan, May 30, 1999.

2. Fo, Improvisation during a lecture on Leonardo, Milan, May 31,1999.

3. Ibid.

4. Felice Cappa, interview with the author, Milan, June 5, 1999.

5. Fo, "*Lezione sul cenacolo*," unpublished ms., p. 2.

6. Ibid.

7. Fo, improvisation during lecture on Leonardo.

8. Fo, "*Lezione sul cenacolo*," unpublished ms., p. 3.

9. Ibid., p. 4.

10. Ibid., pp. 4–5.

11. Ibid., p. 11.

12. Ibid., p. 8.

13. Ibid., p. 9.

14. Fo, "*Lezione sul cenacolo*," second unpublished ms., p. 33.

15. Ibid., p. 34.

16. Ibid., p. 68.

Chapter Five Interlude

1. The lecture was transcribed and published in *Le domeniche d'arte* (Bologna: December, 1999).

Chapter Six

1. Fo, comment on improvisation made at the 1981 session of the International School of Theater Anthropology (ISTA), which was held in Volterra, Italy, and published in Fo, *Fabulazzo*, ed. Lorenzo Ruggiero and Walter Valeri (Milan: Kaos, 1992), p. 103. Fo and Rame have often participated in ISTA sessions organized by Eugenio Barba and the actors of the Odin Teatret, with the collaboration of an international group of scholars.

2. Fo, *Fabulazzo*, p. 121.

3. Ibid., p. 123.

4. Ibid., p. 128.

5. Fo, *Manuale minimo dell'attore* (Turin: Einaudi, 1987), p. 286.

6. Fo, *Fabulazzo*, p. 121.

7. Fo, "Il Primo Miracolo del Bambino Gesu," *Storia della tigre e altre storie* (Milan: La Comune, 1980), pp. 78–81.

8. Ibid., p. 105.

9. Ibid., p. 111.

10. This ending appears in Fo's 1991 performance of the story on the videotape entitled *Monologhi da storia della tigre e Mistero Buffo: Dario Fo 1991*.

11. Fo, *Fabulazzo*, pp 122–23.

12. Fo, "Il Primo Miracolo del Bambino Gesu," p. 113.

13. Fo, prologue to "Tumulto di Bologna," on videotape of 1986 performance in Bologna.

14. Fo, "Tumulto di Bologna," in *Fabulazzo osceno* (Milan: La Comune, 1982), p. 19.

15. Fo, interview with the author, Milan, July 6, 1988.

16. Fo, on the videotape of the 1986 performance of "Tumulto di Bologna" in Bologna.

17. Ibid.

18. Ibid.

19. Fo, interview with author, Delphi, July 2, 2000.

20. Fo, on the videotape *Monologhi da fabulazzo osceno e Mistero Buffo: Dario Fo 1991*.

21. Ibid.

22. Fo, *Manuale minimo dell'attore*, p. 197.

23. Ibid.

24. Ibid.

25. Ibid., p. 199.

26. Fo, *Storia della tigre e altre storie*, p. 27.

27. Fo, *Fabulazzo*, p. 358.

28. Fo, interview with the author, Milan, August 10, 1985.

29. Fo, in videotape of the lecture/demonstration "Trucchi di Mestiere," (1985). From the Fo/Rame archives in Milan.

30. Ibid.

31. Ibid.

32. Fo, Storia della tigre e altre storie, p. 47.

Chapter Seven

1. Fo, "Toto: The Violence of the Marionette and the Mask," trans. Stuart Hood, *Theater XVIII*, no.3 (Summer/Fall 1987), pp. 6–7.

2. See Tom Behan, *Dario Fo: Revolutionary Theatre* (London: Plulto, 2000), pp. 66–68.

3. Fo, Introduction, *Accidental Death of an Anarchist*, adapted by Gavin Richards (London: Pluto, 1980), p. iii.

4. Quoted in Behan, *Dario Fo: Revolutionary Theatre*, p. 68.

5. Fo, on videotape of the 1987 revival of *Accidental Death of an Anarchist*. In the Fo/Rame archive in Milan.

6. Ibid.

7. Fo, Introduction, *Accidental Death of an Anarchist*, p. iii.

8. Fo, *Morte accidentale di un anarchico* (Turin: Einaudi, 1974), pp. 33–34.

9. Ibid.

10. Fo, quoted in Ron Jenkins, "Clowns, Politics, and Miracles," American Theater, June 1986, p. 11.

11. Ibid.

12. Ibid., pp. 11–12.

13. Behan, *Dario Fo: Revolutionary Theatre*, p. 77.

14. Fo, *Marino libero! Marino e innocente!* (Turin: Einaudi, 1998), p. 18.

15. Ibid., fig. 72.

16. Ibid., figs. 30 and 31.

17. Ibid., fig. 88.

18. Fo, interview with the author, Palermo, January 29, 2000.

19. Fo, interview with the author, Milan, June 29, 1999.

20. Ibid.

21. Behan, *Dario Fo: Revolutionary Theatre*, p. 20.

22. Fo, *We Won't Pay! We Won't Pay!*, translated by Ron Jenkins. This and other quotations from this play are taken from a version prepared by Fo and Jenkins for the 1999 revival of the play at the American Repertory Theater, Cambridge, Massachusetts. This version will by published be Theater Communications Group in late 2001.

23. Ibid.

24. Fo with Liugi Allegri, *Dialogo provocatorio sul comic, il tragico, la follia e la ragione* (Rome: Laterza, 1990), p. 116.

25. Ibid., pp. 116–17.

26. Mikhail Bakhtin, *Rabelais and His World* (Bloomington: Indiana University Press, 1984), pp. 88–89.

27. Fo, interview with the author, Milan, June 29, 1999.

Chapter Eight

1. Ruzzante was the pen name of Angelo Beolco, a sixteenth-century actor/writer whom Fo admires as the creator of a *giullare*-like character similar to Harlequin.

2. Fo, in a manuscript translated by Ron Jenkins for the American publication of *Johan Padan and the Discovery of the Americas* (New York: Grove/Atlantic, forthcoming in 2001). All subsequent quotations from the play are from this manuscript.

3. The paintings referred to and reproduced in this chapter are color acrylics from Fo's original sketchbook. Some of these paintings are reproduced in Fo, *Johan Padan* (Turin: Gruppo Abele, 1992).
The paintings are not reproduced in the forthcoming American edition of *Johan Padan*, which does however include a set of Fo's line drawings for the play.

4. Fo, interview with the author, Pisa, February 6, 2000.

5. Ibid.

6. Enrique Pupo-Walker, ed., *Castaways: The Narrative of Alvar Nunez Cabeza de Vaca* (Berkeley: University of California, 1993).

Chapter Nine

1. The official statements of the Swedish Academy translate *"giullare"* as "jester"—perhaps the most appropriate term to be used by an institution whose award was presented to a clown by a king.

2. Press release issued by the Swedish Academy announcing Fo's Nobel Prize, October 9, 1997.

3. Mel Gussow, "The Not-So-Accidental Recognition of an Anarchist," *New York Times*, October 15, 1997.

4. Ugo Ronfani, "Nobel al dinamite per Fo il giullare," *Histrio* no. 4 (1997), p. 7.

5. Jack Lang, "Dario Fo: virtuose de la langue," *Le Journal du Dimanche*, October 12, 1997. Unpaginated clipping from Fo/Rame archive, Milan.

6. Franca Rame, in "Dario Fo: 'Grazie Franca, e tutto merito tuo se ho conquistato il Premio Nobel,'" Gente, October 10, 1997, p. 7.

7. "Ma a qualcuno il premio fa ribrezzo" in *L'Espresso*, October 23, 1997, p. 83.

8. "Vargas Llosa: 'Non se lo merita,'" *La Repubblica*, December 11, 1997, p. 9.

9. "Ma a qualcuno il premio fa ribrezzo," *L'Espresso*, October 23, 1997, p. 83.

10. "Mistero Svedese" in *Corriere della Sera*, October 10, 1997, p. 6.

11. "Carmelo Bene: 'Assurdo, e meglio Platini,'" *Corriere della Sera*, October 10, 1997, p. 11.

12. "Pero in molti hanno gridato allo scandalo," *Oggi*, October 22, 1997, p. 32.

13. "Un Nobel indignante," *Catholic Studies*, November 1997, p. 739.

14. "Ma a qualcuno il premio fa ribrezzo," *L'Espresso*, October 10, 1997, p. 83.

15. "Commosso? Si, ma mi viene da ridere," *Corriere della Sera*, October 10, 1997, p. 9.

16. "Ma a qualcuno il premio fa ribrezzo," *L'Espresso*, October 10, 1997, p. 82.

17. "Giullari di tutti i tempi vi dedico il mio Nobel," *La Repubblica*, October 11, 1997, p. 10.

18. "Comosso? Si, ma mi viene da ridere," *Corriere della Sera*, October 10, 1997, p. 9.

19. "Italy's barbed political jester, Dario Fo, wins Nobel Prize," *New York Times*, October 10, 1997, p. 10.

20. Ronfani, "Nobel al dinamite per Fo il giullare," p. 7.

21. "Il Mistero Buffo del mio Nobel," *L'Espresso*, October 23, 1997, p. 80.

22. Fo, "Contra Jogulatores Obloquentes," in *Les Prix Nobel 1997* (Stockholm: Swedish Academy, 1997), p. 348.

23. "Il Nobel a Dario Fo: un giullare," *Lombardia Oggi*, December 7, 1997, p. 9.

24. Fo, "Contra Jogulatores Obloquentes," p. 348.

25. Ibid.

26. Ibid.

27. Ibid., p. 349.

28. Ibid.

29. Ibid., p. 350.

30. Ibid.

31. Ibid.

32. Ibid., p. 366.

33. Rame, interview with the author, Santa Cristina, June 25, 1999.

34. Fo, "Contra Jogulatores Obloquentes," p. 354.

35. Fo, interview with the author, Santa Cristina, June 25, 1999.

36. Fo, interview with the author, Delphi, July 3, 2000.

37. Rame, interview with the author, Delphi, July 3, 2000.

38. "Il Nobel a Dario Fo: un giullare," p. 9.

LIST OF PLAYS

The collected works of Dario Fo and Franca Rame are published in Italian in a multi-volume series by the Italian publisher Einaudi (Turin).

The collected works of Dario Fo and Franca Rame will be published in English in a multi-volume series by Theater Communications Group (New York)

Currently available English translations include:

Dario Fo: Plays: 1 (edited by Stuart Hood) London, Methuen, 1992.

Dario Fo: Plays: 2 (edited by Stuart Hood) London, Methuen, 1994.

About Face (translated by Ron Jenkins) New York, Samuel French, 1989.

Accidental Death of an Anarchist (adapted by Gavin Richards) London, Pluto, 1980.

Archangels Don't Play Pinball (translated by Ron Jenkins) New York, Samuel French, 1989.

Elizabeth: Almost by Chance a Woman (translated by Ron Jenkins) New York, Samuel French, 1989.

Female Parts (adapted by Olwen Wymark) London, Pluto, 1981.

Johan Padan and the Discovery of the Americas (translated by Ron Jenkins) New York, Grove/Atlantic, 2001.

Mistero Buffo (translated by Ed Emery) London, Methuen, 1988.

The Pope and the Witch, (translated by Joan Holden) New York, Samuel French, 1997.

The Story of the Tiger (translated by Ron Jenkins) in *Master Breasts*, New York, Aperture, 1998.

We Won't Pay! We Won't Pay! & other plays (translated by Ron Jenkins) New York, TCG, 2001.

The following list of stage plays was compiled in part from *Dario Fo: Peoples Court Jester* by Tony Mitchell. (London: Metheun, 1999)

A Finger in the Eye (Il ditto nell'occhio), 1953. A revue in two acts by Franco Parenti, Dario Fo, and Giustino Durano.

Fit to be Tied (I sani da legare), 1954. A revue in two acts by Franco Parenti, Dario Fo, and Giustino Durano.

Thieves, Dummies and Naked Women (Ladri, manichini e donne nude), 1958. Four one-act farces.

Comic Finale (Comica finale), 1958. Four one-act farces.

Archangels Don't Play Pinball (Gli arcangeli non giocano al flipper), 1959. Three-act play.

He Had Two Pistols with White and Black Eyes (Aveva due pistole con gli occhi bianchi e neri), 1960. Three-act play.

He Who Steals a Foot is Lucky in Love (Chi ruba un piede è fortunate in amore), 1961. Two-act play

Isabella, Three Sailing Ships and a Con Man (Isabella, tre caravelle e un cacciaballe), 1963. Two-act play.

Seventh Commandment: Thou Shalt Steal a Bit Less (Settimo: ruba un po' meno), 1964. Two-act play.

Always Blame the Devil (La colpa è sempre del diavolo), 1986. Two-act play.

Throw the Lady Out (La signora è da buttare), 1967. Two-act play.

Grand Pantomime with Flags and Small and Middle-Sized Puppets (Grande pantomima con bandiere e pupazzi picoli e medi), 1968. Two-act play.

Mistero Buffo, 1969. Monologues.

The Worker Knows 300 Words, The Boss Knows 1000—That's Why He's the Boss (L'operaio conosce 300 parole, il padrone 1000—per questo lui è il padrone), 1969. Two-act play.

Chain Me Up and I'll Still Smash Everything (Legami pure che tanto io spacco tutto lo stesso), 1969. Two one-act plays.

I'd Rather Die Tonight If I Had To Think It Had All Been In Vain (Vorrei morire anche stasera se dovessi pensare che con è servito a niente), 1970. Two-act play, subtitled: 'Resistance: the Italian and Palestinian People Speak.'

Accidental Death of an Anarchist (Morte accidentale di un anarachico), 1970. Two-act play.

United We Stand! All together Now! Oops, Isn't That the Boss (Tutti uniti! Tutti insieme! Ma scusa, quello non è il padrone?), 1971. Two-act play, subtitled: "Workers" Struggles 1911–1922.'

Fedayin (Fedayn), 1972. Two-act play, subtitled: 'The Palestinian Revolution through its Culture and Songs.'

Knock Knock! Who's There? Police! (Pum, pum! Chi è? La polizia!), 1972. Two-act play.

The People's War in Chile (Guerra di popolo in Cile), 1973. Two-act play.

We Won't Pay! We Won't Pay! (Non si paga! Non si paga!), 1974. A farce in two acts.

Fanfani Kidnapped (Il Fanfani rapito), 1975. A play in three acts and two interludes.

Mother's Marijuana is the Best (La marijuana della mamma è la più bella), 1976. Two-act play.

It's All About Bed, Home, and Church (Tutta casa letto e chiesa), 1977. Monologues by Dario Fo and Franca Rame.

Story of the Tiger and Other Stories (La storia della tigre e altre storie), 1978. Monologues.

About Face (Clacson, trombette e pernacchi), 1981. Two-act play.

Obscene Fables (Il fabulazzo osceno), 1982. Four monologues.

The Open Couple (Coppia aperata – quasi spalancata), 1983. One-act comedy by Franca Rame and Dario Fo.

Elizabeth: Almost by Chance a Woman (Quasi per caso una donna: Elisabetta), 1986. Two-act play.

Harlequin (Hellequin, Harlekin, Arlecchino), 1985. Two-act play based on lazzi compiled by Ferruccio Marotti and Delia Gambelli.

A Day Like Any Other (Una giornata qualunque), 1986. One-act play by Dario Fo and Franca Rame.

Kidnapping Francesca (Il ratto della Francesca), 1986. Two-act play.

The Pope and the Witch (Il Papa e la strega), 1989. Two-act play.

Hush! We're Falling! (Zitti! Stiamo precipitando!), 1990. Two-act play.

Johan Padan and the Discovery of the Americas (Johan Padan a la descoverta de la Americhe), 1991. Monologue in two parts (with a Prologue).

Seventh Commandment: Steal a Bit Less No. 2 (Settimo: ruba un po' meno no. 2), 1992. A monologue in two acts by Dario Fo and Franca Rame.

Dario Fo Meets Ruzzante (Dario Fo incontra Ruzzante), 1993. Two-act play, based on texts by Angelo Beolco.

Mummy! The Sans-culottes! (Mamma! I sanculotti!),
1993, Two-act play.

Sex? Don't Mind If I Do! (Sesso? Grazie, tanto per gradire!), 1994.
Monologue by Franca Rame, Dario and Jacopo Fo, performed
by Franca Rame.

The Peasants' Bible (La bibbia dei villani), 1996. Monologues.

The Devil with Boobs (Il diavolo con le zinne), 1997. Two-act play.

**Marino is Free! Marino is Innocent! (Marino libero! Marino
è innocente!),** 1998. Monologue in two acts.

Francis, The Holy Fool (Lu Santo Jullare Francesco), 1999.
A monologue.

SELECTED BIBLIOGRAPHY

Tom Behan, **Dario Fo: Revolutionary Theatre,** London, Pluto, 2000.

Marina Cappa & Roberto Nepoti, **Dario Fo,** Rome, Gremese, 1982.

Lanfranco Binni, **Attento te...!,** Verona, Bertani, 1975.

Christopher Cairns, **Dario Fo e la 'pittura scenica': arte teatro regie
1977–1997,** Napoli, Archivio del teatro e dello spettacolo, 2000.

Joseph Farrell, **Dario and Franca,** (Forthcoming)

Joseph Farrell & Antonio Scuderi (eds.) **Dario Fo: Stage, Text and
Tradition,** Carbondale, Southern Illinois University Press, 2000.

David L. Hirst, **Dario Fo and Franca Rame,** London, Methuen, 1989.

Ron Jenkins, **Subversive Laughter,** New York, Free Press, 1994.

Claudio Meldolesi, **Su un comico in rivolta: Dario Fo il bufalo il
bambino,** Rome, Bulzoni, 1978.

Tony Mitchell, **Dario Fo: People's Court Jester,** London, Methuen 1999.

Tony Mitchell, **File on Fo, London,** Methuen, 1989.

Marisa Pizza, **Il gesto, la parola, l'azione: poetica, drammaturgia e
storia dei monologhi di Dario Fo,** Bulzoni, Rome, 1996.

Joel Schechter, **Durov's Pig,** New York, Theater Communications
Group, 1985.

Joel Schechter, **Satiric Impersonations,** Carbondale,
Southern Illinois University Press, 1994.

Antonio Scuderi, **Dario Fo and Popular Performance,**
New York, Legas, 1998.

Chiara Valentini, **La storia di Dario Fo,** Milan, Feltrinelli, 1977.

Walter Valeri (ed.), **Franca Rame: A Woman on Stage,**
West Lafayette, Bordighera, 2000.

BOOKS BY DARIO FO

**Dario Fo and Franca Rame Theatre Workshops at Riverside Studios,
London,** London, Red Notes, 1983.

Dialogo provocatiorio sul comic, il tragico, la follia e la ragione (inter-
viewed by Luigi Allegri), Rome, Laterza, 1990.

Fabulazzo (edited by Lorenzo Ruggiero and Walter Valeri),
Milan, Kaos, 1992.

Federico Fellini & Dario Fo: disegni geniali
(exhibition catalogue) Milan, Mazzotta, 1999.

Manuale minimo dell'attore, Turin, Einaudi, 1987.

Poer Nano (with Jacopo Fo), Milan, Ottavio, 1976.

Pupazzi con rabbia e sentimento, (exhibition catalogue) Milan,
Scheiwiller, 1998.

Il teatro dell'occhio / The Theatre of the Eye
(exhibition catalogue) Milan, Usher, 1984.

Toto: manuale dell'attor comico, Florence, Vallecchi, 1995.

The Tricks of the Trade, London, Methuen, 1991.

La vera storia di Ravenna, Modena, Franco Cosimo Panini, 1999.

Library of Congress Catalog Card Number 2001091301

Hardcover ISBN 0-89381-947-6

Printed and bound by Tien Wah Press (PTE.) LTD., Singapore.

The Staff at Aperture for *Dario Fo and Franca Rame: Artful Laughter* is:

Executive Director Michael E. Hoffman
Editor Melissa Harris
Vice President Production Stevan A. Baron
Production Director Lisa A. Farmer
Associate Art Director Kristi Norgaard
Copyeditors David Frankel, Andrew Hiller
Editorial Assistant Daniel Etra
Editorial Work Scholar Katie Langmore

Aperture Foundation publishes a periodical, books, and portfolios of fine photography and presents worldclass exhibitions to communicate with serious photographers and creative people everywhere. A complete catalog is available upon request.

Aperture Customer Service 20 East 23rd Street, New York, New York 10010. Phone: (212) 598-4205.
Fax: (212) 598-4015. Toll-free: (800) 929-2323.
E-mail: customerservice@aperture.org

Aperture Foundation, including Book Center and Burden Gallery
20 East 23rd Street, New York, New York 10010.
Phone: (212) 505-5555, ext. 300.
Fax:(212) 979-7759. E-mail: info@aperture.org
Visit Aperture's website: www.aperture.org

Aperture Foundation books are distributed internationally through:
CANADA General/Irwin Publishing Co., Ltd., 325 Humber College Blvd., Etobicoke, Ontario, M9W 7C3. Fax: (416) 213-1917.

UNITED KINGDOM, SCANDINAVIA, AND CONTINENTAL EUROPE Aperture c/o Robert Hale, Ltd., Clerkenwell House, 45-47 Clerkenwell Green, London, United Kingdom, EC1R OHT.
Fax: (44) 171-490-4958.

NETHERLANDS, Belgium, Luxemburg: Nilsson & Lamm, BV, Pampuslaan 212-214, P.O. Box 195, 1382 JS Weesp, Netherlands. Fax: (31)29-441-5054.

AUSTRALIA Tower Books Pty. Ltd., Unit 9/19 Rodborough Road, Frenchs Forest, Sydney, New South Wales, Australia. Fax:(61) 2-9975-5599.

NEW ZEALAND Southern Publishers Group, 22 Burleigh Street, Grafton, Auckland, New Zealand. Fax: (64) 9-309-6170.

INDIA: TBI Publishers, 46, Housing Project, South Extension Part-I, New Delhi 110049, India. Fax: (91) 11-461-0576.

For international magazine subscription orders to the periodical *Aperture*, contact Aperture International Subscription Service, P.O. Box 14, Harold Hill, Romford, RM3 8EQ, United Kingdom. One year: $50.00. Price subject to change. Fax: (44) 1-708-372-046.

To subscribe to the periodical *Aperture* in the U.S.A. write Aperture, P.O.Box 3000, Denville, New Jersey 07834. Toll-frée: (866) 457-4603. One year: $40.00. Two years: $66.00.
First Edition
10 9 8 7 6 5 4 3 2 1

BOOK DESIGN BY YOLANDA CUOMO / NYC